Lecture Notes in Computer Science 12324

More information about this series at http://www.springer.com/series/7409

Alexander Nolte · Claudio Alvarez ·
Reiko Hishiyama · Irene-Angelica Chounta ·
María Jesús Rodríguez-Triana ·
Tomoo Inoue (Eds.)

Collaboration Technologies and Social Computing

26th International Conference, CollabTech 2020
Tartu, Estonia, September 8–11, 2020
Proceedings

 Springer

Editors
Alexander Nolte (iD)
University of Tartu
Tartu, Estonia

Claudio Alvarez (iD)
Universidad de Los Andes
Las Condes, Chile

Reiko Hishiyama (iD)
Waseda University
Tokyo, Japan

Irene-Angelica Chounta (iD)
University of Tartu
Tartu, Estonia

María Jesús Rodríguez-Triana (iD)
Tallinn University
Tallinn, Estonia

Tomoo Inoue (iD)
University of Tsukuba
Tsukuba, Japan

ISSN 0302-9743   ISSN 1611-3349   (electronic)
Lecture Notes in Computer Science
ISBN 978-3-030-58156-5   ISBN 978-3-030-58157-2   (eBook)
https://doi.org/10.1007/978-3-030-58157-2

LNCS Sublibrary: SL3 – Information Systems and Applications, incl. Internet/Web, and HCI

This Springer imprint is published by the registered company Springer Nature Switzerland AG
The registered company address is: Gewerbestrasse 11, 6330 Cham, Switzerland

Preface

This volume contains the papers presented at the 26th International Conference on Collaboration Technologies and Social Computing (CollabTech 2020).

The conference was originally planned to take place in Tartu, Estonia. However, due to the COVID-19 outbreak that sadly marked the first half of the year, CollabTech 2020 was held following an online-only format during September 8–11, 2020.

CollabTech 2020 received 25 submissions, each of which was carefully reviewed by at least three Program Committee members. As a result, the committee decided to accept 10 full and 5 work-in-progress papers. The accepted papers present relevant, timely, and rigorous research related to theory, models, design principles, methodologies, and case studies that contribute to better understanding of the complex interaction between collaboration and technology.

This was the second year that the two major conferences, CollabTech and CRIWG, took place as one merged event focusing on innovative technical + human + organizational approaches to expand collaboration support with an interdisciplinary perspective including computer science, management science, design science, cognitive science, and social science.

As editors, we would like to thank the authors of all CollabTech 2020 submissions and the members of the Program Committee for carefully reviewing the submissions. Our thanks also go to our sponsors who allowed us to make CollabTech 2020 attractive to participants despite the difficulties posed by the global circumstances.

In addition, we attribute the success of the conference to the efforts of the Special Interest Group (SIG) on Groupware and Network Services of the IPSJ, the SIG on Cyberspace of the Virtual Reality Society in Japan, and the SIG on Communication Enhancement of the Human Interface Society.

Last but not least, we would like to acknowledge the effort of the organizers of the conference, and thank the Steering Committee for the opportunity, trust, and guidance they provided during the whole process.

September 2020

Alexander Nolte
Claudio Alvarez
Reiko Hishiyama
Irene-Angelica Chounta
María Jesús Rodríguez-Triana
Tomoo Inoue

Organization

Conference Co-chairs

Irene-Angelica Chounta	University of Tartu, Estonia
María Jesús Rodríguez-Triana	Tallinn University, Estonia
Tomoo Inoue	University of Tsukuba, Japan

Program Co-chairs

Alexander Nolte	University of Tartu, Estonia
Claudio Alvarez	Universidad de los Andes, Chile
Reiko Hishiyama	Waseda University, Japan

Doctoral Consortium Chair

Luis P. Prieto	Tallinn University, Estonia

Registration Chair

Fredrik Milani	University of Tartu, Estonia

Publicity Chair

Benjamin Weyers	University of Trier, Germany

Publication Chair

Leo Siiman	University of Tartu, Estonia

Local Organizing Committee

Anni Suvi	University of Tartu, Estonia

Program Committee

Daniela Caballero	Universidad de Chile, Chile
Dominique Decouchant	UAM Cuajimalpa, Mexico, and LIG de Grenoble, France
Yannis Dimitriadis	University of Valladolid, Spain
Orlando Erazo	Universidad Técnica Estatal de Quevedo, Ecuador

Mikhail Fominykh	Norwegian University of Science and Technology, Norway
Benjamim Fonseca	UTAD, INESC TEC, Portugal
Kinya Fujita	Tokyo University of Agriculture and Technology, Japan
Kimberly García	Siemens, USA
Cédric Grueau	Research Center for Informatics and Information Technologies, Portugal
Naoko Hayashida	Fujitsu Laboratories Ltd., Japan
Atsuo Hazeyama	Tokyo Gakugei University, Japan
Davinia Hernandez-Leo	Universitat Pompeu Fabra, Spain
Thomas Herrmann	University of Bochum, Germany
Valeria Herskovic	Pontificia Universidad Católica de Chile, Chile
Satoshi Ichimura	Otsuma Women's University, Japan
Claudia-Lavinia Ignat	Inria, France
Yutaka Ishii	Okayama Prefectural University, Japan
Kazuyuki Iso	NTT Corporation, Japan
Marc Jansen	University of Applied Sciences Ruhr West, Germany
Ralf Klamma	RWTH Aachen University, Germany
Arianit Kurti	Linnaeus University, Sweden
Thomas Largillier	GREYC, France
Liang-Yi Li	National Taiwan Normal University, Taiwan
Tun Lu	Fudan University, China
Wolfram Luther	University of Duisburg-Essen, Germany
Sonia Guadalupe Mendoza Chapa	CINVESTAV, Mexico
Roc Meseguer	Universitat Politècnica de Catalunya, Spain
Marcelo Milrad	Linnaeus University, Sweden
Mamoun Nawahdah	Birzeit University, Palestine
Sergio Ochoa	Universidad de Chile, Chile
Masayuki Okamoto	Toyota Motor Corporation, Japan
Masaki Omata	University of Yamanashi, Japan
Gerti Pishtari	Tallinn University, Estonia
Elvira Popescu	University of Craiova, Romania
Meeli Rannastu-Avalos	University of Tartu, Estonia
Matías Recabarren	Universidad de los Andes, Chile
Armanda Rodrigues	Universidade NOVA de Lisboa, Portugal
Flavia Santoro	UERJ, Brazil
Claudio Sapateiro	EST-IPS, Portugal
Hidekazu Shiozawa	Tamagawa University, Japan
João Paulo Pereira Sousa	Polytechnic Institute of Bragança, Portugal
Daniel Spikol	Malmö University, Sweden
Shin Takahashi	University of Tsukuba, Japan
Kentaro Takano	Fuji Xerox Co., Ltd., Japan
Andrea Vasquez	Universidad Técnica Federico Santa María, Chile
Bahtijar Vogel	Malmö University, Sweden

Hao-Chuan Wang   University of California, Davis, USA
Takaya Yuizono   Japan Advanced Institute of Science and Technology,
                            Japan
Alejandro Zunino   UNICEN, Argentina
Gustavo Zurita   Universidad de Chile, Chile

Contents

Work-in-Progress Papers

Full Papers

Developing and Evaluating a Hackathon Approach to Foster Cyber Security Learning

Abasi-amefon O. Affia[1]([⊠]), Alexander Nolte[1,2],
and Raimundas Matulevičius[1]

[1] University of Tartu, Tartu, Estonia
{amefon.affia,alexander.nolte,rma}@ut.ee
[2] Carnegie Mellon University, Pittsburgh, PA, USA

Abstract. Securing information systems and teaching people about how to use them securely is one of the significant challenges of the coming years. There is, however, a considerable lack of feasible approaches to train potential future professionals on security. Hackathons appear to be a good approach because studies have found them to not only be useful to teach participants but also to encourage people to explore the security of information systems. Such benefits cannot materialize without careful planning though. In our paper, we propose and evaluate a set of interventions aimed at fostering security learning amongst hackathon participants. Evaluating our approach, we found that emphasizing the need for idea generation, introducing security talks relevant to the ideas generated, interaction with mentors that come from diverse backgrounds, and the introduction of incentives can encourage security learning among participants.

Keywords: Hackathons · Security learning · Action research

1 Introduction

Technological advancements have led to the ubiquitous availability of data and continue to shape digital innovation [7]. Industry experts predict there will be 6 billion internet users by 2022 [23] and nearly 26 billion connected devices by 2020 [13]. The increase in devices significantly expands the attack surface for malicious actors, who are continually developing more advanced and scale able tools to e.g. access sensitive user data. It is thus critical to educate future professionals that can build secure systems and train users to use these systems securely.

We propose to utilize the hackathon format as a way to raise interest among potential future professionals and spread security knowledge to the larger population. Hackathons are time-bounded events during which participants from diverse backgrounds form teams and work on projects that are of interest to them [26]. Hackathons have previously been utilized as a tool for education and

© Springer Nature Switzerland AG 2020
A. Nolte et al. (Eds.): CollabTech 2020, LNCS 12324, pp. 3–19, 2020.
https://doi.org/10.1007/978-3-030-58157-2_1

learning [16,24,27] and in fact, learning has been cited as one of the key motivations for participants to participate [14]. However, there is a need for a hackathon approach that specifically focuses on improving the level of knowledge among those which build or use IT systems.

While learning can be considered an essential part of every hackathon, prior work provides indication that what organizers want participants to learn at a hackathon can be different from what they actually learn or are interested in learning [22]. It is thus necessarily to design a hackathon approach that specifically focuses on activities related to security learning. Addressing this gap we propose and evaluate a hackathon approach anchored around specific interventions by asking the following two related research questions:

RQ$_1$. *How can different interventions at a hackathon influence informal learning about security in a social context?*

RQ$_2$. *How can these interventions be improved?*

To answer these questions, we conducted an action research study of three teams at a security hackathon. The methods and processes to stimulate security learning were delivered as interventions introduced during the hackathon process. We observed all teams and participants at set intervals during the early, mid, and later phases of the hackathon, administered questionnaires and conducted interviews at the end of the event.

Our results indicate that organising idea generation as a separate event before the hackathon, security talks focused on topics relevant to the hackathon projects, mentor feedback to increase interaction, and a competition style that encourages practising security, foster security learning within the social context of a hackathon.

Our findings thus expand the current body of knowledge related to the use of hackathons as social learning opportunities in a specific context. The contribution of this paper is twofold. First, we developed specific interventions (idea generation, security talks, mentor feedback and competition style) that aim to allow interested individuals to learn more about security (**RQ**$_1$). Second, based on our evaluation of the aforementioned interventions we developed suggestions for how hackathons can serve as a means to teach interested individuals in the social context of a hackathon (**RQ**$_2$).

2   Background

In the following section, we will discuss common design aspects that encourage learning at hackathons (Sect. 2.1) and show the security learning research gaps in prior works on security hackathons (Sect. 2.2). This provides a view into our research contribution.

2.1   Hackathon Design Aspects for Learning

Designing hackathons that foster security learning require careful planning to create an environment suitable for informal learning through problem-solving within the hackathon social context [6]. Participants should be able to gain sufficient knowledge about security to explore and contribute to the development of security projects within the tight time constraints of the hackathon [17]. Here, we discuss design aspects that have been found in literature to foster security learning. We will use them as a basis for interventions discussed in Sect. 3.1.

The early part of each hackathon event is typically devoted to **idea generation**. Ideas proposed should be real-world problems that are aligned to the theme of the event. These ideas form the basis of projects that teams will work on during the event [30]. Idea generation allows participants to involve themselves in self-regulated learning from the investigation of the necessary information, and the pursuit of logical inquiry based on knowledge gained [1]. It is thus crucial for hackathons to start with an open idea generation phase [4] where teams can express and refine ideas.

To encourage security learning by solving security issues, it is necessary to provide participants with both domain-specific knowledge. This can help them to better understand the problem context and develop suitable ideas [30]. **Security talks** at a hackathon can provide participants with an understanding of the security domain and allow them to recognise the need for security within the current advances in information systems. Security talks also provide the opportunity for participants to acquire new information [12] relevant to the security project.

One of most prevalent forms of participant support during a hackathon are mentors which commonly provide on-demand feedback and guidance to teams in need [5,28]. **Mentor feedback** can help teams to scope their projects, provide suggestions about how approach a problem, and help with (technical) problems [20]. Mentorship also allows participants to receive learning-oriented support, especially when mentors perceive their role as that of a traditional (workplace or educational) mentor [24].

Although participation in a hackathon is voluntary, specific incentives can encourage individuals to participate. **Competition style** designs can provide incentives to motivate participants to attempt challenging projects that might even be out of their comfort zone/zone of knowledge [11]. Competition based design promotes active-learning where participants learn something new through problem investigation, reconciling new knowledge gained with experience to solve a given problem [30].

2.2 Related Work

Hackathons are intense, uninterrupted and *time-bounded* events, typically of 2–5 days, during which people gather together and form *collocated teams*, in attempts to complete a *project* of interest [18,25]. Although studies on security hackathons exist, most reports focus only on describing the hackathon event itself. Kharchenko et al. [15] presented a case study collection of different security hackathons carried out to facilitate university-industry cooperation. However, they did not report on an evaluation of how different hackathon activities contributed to security learning. Similarly, the paper by Starov et al. [29], reports on a hackathon where students were provided comprehensive knowledge in a particular course (i.e, security), then participated in an idea generation and prototype development training. The emphasis of this study was on start-up development and establishing communication between university and industry. The study did not contain an evaluation of hackathon design aspects that foster security learning nor of learning objectives to be achieved by the hackathon. Lastly, Foley et al. [10] discuss findings from a science hackathon for researchers. During this event, researchers were able to explain their ongoing research in cyber-physical systems (CPS) security based on a shared CPS test-bed. But, the paper does not report on an evaluation of the design aspects that foster security learning.

Our work is thus different from prior studies on hackathons because we aim to develop and introduce selected design aspects that foster security learning as *interventions* specific to the context of a case security hackathon. We evaluate the security learning outcomes of participants as a result of the introduced design aspects and then identify means for improving them.

3   Empirical Method

To answer our two main research questions ($\mathbf{RQ}_1$, $\mathbf{RQ}_2$), we applied an action research approach [21]. This approach appears reasonable because we developed and evaluated interventions from selected design aspects to foster security learning in a hackathon context ($\mathbf{RQ}_1$) with the aim to improve them ($\mathbf{RQ}_2$). In the following we will outline our interventions (Sect. 3.1) before discussing our data collection and analysis approach (Sects. 3.2 to 3.4) in detail.

3.1   Proposed Interventions to Foster Security Learning

In this section we discuss the specifics of the interventions we developed to foster security learning at a hackathon. These interventions to be introduced to the security hackathon are based on the design aspects previously discussed in Sect. 2.1.

Our **idea generation** intervention consisted of two parts. We conducted a dedicated idea generation event before the main hackathon during which participants could discuss ideas and form teams. The dedicated idea generation event gave participants an opportunity to prepare an idea fully so that the participants (or newly formed team) can focus on the project during the main hackathon. Nonetheless, we also conducted an idea generation session for all participants at the beginning of the main hackathon. This provided another opportunity to facilitate idea generation for both participants of the idea generation events and for participants that only attended the main hackathon. The idea generation session at the main event was set up so that participants from both categories can present their idea proposals and additionally learn from mentor feedback.

We also introduced **security talks** during the main hackathon and during the idea generation events. These covered top security trends in IoT, security risk management, and the general aspects of security learning. The talks were aimed to enable participants learn about basic security concepts and techniques. They were also aimed to inspire participants to reflect on their ideas and provide them with a foundation to scope and attempt their projects.

Mentor feedback was the third intervention we introduced to the hackathon design. Mentors were organised in two ways; mentors assigned to teams based on the team's needs and free-flowing mentors with a broad range of security expertise that provide support for multiple teams. Team interaction with mentors provided participants with the opportunity to gain expert feedback and allowed them to incorporate this feedback into building their security project.

Lastly, in the **competition style** intervention, we gave prizes to teams that were seen to have attempted challenging projects. We set this intervention to motivate participants to learn through security investigations to create unique solutions to security problems.

3.2   Setting

In this section, we outline the context and organisation of the hackathon event and related idea generation events we studied. The events were organised as follows:

We first prepared the designed interventions for the hackathon. We then organised idea generation events, bringing together people from diverse backgrounds to generate ideas that aim at tackling security issues. The main hackathon started with an idea generation session which allowed participants who did not attend the dedicated idea generation hackathon event, the opportunity to propose and refine their security ideas based on mentor feedback. Invited security experts delivered planned security talks as additional resources to aid idea generation. Once the idea generation sessions were completed, the participants formed into teams of 5–8 participants per selected idea and mentors were assigned per team.

Team-assigned mentors interacted with their teams providing guidance and feedback concerning the team's security project and team progress. Free-flowing mentors visited teams based on their need. Mentors also provided input during checkpoint sessions were teams gathered to discuss their project progress. Halfway into the hackathon event, an invited security expert presented another security talk on security risk management to provide the participants with more security considerations when building their projects.

At the end of the hackathon, all teams presented their projects and prototypes for evaluation. The hackathon provided live-streamed presentations of the security projects and prototypes to all interested community members. After evaluation, the judges presented incentives in form of prizes to selected winners.

Figure 1 shows the timeline of the hackathon activities, including intervention preparation, idea generation pre-hackathon events and the hackathon event.

3.3   Data Collection

We selected three teams (denoted as A, B, and C) for our data collection. They were selected was based on their participation in the idea generation pre-hackathon events. The selected team characteristics are summarised in Table 1. For each team we collected observational data, questionnaires, and post-hackathon interviews. We will elaborate on how each data point contributes to answering our main research questions.

Fig. 1. Timeline of the hackathon activities

Table 1. Team characteristics

Team	# Team members	Interview participants	Selection criteria
A	6	A01 (team lead), A02 (lead developer)	No participation in idea generation pre-hackathon event
B	6	B01 (team lead), B02 (security expert and developer)	Participation in idea generation pre-hackathon event and continued with the same idea at hackathon
C	5	C01 (team lead), C02 (developer)	Participation in idea generation pre-hackathon event but did not continue with same idea at hackathon

At the hackathon event, we moved between the teams to observe the participants. The observation method included monitoring at intervals and recording the responses of the participants to the discussed interventions. Reactions such as attentiveness to security talks, positive interactions between teams and mentors reported when discussing with a sample of participants, and perceived satisfaction of participants related to their project indicated reactions to respective interventions. We also recorded other aspects that may contribute to understanding the overall hackathon experience of the participants such as their perception about their teamwork, team process, and their satisfaction with their project.

We did not observe all teams throughout the entire duration of the hackathon as we perceived the early, mid and late phases of the hackathon to be most crucial. We use the recorded observations to evaluate if the participants able to achieve learning gains with the introduced interventions as well as other team aspects ($\mathbf{RQ_1}$).

After the hackathon event, we conducted a post-hackathon questionnaire using pre-existing instruments [2, 8, 9] that we adapted to our hackathon study[1]. The questionnaire covered the participants' perception of learning gains from the interventions, learning benefits from completing the security project. We also recorded participants' perception of specific team properties such as size, team familiarity, leadership, skill diversity, product satisfaction and collaboration process. The aim of the questionnaire was to gain additional context related information that might influence the participants' experience during the event.

From the selected teams, we chose 2 participants per team for an interview to discuss the hackathon experience, learning gains at the hackathon, and the hackathon outcome (i.e., security project worked on). These participants were selected because they either held a vital role in the team (i.e., team lead) or by observation, appeared to contribute significantly to the team.

The interviews lasted between 25 and 30 min. A sample of questions asked during the interviews include;

1. How was the hackathon from your perspective in the form of: What did you do after you arrived? How did you see the event play out?
2. Did you attend the idea generation pre-hackathon event? What idea did you develop? How else did you prepare for this hackathon?
3. What were the outcomes as a result of learning? [mentors, security talks, team members, working on the project]
4. How do you perceive the outcome of the hackathon? Were you satisfied? How did you see your teamwork?
5. Did you discover new security knowledge during the hackathon? How did you discover this?
6. What about the continuity of your project? Have you use anything learned during the hackathon already? Are you planning to use it in the future?

The data from the post-hackathon interviews allowed us to evaluate how the different interventions related to security learning thus enabling us to develop suggestion on how to improve the proposed interventions ($\mathbf{RQ_2}$).

3.4 Analysis Procedure

First, we discuss the journeys of each selected team and the impacts of the introduced interventions on each teams based on a combination of observation, questionnaire, and interview results. The questionnaires are used qualitatively as an additional data source to the analysis procedure.

---

[1] Detailed questionnaire information can be found in https://git.io/Jfp55.

We then compared security learning for the teams using Bloom's taxonomy learning dimensions as a basis [3,19]. Bloom's taxonomy describes levels of learning where each category of *remember, understand, apply, analyze, evaluate,* and *create* form the learning dimensions [3,19]. Our application of Bloom's taxonomy is based on data from team observations. A security expert assessed the learning gains for each team. By comparing the teams journeys, we can analyse how the participants encountered and worked with knowledge provided through the interventions.

Lastly, we evaluated how well the interventions worked for the team participants in encouraging perceived security learning using data from the questionnaires and interviews. This also reveals the shortcomings of the introduced interventions in fostering learning, where we suggest improvements to the interventions.

4   Findings

This section outlines the journeys of each selected team, the perception of each learning intervention for each team, and the differences between teams in relation to their learning process. Data collected about the perception of learning from interventions are illustrated in Fig. 2, while Table 2 shows data about team properties (of size, team familiarity, leadership, skill diversity, collaboration process, and product satisfaction).

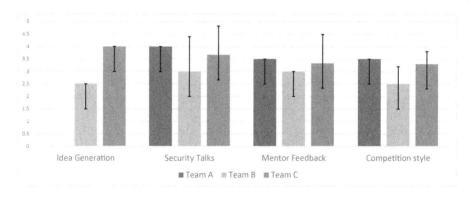

Fig. 2. Questionnaire responses by participants after the hackathon about interventions and satisfaction with learning experience. All responses were given on a 5-point scale which were anchored between strongly disagree (1) and strongly agree (5). The bars indicate the mean (m) and standard deviation (SD) for each team.

4.1   Team A

The leader of team A (A01) proposed the idea for the project in the idea generation session at the main hackathon event. A01 derived the idea from *"a security problem from studies"* (A01) of the hackathon and intended to create a

Table 2. Calculated team property data (means, standard deviations, diversity formula, size count) used in qualitative analysis. Mean and standard deviation values are from responses given on a 5-point scale.

Team property	Team A	Team B	Team C
Size[a]	6	6	5
Team familiarity	$m = 1.1, SD = 0.25$	$m = 4, SD = 0.9$	$m = 1, SD = 0$
Leadership	Yes	Yes	Yes
Skill diversity[b]	0.6	0.7	0.4
Collaboration process	$m = 3.8, SD = 0.3$	$m = 4.5, SD = 0.4$	$m = 4, SD = 0.3$
Product satisfaction	$m = 4, SD = 0.9$	$m = 2.9, SD = 2.1$	$m = 3.5, SD = 0.9$

[a]Reported number of participants in a team.
[b]To estimate skill diversity, we calculated similarities in the reported skills within a team and then determined how different they are (by subtracting the similarity value from one).

tool for enterprises to visualize security aspects. A01 formed a diverse (*0.6*) 6-member team. The team members did not know each other before the hackathon ($m = 1.1, SD = 0.25$). "*Ideation continued during the hackathon because the idea was not properly prepared*" (A01), and completed after discussions in the team and mentor feedback. The idea was refined to "*be targeted at company risk management team to help visualise and communicate security risk scenarios to upper management*" (A01).

At the security talk sessions, team A members reported learning gains from the talks ($m = 4, SD = 0$) and showed an understanding of the security domain while moving forward with the project. A01 highlighted on the "*educating experience about risk management and what is missing in the cybersecurity field*" (A01) presented at the security talks.

During the creation of the final product, A01 highlighted that there was "*support by experienced team members to complete tasks*" for the project. The team leader (A01) fostered learning within the team "*holding everything together, monitoring and identifying the needs of each team members for completing tasks*" (A01). A01 described how teamwork grew and how "*everybody was eager to work and contribute in any way they could*"; "*some team members had no prior experience to security, but they tried to learn and contribute*" (A01). A01 also reported that the team members "*went definitely beyond their current skills*" (A01). The team leader (A01) was involved in "*monitoring and identifying the needs of each team members for completing tasks*", and mentors supported these responsibilities were necessary to adjust scoping of the project. A01 presented updates to the mentors about the project progress, getting feedback from mentors about moving forward to the prototype stage. Talking and interacting with mentors was reported to help the team learn more about security ($m = 3.5, SD = 0.7$).

At the end of the hackathon event, team A presented the security prototype to judges for evaluation. Although team A did not win a prize at the competition, the team members reported, a moderate learning experience from building the final product ($m = 3.3$, $SD = 0.7$) as an impact of the competition style design. But, there was a moderate agreement on the satisfaction with the product outcome ($m = 4$, $SD = 0.9$). A01 expressed that there will be no continuation in the project because *"the market value for this type of project"* (A01) was unclear.

4.2   Team B

The leader of team B (B01) presented an idea developed at the pre-hackathon event. B01 highlights that attending the idea generation event provided *"a lot of support to [my] idea"*. The idea developed was to *"make data security more desirable for startups and give them a badge"* (B01), thereby aiming to improve security learning in startups. B01 presented the idea during the idea pitching session of the hackathon event and received feedback by mentors. After idea generation, B01 reports that team formation was easy. This is because B01 *"was familiar with most of the team because [we] studied together at the university"* (B01) ($m = 4$, $SD = 0.9$). B01 formed a diverse (0.7) 6-member team.

At the security talk sessions, B02 explained that these talks were instrumental as the team *"tried to gather all sorts of information on how to secure systems and gained knowledge"* (B02). Team B members reported security gains from the talks ($m = 3$, $SD = 1.4$). Team B participants reported learning experiences from the mentor feedback ($m = 3$, $SD = 0$) as it provided *"an opportunity for [us] to explain our work progress"* (B02). B02 reported that *"different mentors visited multiple times"*, and that the mentors *"visited to guide completing tasks"* (B02), but B01 reported that the multiple visits *"disrupted the flow of tasks"* (B01). B01 reported that mentors specifically provided feedback on the scoping of the project, and refinement of project content.

During the creation of the final product, the team perceived their collaboration process to be efficient ($m = 4.5$, $SD = 0.4$). B01 mentioned that a *"blackboard equipment for documenting the team's process and ideas, allowing [us] to see the big picture"* (B01), thereby aiding collaboration between members of the team and between the team and visiting mentors. On the impact of competition style of the hackathon on team B, there was a moderate learning experience ($m = 2.5$, $SD = 0.7$) from accomplishing the task of building security content for the prototype.

Towards the end of the hackathon event, Team B pitched their project and presented the prototype for evaluation. Team B won a prize for a unique product developed and its perceived usefulness to the security community. Interestingly, there was a moderate satisfaction with the outcome of the project ($m = 2.9$,

$SD = 2.1$). B01 raised an issue with a team member leaving the team unexpectedly halfway through the hackathon with the resources already gathered by the team. Continuation of the project following the competition style intervention was encouraged by the incentive prize awarded to the team project. Although B01 reported that the team intends to continue with the project, we learned from both B01 and B02 that the provided incentive might not be useful to its continuation.

4.3 Team C

The team lead (C01) pitched an idea during the idea generation session of the hackathon event. Although C01 attended the idea generation pre-hackathon event, the idea pitched at the main hackathon event was different from the one C01 worked on during the pre-hackathon event. C01 pitched the idea to *"create a binary betting platform for smart contracts"* (C01) on a blockchain platform. However, mentors provided feedback that the presented idea did not readily provide a project addressing current security issues and asked C01 to think more about potential security aspects of that idea. C01 formed a less diverse (*0.4*) 5-member team, consisting mainly of developers interested in developing a blockchain-based project.

Once team formation was complete, the participants in team C continued idea refinement with the mentor feedback. C02 stated that the initial idea *"didn't seem like a good idea for a security hackathon, so [we] needed to connect it to a security topic"* (C02). Thus, a new idea was formed based on blockchain, where the team decided on *"an availability insurance smart contract for service providers"* (C02). The team leader (C01) provided progress reports on development to the mentors, who contributed feedback on how to enhance the proposed security prototype. The participants of team C reported learning experience from the provided mentor feedback ($m = 3.33$, $SD = 1.15$). Although there were no individual reports from the participants of team C about learning experiences from the security talk sessions, questionnaires responses from team C participants report learning gains from the security talk intervention ($m = 3.67$, $SD = 1.15$).

The participants in team C report security learning experience by working on project tasks ($m = 3.3$, $SD = 0.5$) such as researching the security aspects of the prototype. The team perceived their collaboration process to be efficient ($m = 4$, $SD = 0.3$). C02 highlighted that this was due to the team's high interest in development using blockchain. Towards the end of the event, Team C pitched the final prototype for evaluation. After evaluation, Team C did not win a prize at the event and reported satisfaction with the outcome of the project ($m = 3.5$, $SD = 0.9$). C02 mentioned that there were no intentions of the participants to continue with the project idea.

4.4   Team Comparison

In this section, we compare the learning gains between the teams A, B and C based on the knowledge of the team's activity, and other observations at the hackathon (see Sect. 3.1). Figure 3 shows the learning gains based on Blooms taxonomy. According to our findings, team B showed the most learning gains followed by team A then team C. In the following, we discuss how the teams were observed to use the different interventions in order to achieve learning gains.

Team A was showed the ability to recognise relevant security knowledge and to provide specific security information gained through the security talks. The study participants (A01, A02) were able to recall the security risk management concepts discussed in the security talks, and discussed about these concepts in relation to their security project. Team B also showed the ability to remember security knowledge from the security talks intervention. B01 presented the security idea of a platform that encourages data security, related to security issues raised in the security talks. Team C participants talked about the availability security aspects of blockchain, recalling knowledge from security talk sessions. Teams A, B, and C thus attained the **remember** process category.

Teams A and B showed the ability not only to remember and recall but interpret and explain security concepts. Team A showed an understanding of security issues from the security talks. This understanding is evident in the generation of a security-relevant idea and discussions with mentors on security issues and their impact in a security risk-aware business environment. Team B showed an understanding of security concepts, evident in the generation of a security-relevant project for the start-up environment. Thus the teams' A and B attained the **understand** process category.

Teams A and B were able to apply the security knowledge gained during the idea generation sessions, following mentor feedback and in the process of building a unique security project. Team A (A01) was able to incorporate feedback from mentors to focus on resources to visualise and communicate security risk scenarios. Team B (B01) was able to apply mentor feedback in defining the security aspects within the life-cycle of target start-ups. Team B also showed the application of security knowledge gained by research on the security aspects within start-up life cycles. Team C participants, in interviews, did not readily show the application of gained security knowledge in its process and blockchain based product. Thus, teams A and B attained the **apply** process.

Teams A, B, and C were given the chance to present their developed security prototypes. However, only team B was able to show how the security knowledge gained through interventions related to the overall purpose and structure of their project. Team B respondents presented an analysis of how the introduction of each intervention affected each task, sub-task or process in the development of the final prototype. The team B achieved the **analyse** process.

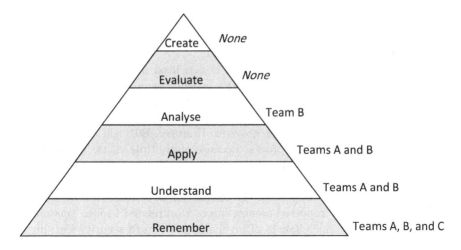

Fig. 3. Team learning comparison

5   Discussion

In this section, we evaluate how the teams A, B, and C benefited from the different proposed interventions. Relating those with the previously discussed differences related to the teams' learning gains allows us to develop improvements for the interventions thus answering $\mathbf{RQ}_2$.

5.1   Evaluation of Interventions

Our findings indicate that Team B benefited the most from the **idea generation** intervention as it was instrumental in creating the security project, and as a result, winning the competition. Of all three teams, team B was able to take the most advantage of this intervention, and having more time to work on their idea, resulted in a more mature security idea they could work on during the main hackathon. Team B reported that this was possible because the team lead (B01) attended the idea generation sessions at the pre-hackathon event and began developing their project idea already then. Although C01 attended the idea generation sessions at the pre-hackathon event, C01 ended up working on a new idea during the main hackathon. Also, none of the participants of team A attended the pre-hackathon event. As such, these teams had fewer chances in involving in as much security learning from idea generation as team B.

Teams A and B benefited most from **security talks** while team C showed little to no benefit according to our findings. This could be because the security talks provided were mainly related to teams A and B's security projects. A01 reported that the security talk on security risk management was relevant to their security risk visualisation project. B01 reported that the security talk on start-up security learning provided the required security knowledge relevant to the team's project. C01 reported that the security talks were not particularly relevant to their blockchain project but were only useful to provide general security knowledge. It thus appears important that talks need to be tailored towards team needs in order to be perceived as useful.

Our findings also indicate that Team B benefited most from the **mentor feedback** intervention in achieving security learning as opposed to other teams. This could be because of the high amount of interaction with diverse mentors. B02 reported that different mentors visited the team at multiple times to provide an expert perspective on work progress. However, B01 said that mentoring became disruptive to the team process because of multiple visits. Teams A and C, showed little benefit from this intervention and did not report as much interaction with diverse mentors as with team B. A01 reported mentor interaction in idea generation and in supporting the completion of set tasks for the security project, while C01 only reported mentor interaction related to idea generation. Thus, reducing the teams' chances of involving in as much security learning as team B. It appears crucial that we should organise mentoring appropriately to ensure an adequate amount of mentor interaction.

Related to the **competition style** intervention, Team B benefited the most. B01 reported that the intervention encouraged rapid knowledge gathering and application of the security knowledge to product creation, thus winning a prize at the hackathon. The perceived benefit could also be as a result of culminating factors including idea generation, team formation, and team properties such as team familiarity, collaboration, satisfaction and leadership, all within the competition constraints. Teams A and C showed little benefit from this intervention. A01 reported that they did not win a prize because too much time was spent on idea generation, causing a race with time to complete the security project adequately. C02 also reported difficulties faced in idea generation.

5.2   Suggestions for Improvement

Based on our analysis we developed the following suggestion to improve the four main interventions introduced in Sect. 3.1 thus answering RQ_2.

Based on our findings, we would suggest supporting teams in **idea generation** to develop ideas before the main event and continue coaching them related to this idea throughout. Changing an idea does not appear to be feasible. For **security talks**, three suggestions can be proposed for future iterations based on our findings. First, the content of the security talks can be more domain-generic. Another option is to appropriately scope the ideas generated at the hackathon to the context of the hackathon. Finally, we develop the security talks only after idea generation is completed, so that the talks are more domain-specific and have maximum effect of offering adequate security knowledge to participants. Based on our findings, we suggest that the **mentor feedback** intervention be handled with excellent coordination not to disrupt the team process. We suggest that a designated member of the team (most likely the team leader) with knowledge of the team's process, stand in between the mentors and the team when necessary, to handle explanations of the teams progress, and what the team needs in mentoring to prevent multiple disruptions.

5.3   Limitations

The aim of our study was to develop and evaluate specific interventions that can foster security learning during a hackathon. While it appeared reasonable to conduct an action research study [21] there are certain limitations associated with this particular study design. We developed specific interventions and studied three teams that participated in a hackathon over a limited period of time that had specific backgrounds and goals for attending the hackathon. Despite selecting teams thoroughly it is not possible to generalize findings beyond our study context since studying a different setting with different teams, during a different hackathon working on different projects might yield different results. Moreover the researchers conducting the study were involved in the planning of the hackathon which can affect the reported findings despite our best efforts to refrain from interfering during the hackathon itself. We also abstained from making causal claims instead providing a rich description of the observed behavior and reported perceptions of teams based on which we discuss differences in how they reacted to the different proposed interventions.

6   Concluding Remarks

In this paper, we reported on findings from an action research study of three teams at a security hackathon. The study aimed to propose and evaluate how specific interventions – namely idea generation, security talks, mentor feedback and a competition-style event – can foster security learning. Our findings indicate that these interventions foster informal learning about security in the social context of a hackathon. Our results also point to suggestions for improvement. These include organising idea generation as a separate event before the hackathon, preparing security talks focused on topics relevant to the hackathon projects, and coordinating mentor feedback to increase mentor-participant interaction.

References

1. Akcay, B.: Problem-based learning in science education. J. Turk. Sci. Educ. **6**(1), 28–38 (2009)
2. Bhattacherjee, A.: Understanding information systems continuance: an expectation-confirmation model. MIS Q. **25**, 351–370 (2001)
3. Bloom, B.S., et al.: Taxonomy of Educational Objectives. vol. 1: Cognitive Domain, pp. 20–24. McKay, New York (1956)
4. Böhmer, A.I., Beckmann, A., Lindemann, U.: Open innovation ecosystem-makerspaces within an agile innovation process. In: ISPIM Innovation Summit (2015)
5. Byrne, J.R., O'Sullivan, K., Sullivan, K.: An IoT and wearable technology hackathon for promoting careers in computer science. IEEE Trans. Educ. **60**(1), 50–58 (2017)
6. Case*, J., Marshall, D.: Between deep and surface: procedural approaches to learning in engineering education contexts. Stud. High. Educ. **29**(5), 605–615 (2004)

7. Davenport, T.H.: Analytics 3.0. Harvard Bus. Rev. **91**(12), 64–72 (2013)
8. van Eemeren, F.H., Garssen, B.: Scrutinizing Argumentation in Practice, vol. 9. John Benjamins Publishing Company, Amsterdam (2015)
9. Filippova, A., Trainer, E., Herbsleb, J.D.: From diversity by numbers to diversity as process: supporting inclusiveness in software development teams with brainstorming. In: 2017 IEEE/ACM 39th International Conference on Software Engineering (ICSE), pp. 152–163. IEEE (2017)
10. Foley, S.N., et al.: Science hackathons for cyberphysical system security research: putting CPS testbed platforms to good use. In: Proceedings of the 2018 Workshop on Cyber-Physical Systems Security and PrivaCy, pp. 102–107. ACM (2018)
11. Grimes, J., Seng, J.: Robotics competition: providing structure, flexibility, and an extensive learning experience. In: 2008 38th Annual Frontiers in Education Conference, pp. F4C–9. IEEE (2008)
12. Horton, M.P.A., Jordan, S., Weiner, S., Lande, M.: Project-based learning among engineering students during short-form hackathon events, vol. 2018. In: ASEE Annual Conference and Exposition, Conference Proceedings (2018)
13. Hung, M.: Leading the IoT, gartner insights on how to lead in a connected world. Gartner Research, pp. 1–29 (2017)
14. Juell-Skielse, G., Hjalmarsson, A., Johannesson, P., Rudmark, D.: Is the public motivated to engage in open data innovation? In: Janssen, M., Scholl, H.J., Wimmer, M.A., Bannister, F. (eds.) EGOV 2014. LNCS, vol. 8653, pp. 277–288. Springer, Heidelberg (2014). https://doi.org/10.1007/978-3-662-44426-9_23
15. Kharchenko, V., Sklyar, V., Brezhnev, E., Boyarchuk, A., Starov, O., Phillips, C.: University-industry cooperation in cyber security domain: multi-model approach tools and cases. In: Proceedings of the University-Industry Interaction Conference: Challenges and Solutions for Fostering Entrepreneurial Universities and Collaborative Innovation, pp. 265–283 (2016)
16. Kienzler, H., Fontanesi, C.: Learning through inquiry: a global health hackathon. Teach. High. Educ. **22**(2), 129–142 (2017)
17. Kollwitz, C., Dinter, B.: What the hack? – Towards a taxonomy of hackathons. In: Hildebrandt, T., van Dongen, B.F., Röglinger, M., Mendling, J. (eds.) BPM 2019. LNCS, vol. 11675, pp. 354–369. Springer, Cham (2019). https://doi.org/10.1007/978-3-030-26619-6_23
18. Komssi, M., Pichlis, D., Raatikainen, M., Kindström, K., Järvinen, J.: What are hackathons for? IEEE Softw. **32**(5), 60–67 (2015)
19. Krathwohl, D.R., Anderson, L.W.: A Taxonomy for Learning, Teaching, and Assessing: A Revision of Bloom's Taxonomy of Educational Objectives. Longman, London (2009)
20. Lara, M., Lockwood, K.: Hackathons as community-based learning: a case study. TechTrends **60**(5), 486–495 (2016). https://doi.org/10.1007/s11528-016-0101-0
21. Lewin, K.: Action research and minority problems. J. Soc. Issues **2**(4), 34–46 (1946)
22. Medina Angarita, M.A., Nolte, A.: Does it matter why we hack?-Exploring the impact of goal alignment in hackathons. In: Proceedings of 17th European Conference on Computer-Supported Cooperative Work. European Society for Socially Embedded Technologies (EUSSET) (2019)
23. Morgan, S.: Humans on the internet will triple from 2015 to 2022 and hit 6 billion. Cybersecurity Ventures, July 2019. https://cybersecurityventures.com/how-many-internet-users-will-the-world-have-in-2022-and-in-2030/
24. Nolte, A., Hayden, L.B., Herbsleb, J.D.: How to support newcomers in scientific hackathons - an action research study on expert mentoring. Proc. ACM Hum. Comput. Interact. **4**(CSCW1), 23 (2020). Article 25

25. Nolte, A., Pe-Than, E.P.P., Filippova, A., Bird, C., Scallen, S., Herbsleb, J.D.: You hacked and now what?:-Exploring outcomes of a corporate hackathon. Proc. ACM Hum. Comput. Interact. **2**(CSCW), 129 (2018)
26. Pe-Than, E.P.P., Nolte, A., Filippova, A., Bird, C., Scallen, S., Herbsleb, J.D.: Designing corporate hackathons with a purpose: the future of software development. IEEE Softw. **36**(1), 15–22 (2018)
27. Porras, J., Knutas, A., Ikonen, J., Happonen, A., Khakurel, J., Herala, A.: Code camps and hackathons in education-literature review and lessons learned. In: Proceedings of the 52nd Hawaii International Conference on System Sciences (2019)
28. Soltani, P.M., Pessi, K., Ahlin, K., Wernered, I.: Hackathon: a method for digital innovative success: a comparative descriptive study. In: Proceedings of the 8th European Conference on IS Management and Evaluation, pp. 367–373 (2014)
29. Starov, O., Kharchenko, V., Sklyar, V., Phillips, C.: Hacking the innovations with university-industry hackathons. In: Academic Proceedings 2015 University-Industry Interaction Conference UIIC 2015, pp. 47–61 (2015)
30. Stoyanov, S., Kirschner, P.: Effect of problem solving support and cognitive styles on idea generation: implications for technology-enhanced learning. J. Res. Technol. Educ. **40**(1), 49–63 (2007)

Augmenting the Human-Robot Communication Channel in Shared Task Environments

Alexander Arntz[1(✉)], Sabrina C. Eimler[1], and H. Ulrich Hoppe[2]

[1] Institute of Computer Sciences, University of Applied Sciences Ruhr West,
Bottrop, Germany
{alexander.arntz,sabrina.eimler}@hs-ruhrwest.de
[2] Department of Computer Science and Applied Cognitive Science,
University of Duisburg-Essen, Duisburg, Germany
hoppe@collide.info

Abstract. Adaptive robots that collaborate with humans in shared task environments are expected to enhance production efficiency and flexibility in a near future. In this context, the question of acceptance of such a collaboration by human workers is essential for a successful implementation. Augmenting the robot-to-human communication channel with situation-specific and explanatory information might increase the workers' willingness to collaborate with artificial counterparts, as a robot that provides guidance and explanation might be perceived as more cooperative in a social sense. However, the effects of using different augmentation strategies and parameters have not yet been sufficiently explored. This paper examines the usage of augmenting industrial robots involved in shared task environments by conducting an evaluation in a virtual reality (VR) setting. The results provide a first step towards an iterative design process aiming to facilitate and enhance the collaboration between human's and robot's in industrial contexts.

Keywords: Human-Robot Collaboration · Virtual reality · Augmentation · Shared task

1 Introduction

Human-Robot Collaboration (HRC) is a promising approach for future industrial production [6] with settings in which human workers and robots work together to achieve a common goal, e.g. an assembling task. The idea is to make production cycles more adaptive, as HRC combines the precision and endurance of industrial robots with the intuition and experience-based decision-making of human workers [22]. While current implementations of this concept delegate the control over the robot to the employee, it is anticipated that robots will be able to act in more adaptive and autonomous ways. This shifts the working relationship from the human operating the robot as a tool, to a shared task

A. Nolte et al. (Eds.): CollabTech 2020, LNCS 12324, pp. 20–34, 2020.
https://doi.org/10.1007/978-3-030-58157-2_2

environment where both parties act collaboratively and contribute specialized skills [8]. However, there are currently no established concepts how these shared task environments involving autonomous robots can be augmented to ensure the acceptance and willingness to collaborate with them. It is assumed that a robot augmented with the capabilities to explain its actions and guide through objectives can diminish the level of uncertainty and contribute to the prevention of stress [23]. Results from a preceding study revealed three augmentation channels desired by the participants: Text-panel, light signals and gestures. Related studies omit the aspect of augmentation channels to inform the human about its characteristics [21,25] and an effective concept to reduce the occurrence of uncertainty and subsequently stress has yet to be explored. This paper evaluated the implementation of augmentation channels for communicating the behavior of an autonomous robot in an authentic VR simulated shared task environment to explore its effects on stress, emotion, presence and acceptance.

1.1 Shared Tasks in Virtual Reality

Involving autonomously acting and adapting robots in a real world shared task environment requires the elaboration of setups that consider restrictive safety precautions to prevent potential harm for participants. The usage of VR provides an alternative approach for evaluating these scenarios as a risk free and cost effective setup in which every parameter can be adjusted to fit the context. Due to this, evaluations involving shared task environments with robots can be standardized in their procedure while monitoring and recording data. Therefore, a VR simulated HRC-centered work-place was created allowing the exploration of human behavior towards collaborative robots and (dis)advantages of certain workplace arrangements in a controlled and replicable setup. Virtual reality has been used in research of industrial working arrangements [21,24], as it allows the representation of any environment, object or context. Nevertheless, the usage of VR in experimental studies requires an appropriate implementation of the interaction and locomotion mechanics as well as a sufficient visual quality to ensure the immersion of the participants, which is necessary to receive accurate behavioral data. To ensure this, the application utilized in this experimental study, used the established recommendations and guidelines for VR.

2   Related Work

Studies investigating the collaboration between human individuals have identified group cognition as an essential criterion for success [13]. The term, proposed by Wegner [34], describes a transactive memory system that contains the shared and organized knowledge of a group of collaborating individuals. Research indicates [29] that the formation of a common mental model, developed through exchange of information, can reduce uncertainty in the decision-making process, as it improves the understanding of individual roles, responsibilities and task distribution [5]. Additionally, findings indicate that the insufficient or inappropriate addressing of information in a collaborative context reduces the likelihood of comprehension about the current context of the task or situation [10], leading to an increased mental workload that can be perceived as stress [1]. Applied to the human-robot interaction, the necessity to explain the robot's current behavior to the human in order to establish a mental model has been recognized [16]. This is amplified when the interaction is conducted with a robot of non-anthropomorphic appearance [11]. Most applications involving automation related shared task environments will make use of industrial robots following an expedient non-anthropomorphic design, so that the individual's ability to recognize the robot's agency becomes more important. This is reinforced by participants' interview statements in a preceding study, suggesting that augmentations by interfaces providing guidance and explanation of the robot's behavior might mitigate stress. Actions of the robot might become more predictable and allow the human to intervene accordingly to ensure accomplishing the goal of the shared task [2]. The robot's ability to provide explanation and guidance is not only beneficial for conveying its current behavior, research exploring human-robot interaction indicates that it also lowers the barrier for individuals to perceive it as a social presence [15]. The social presence has been identified as a direct contributor to a person's enjoyment of interacting with a robot. The experience of less stress, combined with the increased likelihood of perceived social presence should lead to more positive emotions or lower levels of negative emotions (frustration, insecurity) evoked by the robot respectively.

Working steps that are processed in shared task environments can be either divided, overlapping or interdependent, resulting in the human employee to relying on the capabilities of the robot partner for a successful completion. This dependency forms a social structure, which can be either be accepted or rejected by the human. Prior research has shown the influence of the robot's presence for human willingness to interact with it in social contexts [4]. Presence in this context is defined as the "sense of being with another" [28] and, according to Biocca, manifests itself as "the access to the intelligence, intentions, and sensory impressions of another" [7]. While the robot's presence is determined by several factors, its representation mediated through behavior and appearance contributes the most. Non-anthropomorphic designs commonly found in HRC related industrial environments evoke less presence than their anthropomorphic counterparts [17]. However, it has been shown that the influence of physical appearance is mitigated when personified communication channels are applied, as even systems without physical manifestation can be perceived as a social actor [26]. However, the influence of augmentation with explanation and guidance capabilities in shared task environments has yet to be explored.

2.1 Hypotheses and Research Question

To further explore the effect of explanatory and guiding augmentation in shared task environments with non-anthropomorphic robots, the following hypotheses and research question were formed:

- **H1:** The shared task procedure involving the augmented robot-arm is perceived as less stress inducing compared to the condition without augmentation.

– **H2:** The shared task with the augmented robot-arm evokes more positively associated emotions compared to the condition without augmentation.
– **H3:** The augmentation with explanation and guidance channels increase the (social) presence of a robot-arm deployed in a shared task environment.

3   The VR Implementation

The VR-application that serves for the conducted experiment was developed with the goal to replicate a HRC centric workplace as close as possible. It is based on arrangements found in the industry, scientific articles [30] as well as findings acquired in a preceding study [2]. Remarks made by various representatives of enterprises that either use or anticipate to use HRC work-spaces were also incorporated into the design of the environment, i.e. the arrangement of the robot-arm or the ambient soundscape. The VR-application was rendered on an Oculus Rift S and developed with Unity 3D (2018.4.11f1). The robot-arm for the collaboration with the participants was represented by the virtual recreation of a LBR iiwa 7 R800 CR. The behaviour of the robot-arm was determined by an implementation of the Unity Machine Learning-Agents Toolkit, enabling the execution of the work procedure and adaptation to the participant's actions with appropriate reactions in accordance with the ISO TS 15066 guidelines for collaborative robots. Apart from adjusting to the individual work-pace of the participant, this included safety precautions, such as the detection of imminent collisions with the virtual hands of the participant, which resulted in the robot-arm either slowing down and adapt its movement to avoid a potential collision. If the collision is deemed unavoidable, the robot-arm will cease its current motion to protect its human collaboration partner. Although the protection of the human partner is regarded as the highest priority, the latter option is only considered if no alternative evasion is possible. This was implemented to mimic the desire to prevent unnecessary wear on the axis of real industrial robots, due to absorbing the momentum of sudden deceleration. This adaptive movement system prevented the usage of predefined animations, instead the robot-arm used an inverse kinematic system and was able to conduct every action of its real counterpart in terms of speed and movement in seven degrees of freedom, enabling an authentic depiction in virtual reality.

3.1   The Shared Task

The task to be performed in collaboration with the robot-arm involved the manufacturing of pin-back buttons through a Badgematic Flexi Type 900 (59 mm) Button-press, which was accurately recreated for VR in terms of scale and interactive functionality (Fig. 1). This setup provided a shared task that demanded the coordination between the participant and the robot with distinguished roles as well as an inter-dependency for both parties on each other to accomplish the objective. Simultaneously the relative simplicity of the task allowed even participant's without prior knowledge to establish a workflow based on the guidance

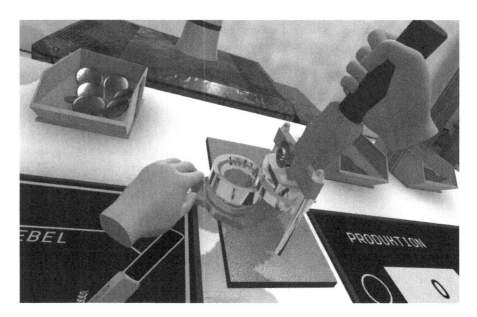

Fig. 1. The Badgematic button-press Flexi Type 900 (59 mm) that was used as the basis for the collaboration task

Fig. 2. The robot-arm extracts a component from one of the storage container while stating: "I pick up the first component"

provided by the robot's augmentation channel. The assembling process of the pin-back buttons itself required nine individual working steps (Table 1), which are divided in five procedures executed by the participants and four by the autonomously working robot-arm (Fig. 2).

Table 1. The collaboration procedure used in the experimental setup.

Working procedure of the participant	Work step
Participant rotate and lock the press platform	2
Participant operate the press lever	3
Participant rotate and lock the press platform	6
Participant operate the press lever	7
Participant rotate and lock the press platform	9
Working procedure of the robot-arm	**Work step**
Robot extract component 1 from its container and inserts into the press	1
Robot extract component 2 from its container and inserts into the press	4
Robot extract component 3 from its container and inserts into the press	5
Robot extract product from the press into the designated container	8

3.2   Augmentation Channels of the Robot-Arm

To explain its actions and provide guidance to the participants, the robot-arm was equipped with three communication interfaces: A text-panel, light-signals and gestures. All three augmentation channels were implemented based on findings from a prior study [2] (Fig. 3(a)). The primary channel was a text-panel, serving both as medium for the robot-arm to explain its actions as well as to provide guidance for the collaboration partner regarding the working procedure. The statements were phrased as a text in natural language, e.g. "I'm gonna put component two in the press now". This implementation follows the recommendations stated in the Guidelines for Human-AI Interaction and allowed the robot-arm to express a variety of comprehensible context-based statements. The phrasing in first-person form was derived from the speech pattern of several voice assistants, such as Amazon Alexa, emulating a personality to reinforce the social presence of the robot-arm. The display containing the text-panel was placed directly in front of the robot to strengthen the association of the statements to the robot-arm. This was emphasized through an illustration of the robot-arm adjacent to a speech-bubble, containing the text-messages (Fig. 3(b)). An additional display was placed right next to button-press, indicating warning signs for imminent collision (Fig. 4(a)) or movement (Fig. 4(b)) and production related information such as production output and remaining time. To complement the augmentation of the display, the robot-arm was equipped with light-signals. Besides being a frequently requested communication method by individuals participating in a preceding study [2], light-signal see usage in almost every industrial environment, e.g. as lamps that light up in case of malfunctions or warnings. These light-signals can be found as augmentation in vicinity of real industrial robots as well, explaining the state of the robot at a glance. A green light indicates that the robot is ready for operation, whereas a red light indicates possible malfunctions. This concept was projected onto the robot-arm which signalled a green light (Fig. 5(a)) when operational for the next task and red (Fig. 5(b)) if the robot detected an imminent collision or error in the working procedure (Fig. 4). Another augmentation, that enabled the robot-arm to explain itself, was the usage of three gestures: standby, action initiating, action termination. The design of gestures followed recommendations stated by [12], after a first self designed implementation was rated to ambiguous by participants [2]. The standby gesture made the robot-arm take a retracted posture, signaling the human collaboration partner that the robot-arm has accomplished its previous task and is now awaiting the human to proceed. In case the human partner ceases to continue the procedure, the robot-arm conducts an action initiating gesture and points towards the object that is required to be operated for the next working step. The opposite of this is an action terminating gesture, in which the robot-arm rotates its head joint to mimic a negating hand gesture with its clamps. These gestures were absent in the condition with no augmentation, in which the robot-arm merely moved and took an arbitrary position based on calculations of the inverse kinematic for the current task instead. The purpose of the gestures was to enable the robot-arm to fit its movement in accordance to social norms, regarding personal space and conformity [19], preventing abrupt movement that was deemed threatening in a prior rendition.

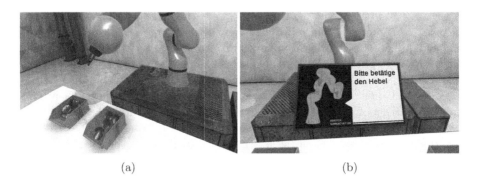

(a)   (b)

Fig. 3. A comparison between the two conditions: (a) The robot-arm without augmentation, (b) The guidance provided by the robot-arm: please use the lever!

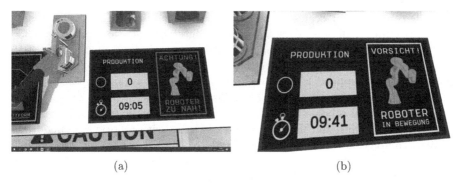

(a)   (b)

Fig. 4. Display with additional explanation: (a) Attention! Robot too close, (b) Caution! Robot is moving

(a)   (b)

Fig. 5. The light-signal on the robot-arm: (a) green for operational, (b) red for collision or malfunction (Color figure online)

4 Evaluation

In an experiment, reactions by participants and the evaluation of the augmented, adaptive version of the robot-arm, were compared with a non-augmented, adaptive version of the robot-arm. Participants were tasked to assemble pin-back button components in collaboration with the robot-arm. In the experimental condition the robot-arm was augmented with a text-panel, light signals, and gestures, giving guidance and explanations to the human collaboration partner about its actions, whereas in the second condition, the communicative augmentation of the robot was absent.

4.1 Measures and Procedure

Participants were invited to take part in a lab experiment. Upon arrival, they signed an informed-consent declaration after going through a briefing about the experiments' purpose. Participants were then asked to fill in the a pre-questionnaire including the Negative Attitudes Towards Robots Scale [27].

The scale contains 3 subscales measured on a 7-point Likert scale (1 = strongly agree, 7 = strongly disagree): "situations and interactions" (5 items, α = .633; e.g. "I would feel nervous operating a robot in front of other people."), "social influence" (5 items; α = .781; "I feel that if I depend on robots too much, something bad might happen."); "emotions in interaction" (3 items; α = .859; e.g. "I feel comforted being with robots that have emotions."). Since prior experience with industrial robots showed to be important in other studies, it was also assessed with 1 item here ("Do you have experience with robotic systems").

After completion, they were introduced to the VR-hardware: The industrial environment with the robot-arm absent was loaded to allow participants a first orientation in the virtual environment and get accommodated to the VR-experience. The scene switched then to the work bench with the robot-arm, which began the procedure at participant's will.

Once the collaboration task was finished, the experimental supervisor released the participant from the VR-hardware and promoted him/her to proceed to the post-questionnaire. The post-questionnaire contained Cohen's Perceived Stress Scale (10 items; α = 0.827) [9] (H1). Participants rated their emotional state using the respective question on the intensity of their frustration ("How insecure, discouraged, irritated, stressed, and annoyed were you?") from the NASA Task Load Index (H2) after they were exposed to the shared task scenario (H2) [14].

To evaluate the robot's presence in a the "sense of being there" (H3), 14 items from the Witmer and Singer's Presence Scale were used [35]. Using a 5-point Likert scale (1 = does not apply at all, 5 = does apply completely), the scale asks into different aspects of presence, e.g. realism, possibility to act, quality of interface and possibility to examine (α = .636). Social presence, in the sense of "being with one another" (H3) was operationalized by self-constructed items assessing participants' evaluation of the quality of the augmentation channels (4 items, α = .853; e.g. "The robot's light-signals were...") and mutuality in interaction (3 items; α = .836). All items were measured on a 5-point Likert scale (1 = very bad; 5= very good).

The experiment closed with a short debriefing that provided participants with additional information regarding the study and thanked them for their participation.

4.2 Results

The sample consisted of N = 80 (40 female), with 40 participants assigned to each of the two conditions. Both conditions consisted of 20 male and 20 female participants. On average, participants were 25 years old (M = 25.31, SD = 6.1). The majority of participants were students from the University of Applied Sciences Ruhr West, 6 of them received course credit for participating in the study. Data were analyzed using SPSS by IBM.

In order to test whether the participants allocated into the different experimental conditions differed in their attitude towards robots before taking the experiment, a t-test was used to investigate the difference in Negative Attitude

Towards Robots. No significant difference was found. Also, participants in the conditions did not report significantly different levels of prior experience with robots.

Hypothesis 1: The shared task procedure involving the augmented robot-arm is perceived as less stress inducing compared to the condition without augmentation.

In order to test H1, an ANCOVA was conducted, using the conditions as independent variable, the Perceived Stress Scale as dependent variable and the mutuality and communication quality as covariates. Significant differences between the conditions emerged ($F(3,78) = 14.93$, $p < 0.01$, $\eta_p^2 = 0.37$), showing that in the augmented condition ($M = 2.15$, $SD = 0.70$) participants experienced less stress than in the non-augmented condition ($M = 2.86$, $SD = 0.6$). Thus, H1 is supported.

Hypothesis 2: The shared task with the augmented robot-arm evokes more positively associated emotions compared to the condition without augmentation.

To investigate H2, the difference between the conditions regarding the frustration (i.e. insecure, discouraged, irritated, stressed, and annoyed) after collaborating with the system was calculated in a t-test. This revealed significant differences $t(78) = -3.396$, $p = .001$), indicating more negative emotions after being exposed to the robot-arm without augmentation ($M = 9.9$, $SD = 5.28$), compared to the augmented condition ($M = 6.05$, $SD = 4.85$). Thus H2 is supported.

Hypothesis 3: Does the augmentation with explanation and guidance channels increase the (social) presence of a robot-arm deployed in a shared task environment?

An ANOVA showed that presence in the "sense of being there" in the environment differed significantly between the conditions ($F(1,37) = 6.07$, $p < 0.02$, $\eta_p^2 = 0.08$). The feeling of presence was higher in the condition with the augmented robot-arm ($M = 4.73$, $SD = 0.55$) compared to the robot-arm without augmentation ($M = 4.34$, $SD = 0.66$). To explore potential differences in the social presence feeling ("sense of being with another"), a MANOVA was conducted including the conditions as independent and perceived quality of communication and mutuality in interaction as dependent variables. The perceived quality of communication differed significantly between the conditions ($F(1,77) = 55.06$, $p < 0.01$, $\eta_p^2 = 0.41$)) and was higher in the augmented version ($M = 3.86$, $SD = 0.65$) compared to condition without augmentation ($M = 2.54$, $SD = 0.91$). Also, mutuality was perceived significantly different ($F(1,77) = 14.41$, $p < 0.01$ $\eta_p^2 = 0.16$) and higher in the condition with the augmented interaction ($M = 4.89$, $SD = 1.3$) than without ($M = 3.74$, $SD = 1.39$). Thus, H3 is supported.

5 Discussion

The importance of communication in collaboration setups between human individuals is already established [33]. This experimental study explores the influence of communicative augmentation in HRC. Results indicate that communication in this context is essential as well and can lead to an increased (social) presence in interacting with the robot-arm, a less stressful working experience and more positive emotions. This can be attributed to the robot-arm informing its intention unambiguously coded via multiple channels, thus supporting the formation of a clear mental model in the recipient [32]. The latter is then able to process the situation and can adapt to the working step conducted by the robot-arm. In contrast, participants of the condition without the augmentation were left to their own interpretation of the situation, due to the lack of the communication interface. This introduces a level of uncertainty into the collaboration process that can lead to stress. Since the majority of participants had no previous experience with industrial-robots, let alone HRC, which might lead to a longer learning process on the capabilities of the robot-arm and the procedure. It can be argued that this delayed or, in some cases, prevented the emergence of a work-flow, resulting in the likelihood of unpleasant feelings and a lower willingness to collaborate with the robot-arm. This coincides with the qualitative data reported in an adjacent study [2]. Although it can be argued that the differences between the conditions are due to the first exposure to a robot-arm, thus denying the necessity of augmentation in HRC for skilled workers in a corresponding situation. Despite the building of a working routine in learned working procedures certainly will help to estimate the behavior of a collaborative robot, the use of AI techniques for adaptation introduces an element of unpredictability. Although more presence was attributed to the robot, the additional layer of presence from the virtual reality has to be considered. Especially novice users tend to experience a greater sense of presence during their first exposure, independent of the content. However, both groups were comparable in their prior experience with VR-devices and participants still attributed more presence in the augmented condition. While an argument can be made that the effects are caused by the selected conditions representing two opposite extremes (all vs. none) of a spectrum of gradual augmentation, it is to mention that the current guidelines used in HRC environments dictate the usage of warning and information channels that are coded through multiple channels [18]. However, a more granular approach, testing the augmentation step wise, could be of interest in future studies. The current guidelines might adjust with technological progress as the introduction of artificial intelligence should equip robots deployed in shared task environments with sophisticated safety procedures, making current regulations obsolete. All in all, future studies will also need to explore long-term effects, e.g. whether workers will get used to text panels, light signals and gestures and might disregard them.

5.1 Limitations

Finally, some limitations need to be mentioned. While a great effort was made, to create an authentic virtual application for the HRC setup, its simulation is only an approximation of a real industrial collaboration scenario. However, related studies made use of virtual simulations in similar cases [21]. Research in the tradition of the Media Equation Theory allows the assumption that humans respond to virtual environments in a way that is comparable to real life situations [31]. Also, VR is accepted as a tool to assess participants' reactions and emotions by exposing them to simulated scenarios [3]. The task used in the experimental study can be seen as a limitation as well, considering that it does not represent a procedure found in a real industrial context. Although, this task is not applicable to all aspects found in shared task environments, alternative considerations, e.g. the assembly of a spring-loaded safety valve, based on the API 526 series [20], have shown to be too complex for many people as they require too much previous knowledge and therefore are not suitable for a first approach of this kind. To get a general evaluation of the collaboration with the augmented robot-arm, a task was selected that allowed the participation of individuals regardless of expertise. This approach can be found in other HRC related studies as well [25]. Another limitation is the composition of the sample. Since most participants were students at the University of Applied Sciences Ruhr West, an affinity towards engineering can be assumed that might be higher than that of the general population. Although these students are currently not occupied in industries prone for HRC, some of them are likely to become exposed to HRC in the future or to be active in designing such scenarios. This makes it valuable to collect their assessment for the design of upcoming HRC setups, to meet the expectations towards such systems.

6   Conclusion

The augmentation of industrial production processes with digital systems is in full motion. It is expected that this will have a major influence on the workforce, as it is not only introducing new production processes but also new concepts of how employees interact with machinery such as robots. Through continuous advancements in artificial intelligence, the concept of equal collaboration between human workers and robotic entities is not some far-fetched vision of the future anymore. The results support the necessity for augmentation with communication channels in these adaptive HRC setups, as they allow for a decreased perceived stress and frustration when collaborating with the robot and contribute to the feeling of working together with the robotic collaboration partner. The implication for the industry is to design future work-arrangements involving HRC with communication based augmentation in mind. Future studies will need to explore further augmentation methods, levels and modalities of augmentation and their influence on productivity and safety. This will contribute to an integrative iterative design process, with the goal to reduce unfit work-place arrangements involving HRC in future production processes.

Acknowledgments. Many thanks go to Dustin Keßler, Dr. Carolin Straßmann, Nele Borgert, Dr. Laura Hoffmann and Sarah Zielinski for their advice, comments to the manuscript and encouragement while conducting this study. Additional thanks go to Dr. Ioannis Iossifidis, Sebastian Doliwa, Mehdi Cherbib, Clarissa Arlinghaus, Stefan Sommer and to all participants contributing to the study as well as to the reviewers.

References

1. Alsuraykh, N.H., Wilson, M.L., Tennent, P., Sharples, S.: How stress and mental workload are connected. In: Mayora, O., Forti, S., Meyer, J., Mamykina, L. (eds.) Proceedings of the 13th EAI International Conference on Pervasive Computing Technologies for Healthcare, pp. 371–376. ACM, New York (2019). https://doi.org/10.1145/3329189.3329235
2. Arntz, A., Eimler, S.C.: Experiencing AI in VR: a qualitative study on designing a human-machine collaboration scenario. In: HCI INTERNATIONAL 2020–22nd International Conference on Human-Computer Interaction, Copenhagen, Denmark (2020)
3. Bailenson, J., Blascovich, J., Beall, A.: Interpersonal distance in immersive virtual environments. Pers. Soc. Psychol. Bull. **29**, 819–833 (2003). https://doi.org/10.1177/0146167203029007002 10.1177/0146167203029007002
4. Bainbridge, W., Hart, J., Kim, E., Scassellati, B.: The effect of presence on human-robot interaction, pp. 701–706 (2008). https://doi.org/10.1109/ROMAN.2008.4600749
5. Banks, A., Millward, L.: Distributed mental models: mental models in distributed cognitive systems. J. Mind Behav. **30**, 249–266 (2009)
6. Bauer, A., Wollherr, D., Buss, M.: Human-robot collaboration: a survey. Int. J. Humanoid Rob. **5**, 47–66 (2008). https://doi.org/10.1142/S0219843608001303
7. Biocca, F.: The cyborg's dilemma: progressive embodiment in virtual environments [1]. J. Comput.-Mediated Commun. **3**(2) (1997). https://doi.org/10.1111/j.1083-6101.1997.tb00070.x
8. Bruemmer, D.J., Few, D.A., Boring, R.L., Marble, J.L., Walton, M.C., Nielsen, C.W.: Shared understanding for collaborative control. IEEE Trans. Syst. Man Cybern. Part A Syst. Hum. **35**(4), 494–504 (2005). https://doi.org/10.1109/TSMCA.2005.850599
9. Chan, S.F., La Greca, A.M.: Perceived stress scale (PSS). In: Gellman, M.D., Turner, J.R. (eds.) Encyclopedia of Behavioral Medicine, pp. 1454–1455. Springer, New York (2013). https://doi.org/10.1007/978-1-4419-1005-9_773
10. Cramton, C.D.: The mutual knowledge problem and its consequences for dispersed collaboration. Organ. Sci. **12**(3), 346–371 (2001). https://doi.org/10.1287/orsc.12.3.346.10098
11. Daugherty, P.R., Wilson, H.J.: Human + Machine: Reimagining Work in the Age of AI. Harvard Business Review Press, La Vergne (2018). https://ebookcentral.proquest.com/lib/gbv/detail.action?docID=5180063
12. Ende, T., Haddadin, S., Parusel, S., Wüsthoff, T., Hassenzahl, M., Albu-Schäeffer, A.: A human-centered approach to robot gesture based communication within collaborative working processes, pp. 3367–3374, September 2011. https://doi.org/10.1109/IROS.2011.6094592
13. Grand, J.A., Braun, M.T., Kuljanin, G., Kozlowski, S.W.J., Chao, G.T.: The dynamics of team cognition: a process-oriented theory of knowledge emergence in teams. J. Appl. Psychol. **101**(10), 1353–1385 (2016). https://doi.org/10.1037/apl0000136
14. Hart, S.G., Staveland, L.E.: Development of NASA-TLX (task load index): results of empirical and theoretical research. In: Human Mental Workload, Advances in Psychology, vol. 52, pp. 139–183. Elsevier (1988). https://doi.org/10.1016/S0166-4115(08)62386-9

15. Heerink, M., Krose, B., Evers, V., Wielinga, B.: Influence of social presence on acceptance of an assistive social robot and screen agent by elderly users. Adv. Robot. **23**, 1909–1923 (2009). https://doi.org/10.1163/016918609X12518783330289
16. Hellström, T., Bensch, S.: Understandable robots. Paladyn J. Behav. Robot. **9**, 110–123 (2018). https://doi.org/10.1515/pjbr-2018-0009
17. Hoffman, G., et al.: Robot presence and human honesty: experimental evidence, vol. 2015, March 2015. https://doi.org/10.1145/2696454.2696487
18. ISO: Iso 10218–1:2011 (2011). https://www.iso.org/standard/51330.html. Accessed 13 Mar 2020
19. Koay, K.L., et al.: Initial design, implementation and technical evaluation of a context-aware proxemics planner for a social robot. In: Kheddar, A., et al. (eds.) Social Robotics. Lecture Notes in Computer Science, vol. 10652, pp. 12–22. Springer, Cham (2017). https://doi.org/10.1007/978-3-319-70022-9_2
20. Leser: Safety valve (2020). https://www.leser.com/de-de/produkte/api/type-526/. Accessed 28 Mar 2020
21. Matsas, E., Vosniakos, G.-C.: Design of a virtual reality training system for human–robot collaboration in manufacturing tasks. Int. J. Interact. Des. Manuf. (IJIDeM) **11**(2), 139–153 (2015). https://doi.org/10.1007/s12008-015-0259-2
22. Müller-Abdelrazeq, S.L., Schönefeld, K., Haberstroh, M., Hees, F.: Interacting with collaborative robots—a study on attitudes and acceptance in industrial contexts. In: Korn, O. (ed.) Social Robots: Technological, Societal and Ethical Aspects of Human-Robot Interaction. HIS, pp. 101–117. Springer, Cham (2019). https://doi.org/10.1007/978-3-030-17107-0_6
23. Mumm, J., Mutlu, B.: Human-robot proxemics. In: Billard, A., Kahn, P., Adams, J.A., Trafton, G. (eds.) Proceedings of the 6th international conference on Human-robot interaction - HRI 2011, p. 331. ACM Press, New York (2011). https://doi.org/10.1145/1957656.1957786
24. Müller, S.L., Schröder, S., Jeschke, S., Richert, A.: Design of a robotic workmate. In: Duffy, V.G. (ed.) DHM 2017. LNCS, vol. 10286, pp. 447–456. Springer, Cham (2017). https://doi.org/10.1007/978-3-319-58463-8_37
25. Müller-Abdelrazeq, S.L., Stiehm, S., Haberstroh, M., Hees, F.: Perceived effects of cycle time in human-robot-interaction. In: 2018 IEEE Workshop on Advanced Robotics and its Social Impacts (ARSO), pp. 25–30. IEEE (27092018–29092018). https://doi.org/10.1109/ARSO.2018.8625819
26. Nijholt, A.: Disappearing computers, social actors and embodied agents. In: Sourin, A., Soon, S.H., Kunii, T. (eds.) 2003 International Conference on Cyberworlds, pp. 128–134. IEEE Computer Society, Los Alamitos (2003). https://doi.org/10.1109/CYBER.2003.1253445
27. Nomura, T., Suzuki, T., Kanda, T., Kato, K.: Measurement of negative attitudes toward robots. Interact. Stud. **7**(3), 437–454 (2006)
28. Oh, C.S., Bailenson, J.N., Welch, G.F.: A systematic review of social presence: definition, antecedents, and implications. Front. Robot. AI **5** (2018). https://doi.org/10.3389/frobt.2018.00114
29. Peltokorpi, V., Hood, A.C.: Communication in theory and research on transactive memory systems: a literature review. Top. Cogn. Sci. **11**(4), 644–667 (2019). https://doi.org/10.1111/tops.12359
30. Philipsen, M., Rehm, M., Moeslund, T.: Industrial human-robot collaboration, pp. 35–38, July 2018. https://doi.org/10.21437/AI-MHRI.2018-9

31. Reeves, B., Nass, C.: The Media Equation: How People Treat Computers, Television, and New Media Like Real People and PLA. Bibliovault OAI Repository. The University of Chicago Press, Chicago (1996)

32. Schmidtler, J., Hoelzel, C., Knott, V., Bengler, K.: Human centered assistance applications for production. In: 5th International Conference on Applied Human Factors and Ergonomics, Krakow, Poland, July 2014. https://doi.org/10.13140/RG.2.1.1608.7203

33. Shah, J., Wiken, J., Williams, B., Breazeal, C.: Improved human-robot team performance using chaski, a human-inspired plan execution system. In: Billard, A., Kahn, P., Adams, J.A., Trafton, G. (eds.) Proceedings of the 6th International Conference on Human-Robot Interaction - HRI 2011, p. 29. ACM Press, New York (2011). https://doi.org/10.1145/1957656.1957668

34. Wegner, D.M., Erber, R., Raymond, P.: Transactive memory in close relationships. J. Pers. Soc. Psychol. **61**, 923–929 (1991)

35. Witmer, B.G., Jerome, C.J., Singer, M.J.: The factor structure of the presence questionnaire. Presence Teleoperators Virtual Environ. **14**(3), 298–312 (2005). https://doi.org/10.1162/105474605323384654

Preliminary Utility Study of a Short Video as a Daily Report in Teleworking

Zhen He[1], Xinwei Dai[1], Toshihiko Yamakami[2], and Tomoo Inoue[1(✉)]

[1] University of Tsukuba, Tsukuba, Ibaraki 3058550, Japan
inoue@slis.tsukuba.ac.jp
[2] ACCESS, Tokyo 1010022, Japan

Abstract. Modern corporate activities are increasingly moving from the traditional way to teleworking. However, as teleworking spreading, the problem of declining employee engagement among teleworkers also comes to the fore. To address this issue, we propose a new approach based on the concept of interactive people analytics. It uses daily video reports to increase interaction between organization members in teleworking, and by analyzing video reports it is expected to detect changes in employee engagement for its maintenance. In this paper, a utility study of using a short video as a daily report in teleworking is presented as well. From the analysis of paralinguistic cues of collected video report samples with corresponding ratings on engagement, it is found there exists relation between paralinguistic cues and engagement in the video.

Keywords: Engagement · Telework · Remote work · Interactive people analytics · Nonverbal · Paralinguistic cue

1 Introduction

The traditional mode of working is undergoing change. Over the past decade, communications technology has evolved rapidly. Various online interactive tools have continued to emerge. By using the Internet, people can communicate with others anytime and anywhere, freeing them of time and space constraints. Moreover, the constant updating of functions brings online communication closer to real-time face-to-face communication, making it effective. Therefore, increasingly sophisticated online interactive technologies are beginning to be accepted by the public and becoming trendy. This trend has also brought change to modern corporations. Recent corporate activity is increasingly moving away from the traditional working mode of coming to work in the same place and at the same time. Using online interactive technologies, a new working mode has emerged, and that is teleworking.

Teleworking, also known as telecommuting or virtual work, has been defined as a work mode that involves using communication and computer technologies to work from home or another location away from the traditional office [1]. As an alternative to the traditional mode of work, teleworking has many benefits. For employees, they can complete job requirements without being physically present at an employer's office

© Springer Nature Switzerland AG 2020
A. Nolte et al. (Eds.): CollabTech 2020, LNCS 12324, pp. 35–49, 2020.
https://doi.org/10.1007/978-3-030-58157-2_3

location. Flexible working hours and free workplaces brings the positive effect of reduced work pressure and increased productivity. For companies, they may want to consider teleworking as a means of cost control and potentially, as an alternative to some layoffs [2]. Because of these benefits, it has become popular in modern corporate activities, and its prospects are well worth looking forward to.

However, teleworking also makes organizational management more difficult. Compared to the traditional working mode, teleworking makes the distance between employees and the company increase. The increased distance is not only physical but also psychological, and it can cause adverse effects such as increased role ambiguity and reduced support and feedback, resulting in employee engagement issue [3]. The decline in employee engagement can negatively affect the company in many aspects, so the maintenance of engagement has always been an essential topic in organizational management. In order for teleworking to be more effective, how to deal with its negative relationship to engagement is imperative.

To solve this issue, the concept of interactive people analytics has been proposed [4]. It is using a short video as a daily report in teleworking. Employees record the progress of their day in the form of short videos and report back to managers. We want to understand the changes in reporter's engagement by analyzing the subjective information which unconsciously revealed by the reporters when recording the video. Then managers can give targeted feedback to employees to help them adjust. For teleworking, which is no longer working in the same place, this kind of process can make up for the lacking interaction between the organization members. We hope it can help to decrease the distance between employees and the company and achieve the goal of engagement maintenance.

To investigate the effectiveness of our interactive people analytics approach, in this paper we explored the utility of using a short video as a daily report in teleworking. First, we collected some video report samples as the analytical dataset used in this paper, with the reporters' rating of engagement level and our original scale of each video report. Then we manually extracted the paralinguistic cues from the video reports, which is rich in subjective information. We extracted two kinds of paralinguistic cues here: filled pause and silent pause. Then we analyzed the relationship between the occurrence of paralinguistic cues and the rating results. Our results illustrate that the relationship between engagement and video reports. The occurrence number and duration of filled pause are more significant at lower engagement level. In terms of our original scale, the relationship between rating results and paralinguistic cues reveals the potential for using video reports to understand employees' subjective evaluations.

2 Related Work

2.1 Employee Engagement

Employee engagement is defined as working with passion and willingness to drive organizational goals, theorized in terms of physical, cognitive and emotional factors. For employees and their organizations, engagement can be critical. It can bring a significant effect on productivity, performance, resilience and organizational profitability [5]. Since maintaining high employee engagement can have many positive effects on an organization, how to maintain and improve employee engagement has always been an essential topic in organizational management. Also, there are many studies on employee engagement.

Regarding the factors that affect employee engagement, many studies show executives [6–8] and managers [9, 10] plays an essential role in shaping and enhancing engagement of their daily report. They explain the superiors can have a significant impact on employee engagement. Appropriate feedback from managers can help improve employee engagement. Besides, Muller et al. discussed the influence on the engagement of peers, friends, and managers [11]. They show the impact on employee engagement from three different aspects: peers, friends, and managers. Their re-search gives a more social view of employee engagement, shows an employee's engagement is associated with the engagement of her/his peer, friends, and managers. It shows not only the manager, but the interaction between organizational members is also a crucial factor influence engagement.

In terms of ways to maintain and enhance employee engagement, Mitra et al. discussed the spread of engagement in a large organizational network [5]. They found how engagement and disengagement spread from one employee to another. Their result suggests it is important for organizations to sense and address workplace disengagement promptly to maintain engagement. In addition to the usual approach, Morales et al. discussed civic engagement using gamification [12]. They proposed a gamified volunteer management platform to enhance engagement and satisfaction. Gamification has been employed to enhance user attraction, satisfaction, and retention in a wide variety of applications, they offer a new perspective on enhancing engagement. Previous studies have discussed the factors that affect employee engagement from various perspectives and have given many ways to increase engagement. However, there is limited research on the increase in employee engagement under teleworking condition.

2.2 People Analytics

From the perspective of organizational management, in this data-centric era, various data collected by various sensors constitute a vast data set to support human re-source management. People analytics is one of such trends and deal with human resources data analytics. Waber combined human resource management and big data and presented the concept of people analytics [13], it can be described as using data analytics to improve organization and human resource management, which is fully data-centered, and always needs unbiased and consistent measurement. It suggests using sensor and analytics to understand how employee work and collaborate, and building a more effective, productive and positive organization.

Regarding the practical use of people analytics in organizational management sight, Xu et al. proposed an approach that enables data mining in inter-company talent transitions using an online business social network [14]. They create a job transition network to extract the characteristics of talent circle. Based on this, they developed a talent circle model and design a talent exchange prediction method for talent recommendation. Roy et al. proposed a conceptual ontology to evaluate human factors [15]. They applied data mining techniques on email corpus, using sentiment analysis to evaluate six components of human resource constructs: performance, engagement, leadership, workplace dynamics, organizational developmental support, and learning and knowledge creation. These studies all illustrate that people analytics techniques can help organizational management become effective. For teleworking, how to leverage people analytics technology has not been explored in depth. On the other hand, engagement as a subjective state related to emotions, whether the objective data-based people analytics technology is suitable, should be discussed again.

2.3 Paralinguistic Cues

Speech information includes verbal and non-verbal information that includes paralanguage. Unlike verbal information, paralinguistic information is content-free, but it plays an essential role in speech communication. It is informative and can help us to understand what is hidden behind the speech. Paralinguistic information always presents as paralinguistic cues in speech. Paralinguistic cues can add context to an utterance, such as information on the way the speaker feels punctually. By analyzing these cues overtime during the interaction, one also gets some hints about the emotional profile of the speaker [16].

Paralinguistic cues contain many categories, including filled pause, silent pause, repetition, pitch, speech rate, energy, loudness, and so on [17]. About their meaning, many prior studies have shown the paralinguistic cues is closely related to the subjective states such as emotion, mental state. Wang et al. showed the relationship be-tween speech rate and emotional mood [18]. Their results showed that when people are under the conditions of happy, angry, scared, and other exciting moods, their speakings naturally become faster. Conversely, negative moods like sad or boring lead to speaking slower. Goto et al. proposed that filled pause is also as having to do with the mental state of the speaker [19]. The results explored that speakers unconsciously use filled pauses to express mental states such as diffidence, anxiety, hesitation, and humility, also to express different thinking states, such as retrieving information from memory. Besides, Lee et al. discussed the connection between the silent pause and the speaker's state of stress [20]. When the speaker is stressed, he/she uses unconsciously more silent pauses during speech than when he is non-stressful, and the duration of silent pauses are also longer than usual. Although the relationships between subjective states such as mood and mind and paralinguistic cues have been addressed a lot in previous studies, the relationship between paralinguistic cues and employee engagement remains unmentioned.

3 Proposal

3.1 Interactive People Analytics

As mentioned before, people analytics is deeply data driven. However, it can be criticized how it is reliable to measure and evaluate subjective mental state or engagement of employees only from such objective data. Instead, previous study has pro-posed the concept of interactive people analytics [4]. Interactive people analytics is defined as data analytics to focus interaction with organization members to improve engagement and organizational goal achievement. It enhances people interaction during the data gathering and provide feedback for further interaction.

People analytics requires unbiased and consistent measurements. In many cases, it is not easy to assure these conditions. In contrast, interactive people analytics emphasizes human centeredness, which aims at introducing intended biases into the measurement. It also discusses that the active reporting by people itself can change or can be a trigger to change them into the direction they wish. It allows biased and intended interaction for positive organizational development.

3.2   Using a Short Video as a Daily Report

To implement the concept of interactive people analytics, we propose a new approach by using a short video as a daily report in telework. Employees record and upload video reports, and due to the content, mangers give feedbacks. Through this process, the interaction between organizational members in teleworking can be realized. Reporting in video form achieves the human-centered goal while collecting data. Further analysis of the video reports may make it possible to capture changes in employee engagement. Screen out employees whose engagement is declining, then based on the content managers give targeted and appropriate feedback, to increase the interaction with them to help them adjust. Finally, the goal of maintaining employee engagement can be achieved.

Our approach has many benefits. First, recording video reports do not require a specific recording place or recording device. It can be done anytime, anywhere just using mobile device such as mobile phone. A short video report for about 30 s a day also does not bring a huge burden on employees. Compare with traditional text format report, analyze video reports is easier to understand changes in engagement. The previous study shows that using video is better than text to let the user engage emotionally in the content [21]. Therefore, video contains much subjective information than text, which is closely related to engagement. Take video reports as a daily routine can also play a role in self-management. Other study shows that employees using more self-management strategies can help them improve their engagement [22]. A regular review of previous video reports can empower introspection and maintain their engagement.

According to our hypothesis, when employee engagement changes, video report content also changes accordingly. For example, assuming an employee's work is not going well, resulting in a decline in his engagement. Then his report may also contain much information, like more pauses during reporting than normal. If our hypothesis is correct, then it proves the utility of our approach. Therefore, in the remaining part of this paper, we conduct a utility study for our approach. Focus on the relationship between engagement and video reports.

4   Utility Study of Daily Video Report

4.1   Material

Daily Video Report Dataset. To investigate the utility of short videos as daily reports, we first collected sample daily video report reports, and build a dataset used for further analysis. The sample video reports were all recorded by a male Japanese employee in his 50 s [4]. He works for an IT company based in Tokyo, Japan, and involved in development-related work contexts. He persistently recorded video reports for over two years from April 2017 to May 2019, finally recorded a total of 418 video reports, 142 in 2017, 194 in 2018, and 82 in 2019. He recorded video reports using the front camera of his smartphone and reported that day's work progress in Japanese. After finished recording, then uploaded it to Google Photo. The example of the daily video reports is shown in Fig. 1. We used all of 418 videos for investigation without any screening.

Specifically, his recording process for each video report was as follows. First, before recording started, the reporter spent around one minute to complete a simple text summary by reviewing what he had done in the day. After that, he sat in front of the camera and started reporting for around 30 s. During the recording, his upper body was in the camera frame. The report content included items such as the date, the progress of ongoing projects, business meetings attendance, future work schedule, problems encountered in work, and other matters related to his work.

Video reports in this dataset have the following features. Due to the report content, the reporters almost always maintained a neutral tone when speaking. Likewise, his expression kept serious and almost unchanged. Besides, the reporter was not tele-working. Although there was no restriction on recording place, most of the reports were recorded in his workplace. Because of this, they did not contain loud voice.

Rating of the Engagement Level. After obtaining sample video reports, we measured the level of engagement of this reporter. Employee engagement is an abstract and subjective state that is difficult to measure directly. Thus, we investigated the engagement level using a questionnaire. The UWES-3 (Utrecht work engagement scale-3) self-report questionnaire was used in our study [23]. The UWES is based on in-depth interviews and was introduced as a 17-item self-report questionnaire that includes three dimensions: vigor, dedication, and absorption. In order to reduce the demand placed on the reporter, we used a shortened version of the questionnaire: UWES-3. It only has three questions, which brings a small burden on the reporter. For the scoring scale, each question needs to be rated on a scale from 0 to 6. A reporter recorded all the video reports first. This time he rated his daily video engagement level based on the video reports' content and his memory at a later date.

Rating by Original Scale. In addition to the rating by the known engagement level, rating by the following original scale was asked. This is to explore what video reports can convey other than the known engagement level. The rating was also conducted at a later date. Our original scale consists of the following three items:

1. Satisfaction. This item refers to the degree the reporter is satisfied with his work. Rating consists of high, medium, and low.
2. Clarity. Clarity here refers not to the clarity of sound in the video, but the clarity of the reported content. Specifically, the item is to evaluate whether a report contains the clearly observable progress of the work. Rating consists of high, medium, and low.

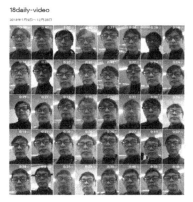

Fig. 1. Example of daily video report samples.

3. Assessment. This item refers to the degree the content includes self-assessment aspects. Specifically, some tasks are routine and some are not. Routine tasks typically require less self-assessment, while non-routine tasks require more self-assessment such as recognition of achievement or recognition of problems. Rating consists of three categories of high, medium, and low.

4.2 Method

We were interested in the relationship between the paralinguistic cues in the video reports and the ratings. We conducted these steps to the material. We extracted para-linguistic cues from the daily video report dataset, and focused on two kinds of para-linguistic cues: filled pause and silent pause, as these two were observed much more than other paralinguistic cues. For the ratings, we tallied the results for each item and the videos were divided into groups. The details are is described as follows.

Paralinguistic Cues Extraction. Previous study proves the mental state affects the occurrence of filled pauses [19]. Speakers unconsciously use pauses to express mental states. In our daily video report data set, filled pauses also frequently appear, and we want to explore whether the occurrence of filled pause is related to our rating results. We counted the frequency of filled pauses, and the rate of filled pause duration for each video report. We used ELAN software to mark the filled pauses in each video report manually to two decimal places in second. The counting rule of filled pauses we use is to count typical Japanese fillers such as/ee-/,/maa-/,/ano-/, and most word-lengthening sounds as the filled pause [19]. On the other hand, we counted the duration of each video from the beginning of the reporter's speech to the end of the last sentence, called actual speech duration. Based on the actual speech duration of each video report, we normalize the data to the result of the frequency of filled pause (times/min) and the rate of filled pause duration in percentage (%).

When in the case of high mental stress, it is easy to have more pauses during speaking [20]. Because each video report is only around 30 s in our case, several seconds of silent pause may contain a wealth of information. What is more, as the reporter conducted the text summary before recording the video report, it may not be normal to have a long duration of silence or frequent silent pauses. We also calculated the frequency of silent pause and the rate of silent pause duration for each video report. Here we counted the silent pauses of more than 1.0 s duration.

Video Grouping According to the Rating. For engagement item, the average score of the 418 ratings was 2.31. Regarding the total 418 samples, we first arranged the rating results in descending order. Then divided them into two groups with the same number of samples by the order, called the high engagement group (209 samples) and the low engagement group (209 samples).

For the original scale, videos were directly divided into groups according to the rating of three categories. For the satisfaction, 67 videos went to high, 124 to medium, and 227 to low. For the clarity, 181 to high, 225 to medium, and 12 to low. For the assessment, 67 to high, 22 to medium, and 329 to low.

Regarding the analysis, we first calculated the mean (M) of different paralinguistic cues in each group for each rating item, including both the mean number of occurrences and mean duration, and the corresponding standard deviation (SD). Then we conducted one-way analysis of variance (ANOVA) by SPSS to check whether there is a statistically significant difference between groups. Furthermore, we conducted Fishers Least Significant Difference (LSD) to determine whether there was a statistically significant difference between each two groups in the original scale.

4.3 Results

Engagement Level. We explored the effect of different engagement levels on filled pause in video reports. The relationship between filled pause and engagement levels is shown in Fig. 2. One-way ANOVA found significant difference of frequency of filled pause between engagement levels where low engagement level had more frequent filled pause (F = 14.143, p = .000). It also found significant difference in the rate of filled pause duration between engagement levels where low engagement level had higher rate of filled pause duration (F = 6.163, p = .013).

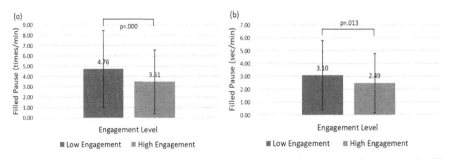

Fig. 2. (a) The relationship between engagement level and filled pause frequency. (b) The relationship between engagement level and filled pause duration.

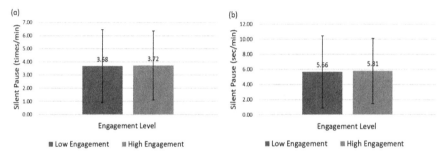

Fig. 3. (a) The relationship between engagement level and silent pause frequency. (b) The relationship between engagement level and silent pause duration.

The relationship between silent pause and engagement levels is shown in Fig. 3. With one-way ANOVA, we did not find significant difference of frequency of silent pause (F = .027, p = .869) and the rate of silent pause duration (F = .114, p = .736) between engagement levels.

Satisfaction. Figure 4 shows the relationship between satisfaction levels and filled pause. One-way ANOVA did not find significant difference of frequency of filled pause between satisfaction levels (F = 2.155, p = .117). Meanwhile, it found marginally significant difference of duration rate of filled pause between satisfaction levels (F = 2.864, p = .058) where high satisfaction level had lower duration rate of filled pause. With further LSD, differences were found between low and high (t = 2.167, p = .031), and between medium and high (t = 2.252, p = .025).

Figure 5 gives the relationship between satisfaction levels and silent pause. One-way ANOVA found marginally significant difference of frequency of silent pause between satisfaction levels (F = 2.684, p = .069) where high satisfaction level had less frequent silent pauses. With further LSD, the difference was found between medium and high (t = 2.289, p = .023). On the other hand, it did not find significant difference of duration rate of silent pause between satisfaction levels (F = .921, p = .399).

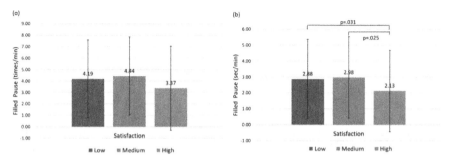

Fig. 4. (a) The relationship between satisfaction level and filled pause frequency. (b) The relationship between satisfaction level and filled pause duration.

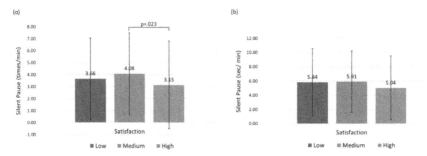

Fig. 5. (a) The relationship between satisfaction level and silent pause frequency. (b) The relationship between satisfaction level and silent pause duration.

Clarity. The relationship between clarity levels and filled pause is shown in Fig. 6. One-way ANOVA found significant difference of frequency of filled pause between clarity levels ($F = 30.664$, $p = .000$) where high clarity level had less frequent filled pause. With further LSD, differences were found between low and high ($t = 3.096$, $p = .002$), and between medium and high ($t = 7.643$, $p = .000$). It also found significant difference of duration rate of filled pause between clarity levels ($F = 43.963$, $p = .000$) where high clarity level had lower duration rate of filled pauses. With further LSD, differences were found between low and high ($t = 4.389$, $p = .000$), and between medium and high ($t = 8.957$, $p = .000$).

The relationship between clarity levels and silent pause is shown in Fig. 7. One-way ANOVA did not find significant difference of both frequency of silent pause ($F = .487$, $p = .615$) and duration rate of silent pause ($F = 1.738$, $p = .177$) between clarity levels.

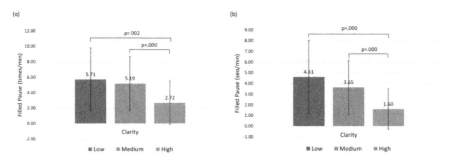

Fig. 6. (a) The relationship between clarity level and filled pause frequency. (b) The relationship between clarity level and filled pause duration.

Assessment. Figure 8 presents the relationship between assessment levels and filled pause. One-way ANOVA found marginally significant difference of frequency of filled pause between assessment levels ($F = 2.465$, $p = .086$) where high assessment level had less frequent filled pauses. With further LSD, the difference was found between low and high ($t = 2.210$, $p = .028$). By contrast, it did not find significant difference of duration rate of filled pause between assessment levels ($F = 1.599$, $p = .203$).

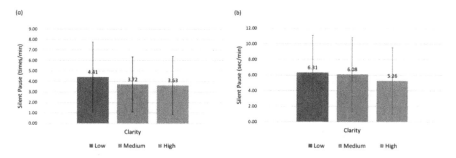

Fig. 7. (a) The relationship between clarity level and silent pause frequency. (b) The relationship between clarity level and silent pause duration.

Figure 9 shows the relationship between assessment levels and silent pause. One-way ANOVA found significant difference of frequency of silent pause between assessment levels (F = 4.233, p = .015) where low assessment level had less frequent silent pause. With further LSD, the difference was found between low and high (t = −2.689, p = .007). It also found significant difference of duration rate of silent pause between assessment levels (F = 8.489, p = .000) where low assessment had lower duration rate of silent pause. With further LSD, differences were found between low and medium (t = −2.552, p = .011), and between low and high (t = −3.481, p = .001).

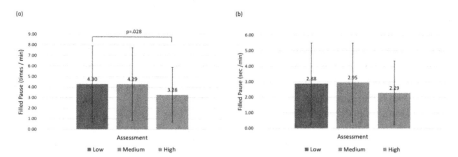

Fig. 8. (a) The relationship between assessment level and filled pause frequency. (b) The relationship between assessment level and filled pause duration.

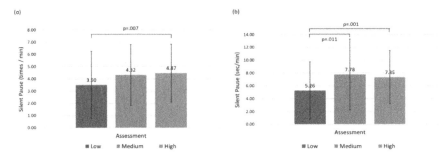

Fig. 9. (a) The relationship between assessment level and silent pause frequency. (b) The relationship between assessment level and silent pause duration.

5 Discussion

5.1 Summary of Results

To summarize the analysis results on engagement, the frequency and duration rate of filled pause was significantly higher in low engagement level than in high engagement level. On the contrary, we did not find any relationship between silent pause and engagement levels.

In terms of our original scale, we did not find the relationship between the frequency of filled pause and satisfaction levels. Meanwhile, the duration rate of filled pause was significantly higher in low and medium satisfaction levels than in high satisfaction level. Also found was that silent pause was more frequent in medium satisfaction level than in high satisfaction level.

On the clarity item, the frequency and duration rate of filled pause was significantly higher in low and medium clarity levels than in high clarity level. We did not find relationship between silent pause and clarity levels.

Regarding the assessment item, the frequency of filled pause was significantly higher in low assessment level than in high assessment level. The frequency of silent pause was significantly lower in low assessment level than in high assessment level. The duration rate of silent pause was significantly lower in low assessment level than in medium and high assessment levels.

5.2 Findings

Among all the results, we found significant effects of some items on paralinguistic cues. It might be an indication of decline of engagement when longer filled pauses are found more frequently in the longitudinal video reports.

Meanwhile, low clarity reports in their contents are likely to have more frequent and higher duration rate of filled pauses. Then frequent and long filled pauses are not necessarily caused by low engagement. They might be caused by reporting not very clear tasks and so on. Thus when longer filled pauses are found more frequently in the longitudinal video reports, we should be also aware if it comes from the reporter's engagement level or from unclear characteristics of the reported tasks, or unclear understanding of the tasks by the reporter.

Moreover, we found high assessment reports had more frequent and higher duration rate of silent pauses. This result proves it is possible to understand employees' self-assessment by analyzing video reports. Which level of self-assessment is con-ducted by the employee can be understood by analyzing their silent pause in their video reports.

5.3 Limitations and Future Works

The study reported in this paper has some limitations. The video report data we used for analysis this time is from one single reporter, which makes it hard to generalize our findings. People's penchant for expressing their subject evaluation or engagement through paralinguistic cues might vary from person to person. Thus, it is not clear if the analysis of the paralinguistic cues of other people can determine their engagement in the same way. The collection and analysis of video reports from other re-porters should be considered in the imminent future. Besides, all ratings in this study conducted at a later date, which is possible to influence the accuracy of rating results. The later ratings might not truly show the reporter's evaluation at the time. Therefore, the real-time rating should also be conducted in future work. In this study, we dis-cussed two paralinguistic cues, filled pause and silent pause, because these two were observed much more than other paralinguistic cues in our dataset. The relationship between various paralinguistic cues can also be considered as a part of future work.

About our rating items, in order to reduce the reporter's burden, we used the UWES-3 questionnaire, the short version of UWES, in this study. Indeed, the reporter can finish only three questions in a short time, but the limited questions may make it harder to understand the subtle changes in engagement. Using the complete version of UWES or other employee engagement scales can be an option in future works. Also, in this study we did not use standardized questionnaires to measure satisfaction, clarity, and assessment. Hence the rating result can be ambiguous and subjective. We aim to study this further to tease out the relationship between these engagement-related items and paralinguistic cues.

5.4 Design Implications for Organizational Structure

Although this study is preliminary, and is supported by not a very solid result because of its data size, we found there would be relationships between paralinguistic cues and engagement in the video. In particular, our results demonstrated that it is possible to use video reports to understand changes in employee engagement. This proves it is useful to address the engagement issue in teleworking by using our approach.

Maintaining a high-level engagement is critical in collaborative work especially when working remotely, and in enterprises. Traditionally teleworking has had issues concerning awareness, communication opportunity and so forth, which resulted in the maintenance of engagement. To address this issue, we propose more active use of video technology in computerized organizational settings. By this study, this claim can be supported in that using video together with analytical computing is helpful for increasing awareness of teleworkers' inner feelings of engagement.

Whether like it or not, teleworking has been increasing in organization. Organizational structure should be and will be designed incorporating teleworking environment. The interactive people analytics could be a nerve of such novel organizations.

6   Conclusion

In this paper, we propose a new approach based on the concept of interactive people analytics to address the engagement issue in teleworking. We propose to use a short video as a daily report to increase interaction between organizational members in teleworking, and by analyzing the video report, it is possible to understand changes in employee engagement. To investigate the utility of our approach, we first collected video report samples to construct a dataset for analysis and obtained the rating results of the engagement level and our original scale from the reporter. Next, we extracted paralinguistic cues from the video report, which are informative and closely related to the subjective state of the reporter. We extracted two paralinguistic cues of filled pause and silent pause. Then we analyzed the frequency and duration of each paralinguistic cue for different rating items. In engagement item, our results illustrated the relationship between engagement and video reports; frequent and longer filled pause occurred in lower engagement. It shows the utility of using daily video report to understand engagement changes. For our original scales, the results show the relationships between subjective evaluation and video reports. They gave possibility of using daily video reports to understand employees' job satisfaction, the completeness of the reported content, and how they conduct self-assessment in daily work. Our results suggest using a short video as a daily report in teleworking is an essential way to ad-dress engagement problem and support effective organizational management.

References

1. Bailey, D.E., Kurland, N.B.: A review of telework research: Findings, new directions, and lessons for the study of modern work. J. Organ. Behav. Int. J. Ind. Occup. Organ. Psychol. Behav. **23**(4), 383–400 (2002)
2. Raiborn, C., Butler, J.B.: A new look at telecommuting and teleworking. J. Corp. Account. Finan. **20**(5), 31–39 (2009)
3. Sardeshmukh, S.R., Sharma, D., Golden, T.D.: Impact of telework on exhaustion and job engagement: a job demands and job resources model. New Technol. Work Employ. **27**(3), 193–207 (2012)
4. Yamakami, T.: Toward interactive people analytics: a new approach to leverage organizational engagement. In: KICSS2019 (2019)
5. Mitra, T., et al.: Spread of employee engagement in a large organizational network: a longitudinal analysis. In: Proceedings of the ACM on Human-Computer Interaction, CSCW, vol. 1, pp. 1–20 (2017)
6. Venkatesh, A.N.: Employee engagement through leadership. Am. Int. J. Res. Humanit. Arts Soc. Sci. **9**(4), 333–336 (2014)
7. Wiley, J.W.: The impact of effective leadership on employee engagement. Employ. Relat. Today **37**(2), 47–52 (2010)

8. Wiley, J.W., Brenda, J.K., Anne, E.H.: Developing and validating a global model of employee engagement. In: Handbook of employee engagement: Perspectives, issues, research and practice, pp. 351–363 (2010)
9. Donaldson-Feilder, E., Rachel, L.: Positive manager behaviour for engagement and wellbeing. In: Flourishing in Life, Work and Careers. Edward Elgar Publishing, Cheltenham (2015)
10. Luthans, F., Peterson, S.J.: Employee engagement and manager self-efficacy. J. Manag. Dev. **21**(5), 376–387 (2002)
11. Muller, M., et al.: Influences of peers, friends, and managers on employee engagement. In: Proceedings of the 19th International Conference on Supporting Group Work (2016)
12. Morales, L., et al.: Toward an open platform for organized, gamified volunteerism. In: Companion of the 2017 ACM Conference on Computer Supported Cooperative Work and Social Computing (2017)
13. Waber, B.: People Analytics: How Social Sensing Technology will Transform Business and what it Tells us About the Future of Work. FT Press, Upper Saddle River (2013)
14. Xu, H., et al.: Talent circle detection in job transition networks. In: Proceedings of the 22nd ACM SIGKDD International Conference on Knowledge Discovery and Data Mining (2016)
15. Gelbard, R., et al.: Sentiment analysis in organizational work: towards an ontology of people analytics. Expert Syst. **35**(5), e12289 (2018)
16. Delaborde, A., Devillers, L.: Use of nonverbal speech cues in social interaction between human and robot: emotional and interactional markers. In: Proceedings of the 3rd International Workshop on Affective Interaction in Natural Environments (2010)
17. Johar, S.: Paralinguistic profiling using speech recognition. Int. J. Speech Technol. **17**(3), 205–209 (2014). https://doi.org/10.1007/s10772-013-9222-4
18. Wang, Y., Hu, W.: Speech emotion recognition based on improved MFCC. In: Proceedings of the 2nd International Conference on Computer Science and Application Engineering (2018)
19. Goto, M., Itou, K., Hayamizu, S.: A real-time filled pause detection system for spontaneous speech recognition. In: Sixth European Conference on Speech Communication and Technology (1999)
20. Lee, M., et al.: Exploring moral conflicts in speech: multidisciplinary analysis of affect and stress. In: 2017 Seventh International Conference on Affective Computing and Intelligent Interaction (ACII). IEEE (2017)
21. Yadav, A., et al.: If a picture is worth a thousand words is video worth a million? Differences in affective and cognitive processing of video and text cases. J. Comput. Higher Educ. **23**(1), 15–37 (2011)
22. Breevaart, K., Bakker, A.B., Demerouti, E.: Daily self-management and employee work engagement. J. Vocat. Behav. **84**(1), 31–38 (2014)
23. Schaufeli, W.B., et al.: An ultra-short measure for work engagement: the UWES-3 validation across five countries. Eur. J. Psychol. Assess. **35**(4), 577 (2019)

What Do We Know About Hackathon Outcomes and How to Support Them? – A Systematic Literature Review

Maria Angelica Medina Angarita[1]([envelope]) and Alexander Nolte[1,2]([envelope])

[1] University of Tartu, Tartu, Estonia
{maria.medina,alexander.nolte}@ut.ee
[2] Carnegie Mellon University, Pittsburgh, PA, USA

Abstract. Hackathons are time-bounded events where participants gather in teams to develop projects that interest them. Such events have been adopted in various domains to generate innovative solutions, foster learning, build and expand communities and to tackle civic and ecological issues. While research interest has also grown subsequently, most studies focus on singular events in specific domains. A systematic overview of the current state of the art is currently missing. Such an overview is however crucial to further study the hackathon phenomenon, understand its underlying mechanisms and develop support for hackathon organizers, in particular related to the sustainability of hackathon outcomes. This paper fills that gap by reporting on the results of a systematic literature review thus providing an overview of potential hackathon outcomes, design aspects and connections between them that have been addressed in prior work. Our findings also outline gaps in prior work e.g. related to the lack of work focusing on hackathon outcomes other than hackathon projects.

Keywords: Hackathon · Hackathon design aspects · Hackathon outcomes

1 Introduction

Hackathons are time-bounded, themed events where participants with diverse interests, expertise and goals form teams to work on projects that interest them [37]. Starting in the early 2000s, the popularity of hackathons has seen a steep increase in recent years. The largest hackathon league, Major League Hacking (MLH) alone, hosts more than 200 hackathons annually, involving around 65.000 students[1].

The growing popularity of hackathons has subsequently also led to an increased interest in research as evidenced by a large number of publications on the topic. Most research on hackathons, however, currently focuses on studying singular events in specific domains covering aspects such as how to organize a hackathon [37] and how teams self-organize [49]. A systematic overview of the current state of the art about hackathons

---

[1] https://mlh.io/about.

© Springer Nature Switzerland AG 2020
A. Nolte et al. (Eds.): CollabTech 2020, LNCS 12324, pp. 50–64, 2020.
https://doi.org/10.1007/978-3-030-58157-2_4

is missing. Such an overview is crucial as a basis to further study the hackathon phenomenon, understand its underlying mechanisms, and develop support for hackathon organizers and participants. Our work aims to address this gap.

In this paper, we particularly focus on the sustainability of hackathon outcomes. As hackathon outcomes, we perceive the diverse direct results of a hackathon, such as prototypes, networking, learning and others [21]. The sustainability of these outcomes has not been studied extensively so far despite organizers and participants investing considerable resources to prepare, run, and follow-up on an event. Previous research even suggests that hackathon outcomes are often not sustained at all [11, 31, 49] rendering the investment of resources useless. In order to develop a systematic understanding of how to sustain hackathon outcomes it is first necessary though to understand which outcomes can be reasonably expected. We thus ask the following research question:

RQ1: What hackathon outcomes have been addressed by previous research?

Understanding which outcomes can reasonably be expected is not sufficient to support their sustainability though. It is also necessary to understand which design aspects form the structure of a hackathon. With design aspects, we refer to characteristics of involved individuals and activities before, during and after a hackathon and that shape the format of a hackathon. This leads to the following research question:

RQ2: What hackathon design aspects have been addressed by previous research?

After developing an understanding of potential hackathon outcomes and aspects that might influence its design, we subsequently focus on previously identified relationships to uncover existing gaps in current research. We thus also ask the following question:

RQ3: Which connections between hackathon design aspects and outcomes have been addressed in prior literature?

In order to answer the aforementioned research questions, we conducted a systematic literature review based on the guidelines described by Kitchenham et al. [27]. Our contribution is twofold: We first provide an overview of potential hackathon outcomes, design aspects and connections between them that have been addressed in prior work. We also outline gaps in prior work e.g. related to the lack of work focusing on hackathon outcomes other than hackathon projects.

2 Background

There is prior work in the hackathon domain where researchers created an overview of different types of hackathons. One example of such works is a typology of hackathons developed by Drouhard et al. [15]. They categorize hackathons in either *communal* (towards community nurturing), *contributive* (issue-oriented), or *catalytic* (towards the search for innovation). A similar approach by Starov et al. [45] also distinguishes hackathons depending on their focus, which could be on innovation, education, or communication. These categorizations are useful to orientate the design of a hackathon towards one focus, but they neither provide an overview of different design aspects nor on how such aspects are connected to the sustainability of the outcomes.

Soltani et al. [44] have discussed connections between different design aspects and hackathon outcomes in the healthcare domain. They identified six hackathon success factors which include the clear definition of the problem area, compensations offered to the winning solutions, and entry requirements for participants, among others. Similarly, Pe-Than et al. [37] elaborate on various design choices connected to strategies, and organizational and personal goals in corporate hackathons. They discuss, for instance, that the continuation of work after a hackathon is linked to the organizational goal of increasing the visibility of projects and the personal goals of gaining recognition and fostering the careers of participants. These two pieces of research work derive their insights from six and ten hackathons respectively which took place in specific domains. Our work, in contrast, aims to provide an overview of previously identified hackathon design aspects and outcomes, as well as connections between them, thus providing a solid basis for future work on the sustainability of hackathon outcomes.

3   Methodology

To answer the research questions stated in the introduction we conducted a systematic literature review based on the guidelines proposed by Kitchenham et al. [27]. Our aim was to create an overview of hackathon outcomes (RQ1), hackathon design aspects (RQ2) and potential connections between them (RQ3). In the following sections, we elaborate on the search queries we used (Sect. 3.1), our inclusion and exclusion criteria (Sect. 3.2), and our process of analysis (Sect. 3.3).

3.1   Search Queries

Our search focused on hackathon outcomes (RQ1), we thus used the following main search terms: "hackathon", "codefest" and "coding competition" as synonyms [8] and combined them with "outcome". We also included "guide", "setup", "design" and "setting", referring to the design of a hackathon (RQ2). We performed the searches using Boolean operators tailored to the specific search grammar requirements of each library and sorted the results by relevance[2]. We searched for publications from 2010 to 2020 to focus on the most recent work about hackathons We conducted our search using online libraries proposed by Brereton [7]: IEEExplore, ACM Digital library, and Google Scholar, as well as Scopus and Web of Science. After the initial search, we carried out a preliminary screening based on the title, keywords, and abstracts. The search results from ACM were: 80 (74 after preliminary screening), from Google Scholar: 7315 (258 after preliminary screening)[3], from IEEE Xplore Library: 37 (28 after preliminary screening), from Scopus: 259 (102 after preliminary screening) and from Web of Science: 94 (68 after preliminary screening).

3.2   Inclusion and Exclusion Criteria

After screening, we read the remaining papers in detail and applied the following including and exclusion criteria to select the most relevant works:

---

[2] We e.g. used the following String for the ACM digital library: + (hackathon) + ("outcome" "guide" "setup" "aspect" "design" "setting") + (codefest) + ("outcome" "guide" "setup" "aspect" "design" "setting") + ("coding competition") + ("outcome" "guide" "setup" "aspect" "design" "setting").

[3] We limited our search to the first 30 results pages.

Inclusion Criteria

Only Hackathons. We perceive hackathons as time-bounded, themed events where participants with diverse expertise and goals work in teams on projects that interest them [37] as outlined in the introduction. We only include events that fit this definition. Papers that focus on similar types of events such as workshops or events during which participants work alone, online, or work on a regular project were not included.

Detailed Description of the Hackathon Setup. Papers must include a description of basic hackathon design aspects, such as the number of participants, the agenda, the setup and the main hackathon activities to be included in the analysis.

The Hackathon Is the Main Focus. Papers have to focus on studying a hackathon. Papers that focus on hackathons as a means to study other phenomena will not be included.

Exclusion Criteria

Non-peer Reviewed Work. In order to ensure the quality of the results, we excluded books and book chapters, workshops, theses, institute publications, presentations, posters, monographs, reports, extended abstracts, websites and magazines.

Exploratory Work. We excluded papers with less than 5 pages which report on preliminary or exploratory results.

After applying these inclusion/exclusion criteria, the remaining papers (29 journal papers and 61 conference papers) were included in our analysis. Additionally, 1 paper was added from a snowballing process.

3.3 Data Analysis

In order to identify potential hackathon outcomes (RQ1) and design aspects (RQ2), the main author of the paper extracted relevant information from the remaining papers and iteratively organized them into categories. The categories were then collaboratively evaluated in a series of iterations together with the second author.

First, we extracted the hackathon outcomes and design aspects mentioned in each paper. We then clustered these aspects based on common outcomes and design aspects between different papers and grouped them into categories (e.g. *"visualizations"* and *"documents"* as outcomes). These clusters subsequently formed larger categories (e.g. *"visualizations"* and *"documents"* were merged into the larger cluster of *"non-technical artifacts"*).

We used a similar procedure to identify connections between hackathon outcomes and design aspects (RQ3). We arranged the connections that were discussed in different papers in a table, outlining the hackathon outcomes on one column and the design aspects on the other (see Table 2 for an overview).

4   Findings

In this section, we will discuss hackathon outcomes (RQ1), design aspects (RQ2), and relationships between them (RQ3) that we identified from our literature review. Section 4.1 focuses on hackathon outcomes (RQ1) and Sect. 4.2 on hackathon design aspects (RQ2). In Sect. 5, we address the current understanding in related work about the relationship between design aspects and the sustainability of outcomes (RQ3)[4].

4.1   Hackathon Outcomes (RQ1)

For the purpose of this paper, we differentiate between tangible and intangible hackathon outcomes [46]. Tangible hackathon outcomes include technical and non-technical artifacts, while intangible hackathon outcomes refer to aspects such as learning and networking (see Table 1 for an overview).

Table 1. Overview of identified hackathon outcomes

ID	Hackathon outcomes
Tangible outcomes	
O1	Technical artifacts (e.g. [10, 29, 44])
O2	Non-technical artifacts (e.g. [46, 49])
Intangible outcomes	
O3	Learning (e.g. [10, 21, 29])
O4	Networking (e.g. [10, 21, 29])
O5	Interdisciplinary collaboration (e.g. [10, 47, 49])
O6	Ideas [40, 47]
O7	Entrepreneurship [11, 31]
O8	Fostering existing enterprise [10, 19]
O9	Fostering awareness about hackathon theme [2, 46, 50]

Tangible Hackathon Outcomes
These are the most commonly discussed hackathon outcomes. They include technical artifacts such as new prototypes [5, 44, 49], product features [49] and bug fixes [10, 49]. Tangible outcomes may also include non-technical artifacts such as visualizations [40, 43, 49], new or improved documentation [46] and publications [49].

Intangible Hackathon Outcomes
Intangible hackathon outcomes include participants learning about the main issue of

---

[4] Due to space constraints we only include the most relevant references here. A full list of all references considered in this literature review is available here: https://bit.ly/2CDIezF.

a hackathon [50], new technologies [9, 46], or acquiring industry and in-university skills [33]. Participants can also engage in networking [46] by meeting new people, thus, creating opportunities for collaboration [3, 39]. Both networking and learning can subsequently lead to participants developing new ideas [40, 47]. Other intangible outcomes may include entrepreneurship [11, 31] (i.e. the creation of new startups), fostering existing enterprises [19], and fostering awareness about the theme of a hackathon [2, 50].

4.2 Hackathon Design Aspects (RQ2)

In this section, we elaborate on design aspects of hackathons that have been discussed in prior work thus answering RQ2 (Fig. 1 provides an overview).

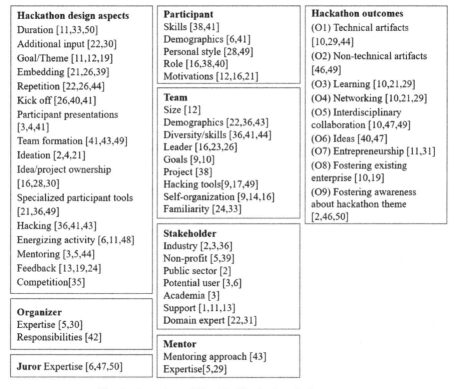

Fig. 1. Overview of identified hackathon design aspects

Hackathons are time-bounded, themed events where participants with diverse interests, expertise, and goals form teams to work on projects that interest them as outlined in the introduction. They can attract diverse **participants** (top-middle in Fig. 1) from different ethnic backgrounds [41], skills [14], education levels [6, 13], and (research) experience [13]. Participants commonly attend hackathons based on individual motivations such as e.g. having fun or learning [40, 50]. Some of them might have previous hackathon experience [29], while others attend a hackathon for the first time. Participants commonly take over a specific role [40] such as team leader, developer, or designer based on prior experience or personal interest.

Participants typically form hackathon **teams** (middle of Fig. 1) which may subsequently consist of participants with different skills [36, 41]. Teams have different sizes that can also fluctuate during the course of a hackathon [14]. Team members can be potential end users of the project they work on during the hackathon [3]. In a team, participants typically agree on the tools [9] they use to work on their project [38] and select a leader [16, 26] for the duration of a hackathon. Some teams form clear objectives and requirements for their project [4, 36] while others choose a less structured approach. Each team's self-organization process can further be influenced by the hackathon venue [36], the size of a team [14], and the guidance they receive [14].

Teams can be supported by **mentors** (bottom in Fig. 1) who help teams achieve their goals by offering advice and directions based on their expertise [5, 29]. For that, different mentors can apply different approaches [43].

A **jury** (bottom-left in Fig. 1) might be formed to evaluate projects at a competitive hackathon. A jury can consist of people with diverse areas of expertise [6, 47, 50] and provide feedback to teams related to their project and choose one or multiple winners.

Stakeholders (middle in Fig. 1) can be involved in hackathons as participants, mentors, jury, or organizers, and can have an active role in the hackathon by being present during the event. They may also contribute by providing financial support [1, 28] typically in exchange for promotional activities.

Hackathon **organizers** (bottom-left in Fig. 1) are in charge of the overall design of a hackathon and use their expertise [5, 30] to design and run them. They have a large array of responsibilities [42] such as marketing an event [6, 17, 48], defining prerequisites for outcomes [42], and recruiting participants [1, 5, 10] based on specific participant selection criteria [5, 10, 22]. They might also provide opportunities for participants to meet prior to the event [13, 17, 26].

Hackathons (top-left in Fig. 1), if organized face-to-face, take place in a venue [21, 36, 41], over a limited period of time [22], with a specific number of participants [20, 41]. A hackathon commonly begins with a kickoff, such as a keynote [41]. Afterwards, participants may can engage in team formation, which could involve different strategies [49]: *open sheepherding*, where participants already come with a project, *selection by organizer*, where teams are formed based on an idea that interests them, and *selection by attraction*, where different ideas are pitched and participants choose the idea they prefer. Ideas for projects could also be proposed by stakeholders and organizers.

After teams are formed, participants commonly begin working on their projects. For that, they could use various techniques such as agile programming [9], rapid iteration [50], and testing [28, 48]. It is also common to run energizing activities [6, 48], breaks [11, 48], and networking activities [11, 33, 48] during a hackathon to lift the moods of the participants.

During hacking, participants typically receive feedback from mentors [44] and sometimes, stakeholders that are also involved in the hackathon [5]. If a hackathon takes place as a competitive event, feedback [24] can also be provided by the jury, who evaluates projects and selects winner teams that receive prizes [29].

5   Discussion

In this section, we elaborate on the current understanding of the relationships between hackathon design aspects and outcomes, thus, answering RQ3. We start by elaborating on connections between hackathon outcomes and design aspects (Sect. 5.1), before outlining activities that have been discussed in prior work related to hackathon outcomes (Sect. 5.2), and addressing gaps in current literature (Sect. 5.3).

5.1   Connections Between Hackathon Outcomes and Design Aspects (RQ3)

The following connections have been found between hackathon outcomes and design aspects and may potentially influence future sustainability (Table 2).

Table 2. Connections between hackathon outcomes and design aspects

ID	Hackathon outcomes	Hackathon design aspects
O1, O2	Technical and non-technical artifacts	Duration [11, 50]
O1	Technical artifacts	Team size [12]
O1	Technical artifacts	Stakeholder connection [22, 30, 34]
O1	Wide range of solutions	Participant's skills [41]
O3	Learning and productivity	Duration [33]
O4	Networking	Participant's skills [38]

Technical and Non-technical Artifacts

The following design aspects have been found to be related to the continuation of technical and non-technical artifacts: Hackathon duration, team size, connections with stakeholders and skills of the participants.

Hackathon Duration. Cobham et al. and Nandi and Wilson et al. [11, 50] discuss the relationship between the duration of a hackathon and the quality of the artifacts that the hackathon teams developed. Cobham et al. [11] argue that the duration of 48 h allowed for periods of rest and relaxation, while still leaving sufficient time for participants to develop elaborate prototypes. Wilson et al. [50], similarly argue that an extended duration allowed participants *"to develop their ideas, flesh them out more fully in their pitches, and engage other groups with questions, ideas, and feedback"* [50].

Team Size. Cobham et al. [12] reported difficulties related to self-organization, task distribution and payment [12] for a winning team composed of 11 participants. In this case, there were more team members than tasks needed to be completed, which meant that *"too often some members were idle awaiting others to complete dependent tasks"* [12]. It would thus seem that a sustainable hackathon team requires that each member contributes equally to the development of the project using appropriate task assignment and management.

Connections with Stakeholders. Linnell et al. [30] found that a strong relationship between hackathon organizers and potential users can ensure that *"the systems built will genuinely meet the needs of the clients"* [30], which could potentially lead to the sustainability of technical artifacts. Similarly, Gama et al. [22] found that *"having a person from the target audience made the participants more confident about their app than in the previous hackathon"* [22] thus drawing a potential connection between stakeholder input and the quality of the technical artifact developed during the hackathon. Nolte et al. [34] also reported that connections between stakeholders and hackathon teams can contribute to project continuation.

Skills of the Participants. Rosell et al. [41] found that allowing for a high degree of diverse participants resulted, in turn, in a wide range of diverse solutions.

Learning
Learning as an outcome has not been extensively studied in the context of research on hackathons. Gama et al. [21] however highlight that while participants *"break barriers to learn other technologies"*, learning at the hackathon occurred superficially *"due to the short time frame"* thus pointing to the necessity for participants to continue learning after an event has ended.

Networking
Pirker et al. [38] found that *"programmers, hardware experts, or 2D artists are growing their social network slower"* [38] compared to audio engineers and other participants with different skill sets. They have also claimed that further investigation is necessary to identify the cause.

5.2 Activities to Sustain Hackathon Outcomes

There are reports of approaches to sustain hackathon outcomes after a hackathon has ended. For instance, in order to sustain the development of technical artifacts that were created in the hackathon, organizers have offered: Coaching and mentoring to the winning teams [1, 35], a showcase of technical artifacts developed during an event at a forum [1], post-hackathon prizes [31, 35], the release of the productive version of technical artifacts [1, 20], recruitment of new team members [35], and grant writing [35].

However, little is known about the long-term impact that these post-hackathon activities had on outcome sustainability. There is still a need to e.g. understand effective mentoring approaches that could be applied after a hackathon ends. Moreover, most prior work on continuation focuses on hackathon projects, while how to sustain, for example, interdisciplinary collaboration is still not well understood.

It might also be important to consider different types of awards for winning teams. It is still unclear if different types of awards would lead to different levels of commitment and engagement from participants. To date, if hackathon organizers were to choose between different types of awards, there are limited insights into the extent to which each type could encourage participants to e.g. continue working on their projects.

In order to sustain networking after the hackathon had ended, participants can join a mailing list [46], but the extent to which a mailing list can sustain networking remains questionable. The lack of studies about sustaining networking for participants has also been addressed by Trainer et al. [49] who proposed three ways to support networking: (1) collecting data from mailing lists and source code-depositories (contributors and number of contributions) to *"construct social networks representing the social structure of a hackathon"* [49], (2) finding connections with people outside the hackathon i.e. to find stakeholders outside the environment of the hackathon to reveal a potential network amongst participants, stakeholders and end users, and (3) *"focus[ing] on practices and technologies for hackathon participants"* [49], where a certain technological tool could be used, for example, to share pictures of the event towards *"repeated exposure"*, which can fortify already established social ties.

In order to retain and expand the awareness of the theme of the hackathon, organizers have advertised outcomes [48] by e.g. presenting technical artifacts at a fair [20]. They have also encouraged participants to report and present their outcomes at conferences and workshops [9]. Albeit these pursuits have been perceived as successful or effective, there is limited evidence towards their feasibility as of this point.

While the impact of different activities is still unknown, it has been suggested that entrepreneurship can be successfully sustained by involving participants in business accelerators and entrepreneurial bootcamps [35]. The feasibility of this approach has not been extensively studied yet.

In addition to preparing activities to sustain the outcomes after the hackathon ends, there has been cases where organizers prepare activities before the hackathon begins. For instance, Nolte et al. [34] reported that preparation prior to a hackathon can influence the continuation of hackathon projects [34]. They particularly pointed towards teams discussing projects with related stakeholders prior to an event and teams engaging in expertise focused learning. Moreover, Rosell et al. [41] found that *"pre-hackathon training and orientation sessions"* allowed participants *"to feel comfortable with the technology"* during the hackathon. Finally, Trainer et al. [49] reported that participants meeting before a hackathon can foster team familiarity and collective task creation before forming teams.

5.3 Gaps in Previous Work on Hackathon Outcome Sustainability

While various connections have been identified between hackathon outcomes and design aspects (c.f. sect. 5.1), there are also considerable gaps in current research related to the sustainability of hackathon outcomes (for an overview, see Fig. 2).

There are limited insights into how **the goals of the participants** could affect, for instance, ideation, team formation, or hacking. It is still uncertain how participant goals [32] relate to their behavior during hackathons and how their individual goals can affect the sustainability of outcomes.

The **goals of hackathon organizers** also certainly affect the design of a hackathon which can potentially influence the sustainability of hackathon outcomes [5, 30]. But there is limited evidence related to how their goals can affect design decisions and in turn influence the sustainability of hackathon outcomes.

Mentors in hackathons have also not been extensively studied yet. While scholars recognize their importance, current research work focuses on their expertise and mentoring approach [5, 29, 43] without elaborating on their goals, previous hackathon

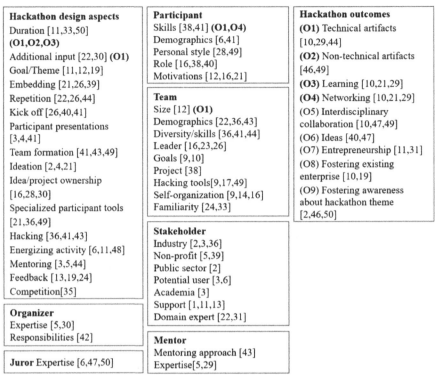

Hackathon design aspects
Duration [11,33,50] **(O1,O2,O3)**
Additional input [22,30] **(O1)**
Goal/Theme [11,12,19]
Embedding [21,26,39]
Repetition [22,26,44]
Kick off [26,40,41]
Participant presentations [3,4,41]
Team formation [41,43,49]
Ideation [2,4,21]
Idea/project ownership [16,28,30]
Specialized participant tools [21,36,49]
Hacking [36,41,43]
Energizing activity [6,11,48]
Mentoring [3,5,44]
Feedback [13,19,24]
Competition[35]

Organizer
Expertise [5,30]
Responsibilities [42]

Juror Expertise [6,47,50]

Participant
Skills [38,41] **(O1,O4)**
Demographics [6,41]
Personal style [28,49]
Role [16,38,40]
Motivations [12,16,21]

Team
Size [12] **(O1)**
Demographics [22,36,43]
Diversity/skills [36,41,44]
Leader [16,23,26]
Goals [9,10]
Project [38]
Hacking tools[9,17,49]
Self-organization [9,14,16]
Familiarity [24,33]

Stakeholder
Industry [2,3,36]
Non-profit [5,39]
Public sector [2]
Potential user [3,6]
Academia [3]
Support [1,11,13]
Domain expert [22,31]

Mentor
Mentoring approach [43]
Expertise[5,29]

Hackathon outcomes
(O1) Technical artifacts [10,29,44]
(O2) Non-technical artifacts [46,49]
(O3) Learning [10,21,29]
(O4) Networking [10,21,29]
(O5) Interdisciplinary collaboration [10,47,49]
(O6) Ideas [40,47]
(O7) Entrepreneurship [11,31]
(O8) Fostering existing enterprise [10,19]
(O9) Fostering awareness about hackathon theme [2,46,50]

Fig. 2. Overview of hackathon design aspects and previously addressed connections between them. The code of the outcome (e.g. O1) placed next to a design aspect represents a potential connection with that outcome and that hackathon design aspect.

experience and background and the potential effects of these on their mentoring approach and subsequent hackathon outcomes.

Moreover, hackathons are sometimes conducted repeatedly. This allows organizers to learn and improve their design. However, it is still unclear how **the repetition of a hackathon** can influence the sustainability of hackathon outcomes.

Hackathons can also be included as a part of a series of events. For instance, at the beginning of a project for development of the skills of the participants, towards the middle for data analysis, or towards the end [23]. However, the influence **of being part of a series of events** on hackathon sustainability is still unknown.

The ideas, and therefore, projects that come as a result of hacking may belong to the participants, but also to the organizers, or stakeholders. How the perceived **ownership of an idea** can potentially influence outcome sustainability is not well understood. Moreover, Filippova et al. [18] found that *"brainstorming impacts satisfaction with outcome indirectly by increasing clarity of goals"* [18], however, details regarding the particulars of the **ideation** process during hackathons are still missing.

While Ghouila et al. [23] and Ferguson et al. [17] mentioned that participants would have wanted more time for improving the quality of their final projects, the impact of different **hackathon durations** remains understudied. In addition, Ghoulia et al. [23] stated that by establishing a strong **intrateam relationship**, teams may be more likely to continue working together after the hackathon ends. They do however not provide any specifics related to the tools or methods that could be used to support the sustainability of connections made during a hackathon. The lack of **specific tools to support intrateam communication** has also been addressed by Hou and Wang [25]. They stated that a CSCW system is necessary in hackathons for expert collocation and knowledge sharing. Likewise, Karlsen and Løvlie [26] mentioned the importance of providing participants with tools to support collaboration. Similarly, Trainer et al. [49] addressed the importance of tools to *"support preparation and bring the results into the hackathon in a usable form"* [49] as well as tools to capture the progress made at the hackathon to seamlessly continue it afterwards.

While previous research work has mainly focused on the potential sustainability of technical artifacts, little attention has been payed to the sustainability of non-technical artifacts, ideas, interdisciplinary collaboration and fostering existing enterprise.

5.4 Limitations

Since the aim of our study was to develop a systematic overview of the current state of the art related to hackathon outcomes, hackathon design aspects and their interconnection, we chose to use conduct a systematic literature review. Despite following well established guidelines this study design has inherent limitations. It only allows us to discover published academic work thus leaving out potentially interesting insights from practitioners that have not been published yet. Moreover, the review was conducted by a group of researchers which makes it subject to interpreter bias. We attempted to mitigate this bias by collaboratively analyzing the identified paper over multiple iterations. Finally, we limited out search to a specific subset of online libraries, using specific search strings and filtering our findings based on specific inclusion and exclusion criteria. Different sources, search strings and inclusion and exclusion criteria might have yielded different results.

6 Conclusion and Future Work

We conducted a systematic literature review to identify previously addressed hackathon outcomes, hackathon design aspects and the connections between them. Based on our findings we developed an overview of previously addressed hackathon outcomes (Table 1), and hackathon design aspects (Fig. 1), discussed their connections and identified gaps in prior literature (Sect. 5). We found that most research work focuses on the sustainability of technical artifacts, while there are other kinds of hackathon outcomes left unstudied. Moreover, many design aspects such as the goals of participants, organizers and mentors have not been explored in relationship to hackathon outcomes.

To expand our work we are currently planning an interview study with hackathon organizers, mentors and participants to identify potential outcomes and design aspects that have not been addressed by prior research. Combining the findings from the planned study and the findings presented in this paper we will develop a model of interconnected factors that can foster the sustainability of hackathon outcomes.

References

1. Alba, M., et al.: Synergy between smart cities' hackathons and living labs as a vehicle for accelerating tangible innovations on cities. In: 2016 IEEE International Smart Cities Conference (ISC2), Trento, pp. 1–6. IEEE (2016)
2. Amugongo, L.M., et al.: Increasing open data awareness and consumption in Namibia: a hackathon approach. In: Cross Media, Berlin, p. 13 (2015)
3. Angelidis, P., et al.: The hackathon model to spur innovation around global mHealth. J. Med. Eng. & Technol. **40**(7–8), 392–399 (2016)
4. Aryana, B., et al.: Strategies for empowering collective design. Des. J. **22**(Sup1.), 2073–2088 (2019)
5. Birbeck, N., et al.: Self Harmony: rethinking hackathons to design and critique digital technologies for those affected by self-harm. In: Proceedings of the 2017 CHI Conference on Human Factors in Computing Systems - CHI 2017, Denver, Colorado, USA, pp. 146–157. ACM Press (2017)
6. Boisen, K., Boisen, A., Thomsen, S., Matthiesen, S., Hjerming, M., Hertz, P.: Hacking the hospital environment: young adults designing youth-friendly hospital rooms together with young people with cancer experiences. Int. J. Adolesc. Med. Health **29**(4), 1–6 (2015)
7. Brereton, P., et al.: Lessons from applying the systematic literature review process within the software engineering domain. J. Syst. Softw. **80**(4), 571–583 (2007)
8. Briscoe, G., Mulligan, C.: Digital Innovation: The Hackathon Phenomenon, p. 13. Creativeworks London (2014)
9. Chandrasekaran, S., et al.: Best practices in running collaborative GPU hackathons: advancing scientific applications with a sustained impact. Comput. Sci. Eng. **20**(4), 95–106 (2018)
10. Chandrasekaran, S., et al.: The OLCF GPU hackathon series: the story behind advancing scientific applications with a sustained impact. In: EduHPC-17: Workshop on Education for High-Performance Computing (2017)
11. Cobham, D., et al.: From appfest to entrepreneurs: using a hackathon event to seed a university student-led enterprise. In: International Technology, Education and Development Conference, Valencia, Spain, March 2017
12. Cobham, D., et al.: From hackathon to student enterprise: an evaluation of creating successful and sustainable student entrepreneurial activity initiated by a university hackathon. In: International Conference on Education and New Learning Technologies, Barcelona, Spain, March 2017
13. Dainotti, A., et al.: The BGP hackathon 2016 report. SIGCOMM Comput. Commun. Rev. **46**(3), 1–6 (2018)
14. Day, K., et al.: How do the design features of health hackathons contribute to participatory medicine? AJIS. **21**, 1–14 (2017)
15. Drouhard, M., et al.: A typology of hackathon events. In: Conference on Computer-Supported Cooperative Work and Social Media (2017)
16. Farhan, E., Kocher, M.: Big Team Game Jams: a framework to emulate big production using game jams with big teams. In: Proceedings of the International Conference on Game Jams, Hackathons, and Game Creation Events - GJH&GC 2016, San Francisco, CA, USA, pp. 1–7. ACM Press (2016)
17. Ferguson, A.L., et al.: Conference report: 2018 materials and data science hackathon (MATDAT18). Mol. Syst. Des. Eng. **4**(3), 462–468 (2019)
18. Filippova, A., et al.: From diversity by numbers to diversity as process: supporting inclusiveness in software development teams with brainstorming. In: 2017 IEEE/ACM 39th International Conference on Software Engineering (ICSE), Buenos Aires, pp. 152–163. IEEE (2017)

19. Flores, M., et al.: How can hackathons accelerate corporate innovation? In: Moon, I., Lee, G.M., Park, J., Kiritsis, D., von Cieminski, G. (eds.) APMS 2018. IAICT, vol. 535, pp. 167–175. Springer, Cham (2018). https://doi.org/10.1007/978-3-319-99704-9_21

20. Frey, F.J., Luks, M.: The innovation-driven hackathon: one means for accelerating innovation. In: Proceedings of the 21st European Conference on Pattern Languages of Programs - EuroPlop 2016, Kaufbeuren, Germany, pp. 1–11. ACM Press (2016)

21. Gama, K., et al.: Hackathons in the formal learning process. In: Proceedings of the 23rd Annual ACM Conference on Innovation and Technology in Computer Science Education - ITiCSE 2018, Larnaca, Cyprus, pp. 248–253. ACM Press (2018)

22. Gama, K., et al.: Mapathons and hackathons to crowdsource the generation and usage of geographic data. In: Proceedings of the International Conference on Game Jams, Hackathons and Game Creation Events 2019 - ICGJ 2019, San Francisco, CA, USA, pp. 1–5. ACM Press (2019)

23. Ghouila, A., et al.: Hackathons as a means of accelerating scientific discoveries and knowledge transfer. Genome Res. 28(5), 759–765 (2018)

24. Horton, P.A., et al.: Project-based learning among engineering students during short-form hackathon events. In: American Society for Engineering Education Annual Conference & Exposition at, Salt Lake City, UT (2018)

25. Hou, Y., Wang, D.: Hacking with NPOs: collaborative analytics and broker roles in civic data hackathons. Proc. ACM Hum. Comput. Interact. 1(CSCW), 1–16 (2017)

26. Karlsen, J., Løvlie, A.S.: 'You can dance your prototype if you like': independent filmmakers adapting the hackathon. Digit. Creat. 28(3), 224–239 (2017)

27. Kitchenham, B., et al.: Systematic literature reviews in software engineering – a systematic literature review. Inf. Softw. Technol. 51(1), 7–15 (2009)

28. Lara, M., et al.: Peer-led hackathon: an intense learning experience (2015)

29. Lara, M., Lockwood, K.: Hackathons as community-based learning: a case study. TechTrends 60(5), 486–495 (2016). https://doi.org/10.1007/s11528-016-0101-0

30. Linnell, N., et al.: Hack for the homeless: a humanitarian technology hackathon. In: IEEE Global Humanitarian Technology Conference (GHTC 2014), San Jose, CA, pp. 577–584. IEEE (2014)

31. Mantzavinou, A., Ranger, B.J., Gudapakkam, S., Broach Hutchins, K.G., Bailey, E., Olson, K.R.: Health hackathons drive affordable medical technology innovation through community engagement. In: Hostettler, S., Najih Besson, S., Bolay, J.-C. (eds.) UNESCO 2016, pp. 87–95. Springer, Cham (2018). https://doi.org/10.1007/978-3-319-91068-0_8

32. Medina Angarita, M.A., Nolte, A.: Does it matter why we hack? – exploring the impact of goal alignment in hackathons, 16 (2019)

33. Nandi, A., Mandernach, M.: Hackathons as an informal learning platform. In: Proceedings of the 47th ACM Technical Symposium on Computing Science Education - SIGCSE 2016, Memphis, Tennessee, USA, pp. 346–351. ACM Press (2016)

34. Nolte, A., et al.: You hacked and now what?: - exploring outcomes of a corporate hackathon. Proc. ACM Hum. Comput. Interact. 2(CSCW), 1–23 (2018)

35. Olson, K.R., et al.: Health hackathons: theatre or substance? A survey assessment of outcomes from healthcare-focused hackathons in three countries. BMJ Innov. 3(1), 37–44 (2017)

36. Page, F., et al.: The use of the "hackathon" in design education: an opportunistic exploration. In: Engineering and Product Design Education (2016)

37. Pe-Than, E.P.P., et al.: Designing corporate hackathons with a purpose: the future of software development. IEEE Softw. 36(1), 15–22 (2019)

38. Pirker, J., et al.: Social aspects of the game development process in the Global Gam Jam. In: Proceedings of the International Conference on Game Jams, Hackathons, and Game Creation Events - ICGJ 2018, San Francisco, CA, USA, pp. 9–16. ACM Press (2018)

39. Porter, E., et al.: Reappropriating hackathons: the production work of the CHI4Good day of service. In: Proceedings of the 2017 CHI Conference on Human Factors in Computing Systems - CHI 2017, Denver, Colorado, USA, pp. 810–814. ACM Press (2017)
40. Purwanto, A., Zuiderwijk, A., Janssen, M.: Citizens' motivations for engaging in open data hackathons. In: Panagiotopoulos, P., et al. (eds.) ePart 2019. LNCS, vol. 11686, pp. 130–141. Springer, Cham (2019). https://doi.org/10.1007/978-3-030-27397-2_11
41. Rosell, B., et al.: Unleashing innovation through internal hackathons. In: 2014 IEEE Innovations in Technology Conference, Warwick, RI, pp. 1–8. IEEE (2014)
42. Sadovykh, A., et al.: On the use of hackathons to enhance collaboration in large collaborative projects : - a preliminary case study of the MegaM@Rt2 EU project. In: 2019 Design, Automation & Test in Europe Conference & Exhibition (DATE), Florence, Italy, pp. 498–503. IEEE (2019)
43. Safarova, B., et al.: Learning from collaborative integration. In: 33rd eCAADe Conference (2015)
44. Soltani, P., et al.: Hackathon – a method for digital innovative success: a comparative descriptive study. In: Proceedings of the 8th European Conference on Information Management and Evaluation, ECIME 2014 (2014)
45. Starov, O., et al.: Hacking the Innovations with University-Industry Hackathons. University-Industry Interaction Conference (2015)
46. Stoltzfus, A., et al.: Community and code: nine lessons from nine NESCent Hackathons. F1000Res. **6**, 786 (2017)
47. Suominen, A.H., et al.: Educational hackathon: innovation contest for innovation pedagogy. innovation, the name of the game. In: Proceedings of the 2018 ISPIM Innovation Conference (Stockholm), 18 (2018)
48. Tang, T., Vezzani, V.: Fostering a culture of collaboration through playful Design Jams. In: 9th International Conference, Senses & Sensibility 2017: Design Beyond Borders and Rhizomes (2017)
49. Trainer, E.H., et al.: How to hackathon: socio-technical tradeoffs in brief, intensive collocation. In: CSCW (2016)
50. Wilson, J., et al.: Beyond the classroom: the impact of a university-based civic hackathon addressing homelessness. J. Soc. Work. Educ. **55**(4), 736–749 (2019)

Time-Position Characterization of Conflicts: A Case Study of Collaborative Editing

Hoai Le Nguyen⃝ and Claudia-Lavinia Ignat$^{(\boxtimes)}$⃝

Université de Lorraine, CNRS, Inria, LORIA, 54000 Nancy, France
{hoai-le.nguyen,claudia.ignat}@inria.fr

Abstract. Collaborative editing (CE) became increasingly common, often compulsory in academia and industry where people work in teams and are distributed across space and time. We aim to study collaborative editing behavior in terms of collaboration patterns users adopt and in terms of a characterisation of conflicts, i.e. edits from different users that occur close in time and position in the document. The process of a CE can be split into several editing *'sessions'* which are performed by a single author (*'single-authored session'*) or several authors (*'co-authored session'*). This fragmentation process requires a pre-defined 'maximum time gap' between sessions which is not yet well defined in previous studies. In this study, we analysed CE logs of 108 collaboratively edited documents. We show how to establish a suitable 'maximum time gap' to split CE activities into sessions by evaluating the distribution of the time distance between two adjacent sessions. We studied editing activities inside each *'co-author session'* in order to define potential conflicts in terms of time and position dimensions before they occur in the document. We also analysed how many of these potential conflicts become real conflicts. Findings show that potential conflicting cases are few. However, they are more likely to become real conflicts.

Keywords: Collaborative editing · Collaboration patterns · Conflicts · ShareLaTeX

1 Introduction

Today, modern word processors such as Google Docs [8], ShareLaTeX [16], Etherpad [7] are popular with many useful features to support collaborative editing (CE) such as adding comments, in-line communication (chat), revision histories and editing logs. The question *'How people write together'* [14,15] captured the attention of CSCW researchers. Birnholtz et al. [1] reveal that edits and comments in CE often carry social meaning i.e. they can have emotional and relational impact. The authors also pointed out that communication can be used to explain potentially conflicting behaviors and avoid negative relational effect.

© Springer Nature Switzerland AG 2020
A. Nolte et al. (Eds.): CollabTech 2020, LNCS 12324, pp. 65–80, 2020.
https://doi.org/10.1007/978-3-030-58157-2_5

Their follow up research [2] presented an experimental study of group maintenance in collaborative editing using Google Docs. This is the first research that considered to analyse editing logs. The study was separated into an asynchronous phase followed by a synchronous phase. In the asynchronous phase two users separately edited a document on a specific topic and then shared it with the assigned partner who provided feedback and revised the document. The synchronous phase required that the two users edit a shared document summarizing their opinions expressed in their previously written documents. However, the study was controlled by separating the writing activity into asynchronous and synchronous and has not given users the freedom to choose and alternate the writing style. Moreover, the study focused uniquely on the relationship between communication, editing and collaborators social relationships and did not study the editing process of users.

Follow up research studied how people collaboratively edit documents by analysing collaborative editing logs. Sun et al. [17] presented an analysis of collaboration logs over two years of all Google employees using Google Docs suite. They found that collaboration editing has grown rapidly up to 53% during the period they examined and 'concurrent editing is sticky' with 76% of the employees who participated in a 'concurrent session' repeating the activity in the following month. In [9,10] authors studied the effect of delay on the error rate, redundancy and quality of collaboratively produced documents by analyzing logs of real-time collaborative editing tasks using Etherpad. Olson et al. [14] examined the traces of collaborative writing behavior of advanced undergraduates in a project course using Google Docs. They found that 95% of documents have some simultaneous work (i.e. have at least one 'co-authored session'). The study assesses the quality of the collaboratively edited documents and analyses different aspects of CE using the taxonomy of CE [12,15]. D'Angelo et al. [3] analysed the histories of a large collection of documents edited in Etherpad [7] to study how people are writing in the wild and found that simultaneous editing happens very rarely.

Conflict is a common phenomenon in collaboration between groups of people, and conflict management is a key concern in designing collaborative applications [6]. In collaborative editing conflicts occur when users concurrently write in the same part of the document. As stated in [4], syntactic conflicts occur at the system infrastructure level, while semantic conflicts are inconsistencies from the perspective of the application domain. Generally, merging algorithms underlying the application solve the syntactic inconsistency problems in collaborative text editing, but they do not enforce semantic consistency. In [13] authors studied conflicts in asynchronous collaboration over open source software projects that used Git.

We aim to study collaborative editing behavior in terms of patterns of collaboration users adopt such as alternating synchronous and asynchronous collaboration and measuring and comparing user performances during the different collaboration modes. We also aim to study a characterisation of conflicts in terms of time and position in the document.

The process of collaborative editing can be split into several *sessions*, including *single-authored sessions* and *co-authored sessions*. The previous studies did not well define a suitable 'interval' or 'maximum time gap' which is used for this fragmentation process. Moreover, they haven't provided a detailed analysis of editing activities inside these sessions. We particularly aim to analyse *collaborative edits* inside *co-author sessions* and study how users manage 'potential conflict' cases when they edit together in a close period of time and in close parts of the document. For this purpose we define a characterisation of collaborative editing by means of *time-position windows*. Our research questions are listed below:

1. How to choose a suitable 'maximum time gap' to split editing activities into sessions?
2. What is the time-position characterization of editing sessions, namely for 'co-authored sessions'?
3. Inside 'co-authored sessions', how often 'potential conflicts' happen within some time-position extension (condition)?

The rest of the paper is organized as follows. In Sect. 2, we present related approaches which are based on an analysis of the traces of collaborative editing. In Sect. 3, we describe the measurements of our study. We then discuss about our results and conclusion of this study.

2   Related Work

Sun et al. [17] published an in-house study that analysed the logs of activity for all Google employees from 2011 to 2013. They found that on that period, the percentage of new employees who collaborate on Google Docs per month has risen from 70% to 90%. To estimate the percentage of documents which had concurrent editing, they used a *15 minutes interval* to split documents into intervals and consider edits by different users in the same *15 minutes intervals* as concurrent edits. The choice of *15 minutes intervals* is arbitrary. And this approach has edge cases in which two users edit the same document within 15 minutes but they are split into two adjacent intervals and are not counted as concurrent edits. Authors proposed a more accurate approach which is looking for a sequence of edits by different users with the maximum gap of 15 minutes. However this proposed mechanism was not applied.

Olson et al. [14] collected and analysed 96 Google Docs documents written by 32 teams of undergraduate students from the Project Management class in three successive years (2011, 2012 and 2013) at University of California, Irvine. They found that 95% of the documents exhibited some simultaneous work. In fact, they used the approach of [17] with the *7 minutes gap*. To determine the *7 minutes gap*, they examined all documents with *15 minutes gap* and found that 90% of them were 7 minutes or less. In more details, a document consists of many *sessions*. Each *session* combines a series of *slices*. Each *slice* which aggregates a series of keystrokes is generated after a certain of pause or a certain amount of edits. If a *session* was edited by more than one editor, they consider it as a *simultaneous session*. The others are considered as *solo-authored sessions*.

Both studies above focus only on time-dimension of collaborative editing. If two authors edit a document within 7 or 15 minutes gaps, they are considered as having a simultaneous writing session either they can edit in adjacent positions or far different positions. The choices of 7 or 15 minutes gaps are still arbitrary. In another study, Larsen et al. [11] use a mixed methods involving interviews and analysis of the traces of collaborative editing documents (using Google Docs) to outline the role of 'territorial functioning' in CE. On their analysis, they take into account the position-dimension of edits to visualize the 'editing territories' of different authors over the time. However, for the time-dimension, they use the same technique as previous studies of Sun et al. [17] and Wang et al. [18] which is based on the *15 minutes time gap*.

D'Angelo et al. [3] presented a study on how Etherpad, a real-time collaborative editing tool, is used in the wild. They analysed the histories of a large collection of documents (about 14000 pads) in both time and position dimensions. Edits are independently classified as collaborative or not in time, position and time-position. An edit is considered as collaborative in time dimension if it is *close enough in time to an edit applied by a different author*. In this study, they used the *time windows* which are 5, 10 and 60 seconds to determine if an edit is *close enough* or not. And similarly, they used the *position window* of 10, 80, 400 and 800 characters. For two-dimensional analysis (time-position), all pairs of *time/position windows* were used. Results show that about half of the pads were edited by a single author. Asynchronous collaboration in which users edit in close positions of the document but in different times happens often. Simultaneous editing in which users edit in close positions within the same *time window* happens very rarely. Note that they used the proportion of time, position and time-position collaborative edits over the total edits of the documents for their inferences.

While [17] and [14] focus on finding if a document has some *simultaneous sessions* or not, [3] focuses on finding the quantity of *simultaneous edits* of shared editing documents. It presents a more detailed quantitative analysis of *collaborative editing* than the two previous works. However it lacks the overview of how people work together. For example, people can use 'divide and conquer' strategy in which editors work in different parts (positions) of the document [18]. Then it's obviously that the document presents only *time collaborative edits* results on their analysis. Beside, the *5 seconds or 10 seconds time window* is too short to have multiple editing activities. People can stop to discuss or to read the work of the others during several minutes before continue to write. Moreover, when people are free to collaborate, they do not edit simultaneously all the time. There are several *sessions* that they work asynchronously [14].

3   Time and Position Characterisation

We analysed [16] logs which were collected from a ShareLaTeX server used inside an engineering school and anonymized for privacy purpose. Groups of three or four students were assigned a writing task and required to use a shared Share-LaTeX document for their collaborative writing. All editing activities inside the shared document were recorded by ShareLaTeX server from the beginning until the end of the assignment, i.e. from 20-September-2017 to 20-November-2017. Students could collaboratively edit the shared documents while being collocated during their classes or remotely from home. However, users were free to use other coordination tools to coordinate their work. We have not analysed their coordination efforts during the task.

In ShareLaTeX, there are two types of edits which are 'Insertion' and 'Deletion'. They are recorded with the following information: the *timestamp* when they happen, the *position* in the document where they happen, the *user-id* who performs the edit, the *action-type* which determines the type of edit, i.e. an 'Insertion' or a 'Deletion' and the *content* which is inserted or deleted. The *content* of an edit can be a single character or a long string. In addition, a copy-paste action is considered as an 'Insertion'. A modification action is considered as a 'Deletion' of the old content followed by an 'Insertion' of the new content.

We retrieved 1748 documents from the logs. However, 856 documents were created for testing purpose (i.e. they were created and edited by a single user and have none or only one edit action). In the rest 892 documents, only 108 of them were edited by more than one author. As we are focusing on collaborative editing, our analysis was performed on these 108 documents. Table 1 presents the overview of our data in which *'No. of authors'* and *'No. of edits'* are the number of editors and the number of recorded editing activities of each documents. The *'Amount of edit'* is the sum of all *content* edits lengths.

Table 1. Overview of the data: 108 documents

	Min	Max	Average	Std
No. of authors	2	4	2.69	0.87
No. of edits	53	38,329	8,000	10,583
Amount of edit	245	272,935	47,133	56,866

A document can be presented in time-position view (two dimensional view). Figure 1 presents a sample document which is segmented into three *writing sessions* by time dimension. These sessions are classified into *single-author-session* (SAS) and *co-author-session* (CAS) depending on the number of editors of each session. In this sample we have one SAS and two CASs. Note that in a CAS, two or more editors can edit in the same position or in different positions. For a *time dimension* analysis we defined 'internal time distance' (or *internal-distance*) which is the time distance between two adjacent edits in the same session and 'external time distance' (or *external-distance*) which is the time distance between two adjacent sessions in a document.

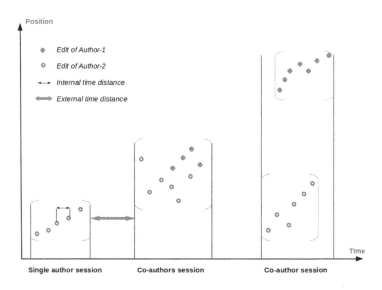

Fig. 1. A document with two authors in time-position view

3.1   Time Dimension

We first borrow the proposed approach of [17] to analyse the 'time dimension' of our data. Instead of using only an *'arbitrary maximum time gaps'*, we try to examine the data with different *'maximum time gaps'*: 15 minutes, 7 minutes, 5 minutes, 2 minutes, 1 minute and 30 seconds. Furthermore, after dividing a document into sessions and classifying the sessions into SASs and CASs, we analysed the differences between CASs and SASs such as: the internal-distance which is the distance between two edits in the same session, the average time which is the average length of sessions, the average number of edits of sessions.

Table 2 presents all the results of our analysis in time dimension. *Doc having CAS(s)* shows the number of documents that have at least one co-author session. The proportion of *Doc having CAS(s)* over all analysed (108) documents is 77.77% with *15 minutes time gap* and downs to 69.44% with *30 seconds time gap*. In comparison to [14] which showed that 95% of documents exhibited some 'simultaneous work' with *7 minutes time gap*, our data set shows that 75.92% of documents have collaborative sessions. Also with this time gap, our analysis shows that the average length of co-author sessions is 2369 seconds (39.5 minutes) and the longest co-author session is 8639 seconds (144 minutes) while they are 9.2 minutes (average) and 74 minutes (longest) in [14].

Table 2. Documents segmentation by different *maximum time gaps*

	Time gaps					
	15mn	7mn	5mn	2mn	1mn	30s
Doc having CASs	84/108	82/108	80/108	77/108	76/108	75/108
Proportion	77.77%	75.92%	74.07%	71.30%	70.00%	69.44%
No. of CASs per doc						
Average	2.3	2.9	3.4	5.8	9.4	14.1
Proportion	28.4%	24.4%	22.7%	17.5%	13.9%	10.7%
Internal-distance						
SASs (Average)	9.61s	6.77s	5.89s	4.04s	2.87s	2.01s
SASs (CI 99%)	[6.56–12.68]	[5.74–7.80]	[5.19–6.61]	[3.73–4.35]	[2.74–3.00]	[1.97–2.07]
CASs (Average)	4.25s	4.19s	4.15s	2.55s	1.78s	1.24s
CASs (CI 99%)	[2.89–5.62]	[2.69–5.70]	[2.71–5.59]	[1.97–3.14]	[1.54–2.02]	[1.13–1.35]
Session length						
SASs (Average)	972s	647s	507s	226s	109s	51s
CASs (Average)	3,314s	2,369s	1,953s	878s	350s	155s
No. of edits						
SASs (Average)	213	170	146	94	60	39
CASs (Average)	2,140	1,841	1,629	961	470	255
CASs (Normalized)	893	787	704	429	214	118

No. of CASs per Doc is the average number of CASs in each document after a segmentation of the document with the given *time gaps*. We also displayed the proportion of CASs over all sessions (CASs and SASs). The smaller *time gaps* given, the more CASs are generated. However, it reduces the proportion of CASs over the total sessions. In another way, the number of CASs increases slower than the number of SASs when the *time gap* decreases.

Internal-distance presents the average internal distance between two edits in the same session (SASs or CASs). For more details, we calculated the confidence interval with 99% of significance (CI 99%) for the internal distance variable. We found that the internal distance of SASs is longer than the internal distance of CASs. In another way, the distance between two edits in single-author sessions is longer than the one in co-authors sessions.

Session length shows the average length in seconds of each session, i.e. how long each session lasts. *No. of edits* is the average number of edits in each session. We found that (with 99% of significance) the average length of CASs is longer than the average length of SASs and also that CASs have larger number of edits than SASs in average. In order to compare *No. of edits* for CASs and SASs, we normalized *No. of edits* of CASs as it includes edits from all collaborators while *No. of edits* of SASs includes only edits of a single editor. Normalized *No. of edits* of each document is calculated by dividing original *No. of edits* to the number of collaborators. Having more edits with shorter distance between edits and longer collaborating time, it significantly gives us a quantitative view that the co-authors sessions are more productive in terms of the quantity of contributions to the documents than the single-author sessions.

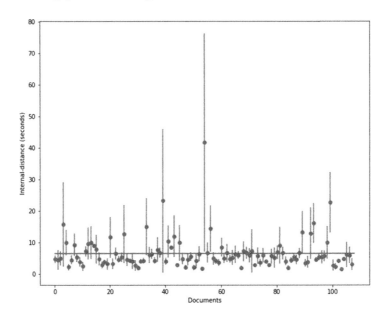

Fig. 2. Time gap = 420s, Average internal-distance with confidence interval CI90

As the *maximum internal-distance* is limited by the *time gap*, it's obviously that the *internal-distance* presented in Table 2 must be shorter than the given *time gap*. However, the result shows that the average *internal-distance* is much shorter than expected. For a better understanding, we calculated the confidence interval of *internal-distance* for each documents with 90% significance. Both SASs and CASs were included in this analysis. Figure 2 presents the results of *420s (7 minutes) time gap* in which all the confidence interval do not reach out 80 seconds and the general average *internal-distance* of all documents is 6.5 second presented by the red line. We can see that the *7 minutes time gap* is not a suitable *time gap* for our corpus. The suitable *time gap* should be shorter than 7 minutes.

In addition, we measured the *external-distances* of *30 seconds time gap* and calculated their distribution in different intervals which are created from *potential time gaps*: [30s, 60s), [60s, 120s), [120s, 180s), [180s, 240s), [240s, 300s), [300s, 420s), [420s, 900s), [900s). In which the left square bracket '[' denotes *'equal or longer than'*, the right round bracket ')' denotes *'shorter than'* and the last interval denotes the *external-distances* which are *'equal or longer than 900 seconds'*. Our suggestion is that if an interval covers more *external-distances* than others, it has much 'potential' to become a suitable *time gap* than others. Figure 3 shows the distribution of *external-distances* in each document. In average, *external-distances* represent 39.73%, 24.58%, 8.98%, 4.37%, 2.53%, 3.03%, 3.98% and 12.80% respectively for the given intervals. This means that if we increase the *time gap* from 30 seconds to 60 seconds, 39.73% of sessions will become part of other sessions because *external-distances* can not be shorter than

60 seconds. If we use 120 seconds *time gap* instead of 30 seconds *time gap*, 64,31 % (39.73% +24.58%) of sessions will be merged into other sessions and so on. From the above results, we can say that the [30s, 60s) and [60s, 120s) intervals have much potential to contain the suitable *time gap* as it covers much more *external-distances* (64,31%) than others. Moreover, we found that the range of *external-distances* is very wide, from 30 seconds to 87 hours (3.6 days). This wide range is due to the fact that collected logs represent the students writing task over a period of two months with an allocated time slot in their schedule of two hours per week, but students could continue the writing outside the allocated time slot.

Summarizing the time-dimension analysis, we found that collaborative editing is usually separated into many editing sessions including *single-author sessions* and *co-author sessions*. The time distance between sessions has a very wide range (up to 87 hours in our case study). To split a document into sessions, a suitable *time gap* needs to be determined. And finally, editors have more editing activities in co-authors sessions than in single-author sessions, i.e. having more contributions when working collaboratively.

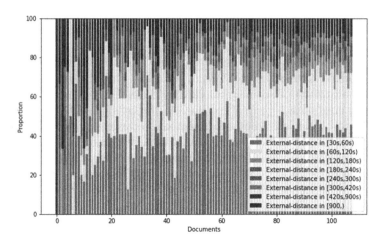

Fig. 3. Time gap = 30s, External-distances distribution

3.2   Time-Position Analysis

The analysis on *time dimension* gives us an overview of how collaborative editing happens over the time. It determines *co-authors sessions* in which the authors write closely together in time. However, it lacks the information about whether or not they write 'closely' in the same part of a document or 'separately' in different parts of it. A more detailed analysis in both time-position dimensions gives us a better understanding about how they write collaboratively.

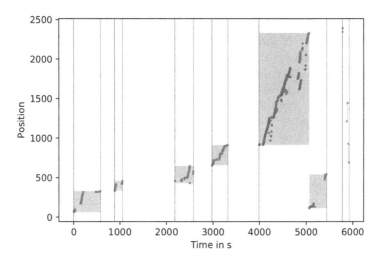

Fig. 4. A real document (id = 59e8f8d98e96ef7e2dc01eb2) presented in time-position view (Color figure online)

As we can see in Fig. 1, edits inside a session can be grouped into differ-ent 'clusters' depending on their time-position distances. In order to explain our time-position analysis we illustrate in Fig. 4 the time-position view of the document with id *59e8f8d98e96ef7e2dc01eb2* from our data corpus. The figure illustrates the notions of session and cluster. A session begins with a vertical blue line and ends with a vertical red line. A cluster is presented as a rectangle filled with light-blue color. Edits are presented as orange and green dots depend-ing on which authors they belong to (called orange author and green author). This document contains about 2500 characters (including white-spaces, empty lines) and was edited in total 6000 seconds by 2246 edit actions (including dele-tion, insertion). In the first 60 minutes, it was edited by the orange author only. Those edits are split into four single-author sessions, the longest time distance between them being about 16 minutes. In the next 25 minutes, the figure illus-trates a co-authors session in which the document was edited collaboratively by two authors (the orange author and the green author). And in the last time slot, the figure illustrates a single-author session of the orange author. In this session, the orange author had edited in three different positions of the document with position-distance larger than 400 characters. Note that in Fig. 4, for the sim-ple presentation, we use large size windows of the form *[time-gap, position-gap]* = *[300seconds, 400 characters]* in order to reduce the number of sessions and clusters.

Edits in a single-author session can be re-edited by another author in another session. However, these two sessions are separated in time so that if conflicts happen, they are asynchronous conflicts. In this analysis, we focus on the cases that two or more authors edit closely together in both time and position. Having a closer look in the co-author session in Fig. 4 which contains two clusters of edits, we can see that these two clusters have edits of both authors. In the bottom right cluster, there is a clear border between edits of two authors. In the top left cluster, besides three borders separating edits of different authors, there are several cases in which one author edited between two continuous edits of another author. We are interested in a characterization of conflicts in these cases where all involved edits are very close together in both time-position dimensions.

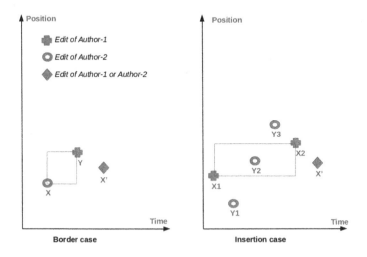

Fig. 5. Illustration of border case and insertion case

We examined two cases in which conflicts potentially happen. The first case called *border case* refers to the switch-point between two adjacent editing-areas which belong to two different authors. Those editing-areas can contain one or more continuous edits. The second case called *insertion case* refers to the case in which one author tries to edit between two continuous edits of another author, i.e. one author tries to insert one or more edits into an editing-area of another author. In both cases, if the time-position distance between those continuous edits is small, conflicts have high potential to happen. Figure 5 presents the illustration of *border case* and *insertion case*. On the left side of Fig. 5, **X, Y** and **X′** are three continuous edits (in time order) of two different authors in which [**X, Y**] form a *border case*. This *border case* can become a *potential border conflict case* if its time-position distance defined by the red rectangle is small. And if the adjacent edit **X′** happens between the positions of **X** and **Y**, it should be classified as a *border conflict*. A formal description of *border conflict* is presented in Definition 3.

On the right side of Fig. 5, $[X_1, Y_1, Y_2, Y_3, X_2, X']$ is a sequence of edits in time order. It means that Y_1, Y_2, Y_3 happen between X_1 and X_2 and X' happens right after X_2. However, in position dimension, the order is different, which is $[Y_1, X_1, Y_2, X', X_2, Y3]$. Focusing on $[X_1, Y_2, X_2]$, we can see that they satisfy both time order and position order. In another way, *Author-2* had inserted an edit into the time-position window formed by two continuous edits of *Author-1*. In the Fig. 5, this time-position window is presented by the red rectangle created by X_1 and X_2. If this window is small and the adjacent edit $\boldsymbol{X'}$ happens between the position of X_1 and X_2, we consider this case as an *insertion conflict*. A formal description of *insertion conflict* is presented in Definition 4.

Definition 1. *A sequence of edits $[X_1, X_2, .., X_n]$ is a **sequence of edits in time order with time-gap t** if $\forall i \in [1, n) : time(X_{i+1}) > time(X_i)$ and time-distance$(X_i, X_{i+1}) < t$.*

Definition 2. *A sequence of edits $[X_1, X_2, .., X_n]$ is a **sequence of edits in position order with position-gap p** if $\forall i \in [1, n) : position(X_{i+1}) > position(X_i)$ and position-distance$(X_i, X_{i+1}) < p$.*

Definition 3. *X is an edit of Author-1, Y is an edit of Author-2 and X' is an edit belonging to one of them. If $[X, Y, X']$ is a sequence of edits in time order with time-gap t and $[X, X', Y]$ is a sequence of edits in position order with position p, $[X, Y]$ then form a **border conflict** within time-position window $[t, p]$.*

Definition 4. *X_1, X_2 are edits of Author-1, $Y_1, Y_2, ...Y_k$ are edits of Author-2 and X' is an edit belonging to one of them. $(Y_i)^+, i \in [1, k]$ is a sub-sequence of edits of Author-2 which has at least one edit. If $[X_1, Y_1, Y_2, ...Y_k, X_2, X']$ is a sequence of edits in time order with time-gap t and $\exists (Y_i)^+$ so that $[X_1, (Y_i)^+, X_2]$ or $[X_2, (Y_i)^+, X_1]$ form a sequence of edits in position order with position p, $[X_1, (Y_i)^+, X_2]$ or $[X_2, (Y_i)^+, X_1)$ then form an **insertion conflict** within time-position window $[t, p]$.*

We use a **[30s, 10c]** time-position window to run our experiments. As we explained in Sect. 3.1, the documents are separated into sessions using a *30 seconds time-gap*. After that, all co-authors-sessions are checked for *border cases* and *insertion cases*. If these *border cases* and *insertion cases* satisfy the selected time-position window which is **[30s, 10c]**, they become *potential border conflicts* and *potential insertion conflicts*. And if one of the involved authors edits right after in the potential-conflict-area, we consider that potential conflict as a conflict. The reason that we choose the **[30s, 10c]** time-position window is that it can allow three or more editing actions and can cover the position distance of two or three words. Table 3 characterizes conflicts for the **[30s, 10c]** time-position window.

The results in Table 3 show the high proportion of potential-conflicts that become conflicts: from 77.53% to 91.51% for *border conflict* and from 88.96% to 100% for *insertion conflict* with significance of CI99%. However, these two types of conflict happen very rarely. It is less than 9.66% for *border conflict* and less than 5.04% for *insertion conflict*. The case of *potential border conflict* that is not a *border conflict* corresponds to the case that the time-position window (the border) of two continuous edits of two authors is larger than the time-position window that we use to determine *border conflict*. And in the case of *potential insertion conflict* that is not an *insertion conflict*, two authors are editing in two different areas which are large enough in position.

Table 3. Border conflict and insertion conflict with **[30s, 10c]** time-position window

	Border conflict	Insertion conflict
Proportion of Potential-conflicts over Consider-cases CI99%	5.7% [1.73–9.66%]	2.27% [0–5.04%]
Proportion of Conflicts over Potential-conflict CI99%	84.52% [77.53–91.51%]	97.22% [88.96–100%]
Average of Time-distance of Conflict cases CI99%	6.17s [3.67–8.68s]	4.06s [0–10.3s]
Average of Position-distance of Conflict cases CI99%	3.43c [2.88–3.98c]	4.15c [2.13–6.17c]

Beside the time-position window *[30s, 10c]*, we also used a smaller window of *[10s, 5c]* and a larger window of *[60s, 20c]* to examine the *border conflict* and the *insertion conflict*. Results are presented in Table 4 and Table 5 respectively. We can see that the *potential border conflict* is affected by the time-position window more than the *potential insertion conflict*. The *potential border conflict* decreases from 5.7% to 3.07% with a smaller window and increases to 9.94% with a larger window. The *potential insertion conflict* has less effects by the size of time-position window. Furthermore, the smaller time-position window decreases the proportion of *border conflict* over *potential border conflict* while the larger window increases it. For the *insertion conflict*, the result is reversed. It means that the smaller the time-position window is, the more likely the *potential insertion conflicts* become real *insertion conflicts*.

Table 4. Border conflict and insertion conflict with **[10s, 5c]** time-position window

	Border conflict	Insertion conflict
Proportion of Potential-conflicts over Consider-cases CI99%	3.07% [0.9–5.23%]	2.13% [0–5.49%]
Proportion of Conflicts over Potential-conflict CI99%	84.04% [76.93–91.16%]	100% [NA]
Average of Time-distance of Conflict cases CI99%	2.59s [1.51–3.68s]	4.34s [0–12.91s]
Average of Position-distance of Conflict cases CI99%	2.23c [1.88–2.57c]	2.3c [0.98–3,62c]

As an implication for design for our study we recommend that awareness mechanisms [5] could be proposed for users when potential conflicts of both types border conflicts and insertion conflicts are detected. Users can get notified

Table 5. Border conflict and insertion conflict with **[60s, 20c]** time-position window

	Border conflict	Insertion conflict
Proportion of Potential-conflicts over Consider-cases CI99%	9.94% [3.95–15.93%]	2.04% [0–4.33%]
Proportion of Conflicts over Potential-conflict CI99%	87.0% [80.98–93.02%]	95.53% [85.05–100%]
Average of Time-distance of Conflict cases CI99%	5.33s [3.16–7.5s]	4.24s [0–9.14s]
Average of Position-distance of Conflict cases CI99%	7.46c [5.96–8.97c]	4.9c [2.41–7.39c]

by means of a 'heat map' that visualizes the recency of editing activities [11] when they write closely in time and position with other users, i.e. when the potential border conflicts and potential insertion conflicts occur.

4 Conclusion

In this paper we studied collaborative editing behavior in terms of collaboration patterns users adopt and in terms of a characterisation of conflicts, i.e. edits from different users that occur close in time and position in the document. By examining different 'maximum time gaps' from 30 seconds to 15 minutes we found that the time distance between sessions (i.e. *'external-distance'*) has a very wide range (up to 87 hours in our case study). By evaluating the distribution of *'external-distance'* of a very small time gap, we can determinate a suitable 'maximum time gap' to split editing activities into single-author sessions and co-author sessions. We found that users are more productive in co-author sessions than in single-author sessions.

In a more detailed analysis of the *co-authors-sessions*, we use a [30 seconds, 10 characters] time-position window to examine the cases in which two authors edit closely together in both time and position. We focus on two cases which potentially result in conflict: *'border case'* and *'insertion case'*. *'Border case'* refers the cases in which two different authors edit in the border of two close editing areas that belong to them. And *'insertion cases'* refers to the cases in which one author does some edits between two continuous edits of another author. The results show that these two cases happen rarely: up to 5.04% for *'insertion cases'* and up to 9.66% for *'border cases'*. It means that people rarely edit closely in both time and position. However, these cases (i.e. the case in which people edit closely) are very likely to become conflicts: 77.53% to 91.51% of *'border cases'* and 88.96% to 100% for *'insertion cases'* result in 'conflict'. From above results, we suggest that collaborative editing tools (ShareLaTeX in this case) should consider to have an awareness mechanism for these two types of 'potential conflicts'.

Acknowledgement. We would like to thank Gérald Oster and Quentin Laporte-Chabasse for their valuable help for the collection of the ShareLaTeX logs.

References

1. Birnholtz, J., Ibara, S.: Tracking changes in collaborative writing: edits, visibility and group maintenance. In: Proceedings of the ACM Conference on Computer Supported Cooperative Work - CSCW, pp. 809–818. ACM (2012). https://doi.org/10.1145/2145204.2145325

2. Birnholtz, J., Steinhardt, S., Pavese, A.: Write here, write now!: an experimental study of group maintenance in collaborative writing. In: Proceedings of the SIGCHI Conference on Human Factors in Computing Systems - CHI, pp. 961–970. ACM (2013). https://doi.org/10.1145/2470654.2466123

3. D'Angelo, G., Di Iorio, A., Zacchiroli, S.: Spacetime characterization of real-time collaborative editing. Proc. ACM Hum. Comput. Interact. **2** (2018). https://doi.org/10.1145/3274310

4. Dourish, P.: Consistency guarantees: exploiting application semantics for consistency management in a collaboration toolkit. In: Proceedings of the ACM Conference on Computer Supported Cooperative Work - CSCW, pp. 268–277. ACM (1996). https://doi.org/10.1145/240080.240300

5. Dourish, P., Bellotti, V.: Awareness and coordination in shared workspaces. In: Proceedings of the Conference on Computer Supported Cooperative Work - CSCW, pp. 107–114. ACM (1992). https://doi.org/10.1145/143457.143468

6. Easterbrook, S.M., Beck, E.E., Goodlet, J.S., Plowman, L., Sharples, M., Wood, C.C.: A survey of empirical studies of conflict. In: Easterbrook, S. (ed.) CSCW: Cooperation or Conflict?. CSCW, pp. 1–68. Springer, London (1993). https://doi.org/10.1007/978-1-4471-1981-4_1

7. Etherpad. Open Source online editor providing collaborative editing in really real-time (2018). https://etherpad.org/

8. GoogleDocs. Create and share your work online (2006). http://docs.google.com

9. Ignat, C.-L., Oster, G., Fox, O., Shalin, V.L., Charoy, F.: How do user groups cope with delay in real-time collaborative note taking. In: Boulus-Rødje, N., Ellingsen, G., Bratteteig, T., Aanestad, M., Bjørn, P. (eds.) ECSCW 2015: Proceedings of the 14th European Conference on Computer Supported Cooperative Work, 19-23 September 2015, Oslo, Norway, pp. 223–242. Springer, Cham (2015). https://doi.org/10.1007/978-3-319-20499-4_12

10. Ignat, C.-L., Oster, G., Newman, M., Shalin, V., Charoy, F.: Studying the effect of delay on group performance in collaborative editing. In: Luo, Y. (ed.) CDVE 2014. LNCS, vol. 8683, pp. 191–198. Springer, Cham (2014). https://doi.org/10.1007/978-3-319-10831-5_29

11. Larsen-Ledet, I., Korsgaard, H.: Territorial functioning in collaborative writing. Comput. Support. Coop. Work. (CSCW) **28**(3), 391–433 (2019). https://doi.org/10.1007/s10606-019-09359-8

12. Lowry, P.B., Curtis, A., Lowry, M.R.: Building a taxonomy and nomenclature of collaborative writing to improve interdisciplinary research and practice. J. Bus. Commun. **41**(1), 66–99 (2004). https://doi.org/10.1177/0021943603259363

13. Nguyen, H.L., Ignat, C.-L.: An analysis of merge conflicts and resolutions in git-based open source projects. Comput. Support. Coop. Work. (CSCW) **27**(3), 741–765 (2018). https://doi.org/10.1007/s10606-018-9323-3

14. Olson, J.S., Wang, D., Olson, G.M., Zhang, J.: How people write together now: beginning the investigation with advanced undergraduates in a project course. ACM Trans. Comput. Hum. Interact. **24**(1) (2017). https://doi.org/10.1145/3038919

15. Posner, I.R., Baecker, R.M.: How people write together (groupware). In: Proceedings of the Twenty-Fifth Hawaii International Conference on System Sciences - HICSS, pp. 127–138. IEEE (1992). https://doi.org/10.1109/HICSS.1992.183420

16. ShareLaTeX. ShareLaTeX, Online LaTex editor (2017). https://www.sharelatex.com/. Accessed 19 Oct 2017

17. Sun, Y., Lambert, D., Uchida, M., Remy, N.: Collaboration in the cloud at Google. In: Proceedings of the 2014 ACM Conference on Web Science - WebSci, pp. 239–240. ACM (2014). https://doi.org/10.1145/2615569.2615637

18. Wang, D., Olson, J.S., Zhang, J., Nguyen, T., Olson, G.M.: DocuViz: visualizing collaborative writing. In: Proceedings of the 33rd Annual ACM Conference on Human Factors in Computing Systems - CHI, pp. 1865–1874. ACM (2015). https://doi.org/10.1145/2702123.2702517

Image-Based Detection Criteria
for Cultural Differences in Translation

Ikkyu Nishimura$^{(\boxtimes)}$(ID), Yohei Murakami(ID), and Mondheera Pituxcoosuvarn(ID)

Faculty of Information Science and Engineering, Ritsumeikan University,
Kusatsu, Shiga, Japan
is0368xk@ed.ritsumei.ac.jp

Abstract. These days, the improved accuracy of machine translation system enable us conduct intercultural collaboration. Even though
machine translation could translate words correctly, we sometimes face
trouble in our communications because we think about different images
for the same word due to our different backgrounds and culture. To make
the machine translation users notice the difference, a previous study proposed a cultural difference detection method based on image feature
similarity. However, the proposal have a deficiency about any similarity
criteria for judging cultural differences. This paper proposes a method for
calculating the criteria for detecting cultural differences. Specifically, a
threshold value is used to determine the presence or absence of a cultural
difference from the image similarity. An experiment compares the detection results with the results of human determination as to the cultural
difference contained in the pair. The experiment changes the threshold
value to determine the optimum threshold value. We prepared 1000 concepts and judged the cultural difference by the proposed method. We
divided the concepts into 200 and verified them by 5-fold cross validation. As a result, the average threshold value closest to human judgement
calculated from validation data was 0.4 and the accuracy for test data
was 80.4%.

Keywords: Intercultural collaboration · Multilingual communication ·
Machine translation · Image feature

1 Introduction

In order to tackle international problems, it is necessary to develop solutions
that transcend language and cultural differences and consider social diversity.
For that, intercultural collaboration is important. The realization of global citizenship education that fosters these abilities is defined as one of the Sustainable Development Goals (SDGs)[1]. For example, each year, NonProfit Organization (NPO) Pangaea holds a summer school called Kyoto Intercultural Summer
Schools for Youths (KISSY[2]), which gathers children using different languages

---

[1] https://sustainabledevelopment.un.org/?menu=1300.

[2] https://www.pangaean.org/web/japanese/general/aboutpangaeaact_jp.html.

© Springer Nature Switzerland AG 2020
A. Nolte et al. (Eds.): CollabTech 2020, LNCS 12324, pp. 81–95, 2020.
https://doi.org/10.1007/978-3-030-58157-2_6

and cultures from various countries. The children collaborates with each other and design proposals that can realize global citizenship education.

However, language and cultural differences make intercultural collaboration difficult. Language differences are being erased by the continual improvements in the quality of machine translation, but misunderstandings still occur due to cultural differences. For example, KISSY uses a unique machine translation tool for conversations, but a word that is unique to a Japanese culture could be translated into a word with quite different connotation, causing misunderstanding. In addition, even if the translation result is theoretically accurate, the nuance intended by the speaker may not caught by the receiver, and the conversation may not be successful.

In order to tackle these problems, a cultural difference detection method based on image similarity has been proposed previously. However, the original version did not introduce a criterion of similarity that would allow the presence or absence of cultural difference to be clearly determined. We rectify this omission by proposing a method to calculating the detection criteria of cultural differences so as to replicate human evaluations. Specifically, a threshold value of image similarity is used to determine the presence or absence of a cultural difference. This approach is confirmed by comparing the differences demonstrated by many image pairs with the results of the human assessed cultural differences. The threshold value is optimized to yield assessments closest to the judgements of people.

The cultural differences perplexing multilingual communication are explained in Sect. 2. The problems and solutions to the current cultural differences are also explained. Section 3 describes the approach of detecting cultural differences by calculating the similarity from the image feature vectors. Section 4 describes the threshold optimization method, which solves the part missing from approach described in Sect. 3. Then, in Sect. 5, we discuss several characteristic patterns resulting in mis-detections.

2   Cultural Differences in Multilingual Communication

2.1   Cultural Differences

Multilingual communication is becoming more effective by improving the translation accuracy of machine translation continues to improve, but there are still many wherein conversations do not turn out well. Cultural differences are the chief cause of communication failures. People have different ways of thinking, values, and images depending on their cultural background, such as the environment they grew up in and the culture they were exposed to. This may cause the listener to imagine something different from what the speaker wants to communicate[1]. Other conversation difficulties include culture specific items, items unique in one culture cannot be fully understood by people of other cultures even if the translation is detailed.

For example, "ゴボウ (*gobou*)" which is often eaten in Japan has the machine translation outputs of "burdock", "great burdock", or "greater burdock".

"ゴボウ(*gobou*)"

"great burdock" "burdock" "greater burdock"

Fig. 1. Example of cultural differences

When Japanese people hear "ゴボウ (*gobou*)", they think of a desirable food (left side of Fig. 1). However, people in many countries other than Japan associate "burdock", "great burdock", or "greater burdock" with the inedible plant above the ground, not its edible root (right side of Fig. 1). The two images triggered by these words are not wrong. Because both are the same plant, the "ゴボウ (*gobou*)" in Japan is the root of the plant that is reminiscent of "burdock", "great burdock", "greater burdock". In Japanese culture, the root of this plant is often eaten, it is recognized as a foodstuff and it has a rootlike appearance. However, because the culture of eating "ゴボウ (*gobou*)" overseas is less popular, the image of vegetation is more often imagined.

2.2   Related Research

Existing research on cultural differences in multilingual communication can be broadly divided into two types: cultural difference analysis based on written knowledge and cultural difference analysis based on image interpretation.

Knowledge-Based Cultural Differences: Yoshino et al. focused on Wikipedia [2]. This research attempted to confirm whether cultural differences could be detected by using the categories used by Wikipedia; the words examined were those manually judged to exist by a questionnaire. Calculating the degree of importance was shown to improve the accuracy of detecting cultural differences. Similar work by Ulrike et al. [3] used Wikipedia to examine the cultural diversity of France, Germany, Japan, and the Netherlands; they investigated the relationship between national culture and computer-mediated communication by assessing the Wikipedia editing operations in the different countries. Their research yielded results that well matched the four dimensions of cultural impact revealed by Hofstede et al. [4]

Images-Based Cultural Differences: Cho Heeryon et al. [5] used pictograms to detect cultural differences. This research focused on pictograms as a communication tool that does not need to use words when people from different cultures communicate a network. Their results showed that pictograms are interpreted differently depending on the culture. Research by Koda et al. [6] focused on avatars, which are often used in online communication in recent years, and determined whether there are cultural differences in the interpretation of avatars' facial expressions. They compared and analyzed the interpretation contents of the avatar's facial expressions between Asia and eight Western countries, and found that there was no cultural difference in the interpretation of negative expressions, unlike the interpretation of positive expressions.

3   Cultural Difference Detection Based on Image Similarity

In order to detect cultural differences, a group of researcher [7] devised a method to automatically determine the presence or absence of cultural differences that used the feature vectors of images associated with the words. Specifically, image search is performed using each word in Japanese and English linked to the same concept in a concept dictionary, and a feature vectors of the acquired images are generated. Then the method calculates the similarity between the vectors and detects the existence of cultural difference based on the similarity (Table 1).

Table 1. Japanese WordNet example

Identifier	Japanese	English	Explanation
11924445-n	ゴボウ, 牛蒡 (gobou)	burdock, clotbur	any of several erect biennial herbs of temperate Eurasia having stout taproots and producing burs

Figure 2 displays a flowchart of a variation of the proposed method. First, extract Japanese and English words that are defined as the expressing the same concept from Japanese version of WordNet [8]. WordNet is an English dictionary created by Princeton University's team, and Japanese WordNet [9] was created by manually associating Japanese with WordNet.

Next, the top 10 images in each source are selected. The acquired images are gray-scaled to eliminate extraneous information and facilitate similarity calculation. An image feature vector is generated from each gray-scaled image by applying Keras VGG16[3]. The feature vector consists of 4 sets of 4 rows with 12 dimensions. Shape a 4 * 4 * 512 vector into a 1row, 8192 dimensional vector. Then, the average of the 10 feature vectors is determined for each language. The resulting pair of averaged image feature vectors obtained from the Japanese and English words is subjected to cosine similarity to calculate the degree of match between the vectors. The system then judges whether there is a cultural

---

[3] https://arxiv.org/abs/1409.1556.

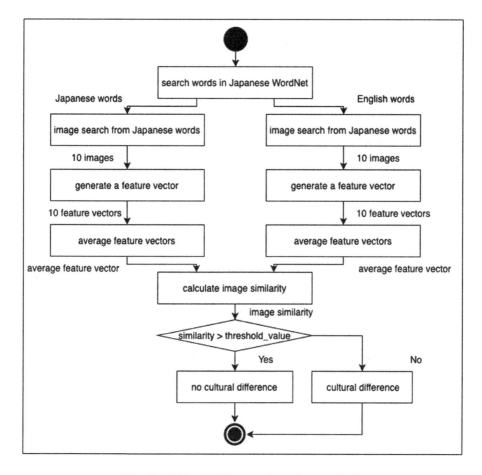

Fig. 2. Cultural difference detection method

difference by reference to a similarity threshold. If the similarity is below the threshold, a cultural difference is deemed to exist, otherwise no cultural difference exists.

4   Threshold Value Optimization

This Section describes a threshold value optimization method that ensures the proposed method can accurately detect the presence or absence of cultural differences.

4.1   Cultural Difference Detection Accuracy

A metric of cultural difference is needed in order to optimize the threshold of cultural difference criteria. As this metric, we use the rate at which the proposed

method matches the judgements of cultural differences made by humans. The
metric is quantified by using the percentage of concurrence between the made
by the proposed method and those made by humans.

Table 2. Judgement comparison

	Cultural difference (Human)	No cultural difference (Human)
Cultural difference (Automated detection)	True	False
No cultural difference (Automated detection)	False	True

From Table 2, the proposed method matches the manual judgement as
regards the presence or absence of cultural differences in two cases:

- Both automated detection and human judge that cultural differences exist.
- Both automated detection and human judge that cultural differences do not
  exist

Those cases are identified as True in Table 2. The accuracy of automated
detection is calculated by the following formula.

$$Accuracy = \frac{\text{Number of synsets classified as True cases}}{\text{Number of synsets classified as True and False cases}}$$

4.2 Threshold Value Optimization

Threshold value is the reference similarity value indicating the presence or
absence of cultural difference. It is necessary to set the threshold appropriately
so that the automated judgement is as accurate as possible. We selected from
the Japanese WordNet 1000 concepts indicating individual objects, and divided
them into 5 groups that have 200 concepts for each to conduct 5-fold cross validation. We calculated the accuracy that is obtained from the 4 validation results,
and determined the threshold that maximized the cultural difference detection
accuracy. The procedure for the optimization of the threshold value is shown in
Fig. 3. In WordNet, a synset is a set of synonyms that belongs to a concept. First,
the initial value of the synset and the threshold were set to 0 and 0.00, respectively. Then the similarities of the 800 synsets (4 groups out of 5 groups) were
calculated using the method described in Sect. 3 with different threshold-values.

First, synset and threshold-value were initialized to 0 and 0.0, respectively.
Synset is the concept and threshold-value is a variable for threshold value. We
chose 4 groups from 5 groups, and those are 800 concepts. Then, the similarity
of the 800 synset instances were calculated using the method in Sect. 3 with
different threshold-values. The threshold value was checked in the range of 0.0
to 1.0 in steps of 0.05. Also, we compared the accuracy of each threshold-value
and took the value with the highest accuracy as the optimal threshold value.
Finally, we averaged the accuracy that is gotten by the 5 patterns of validation
results.

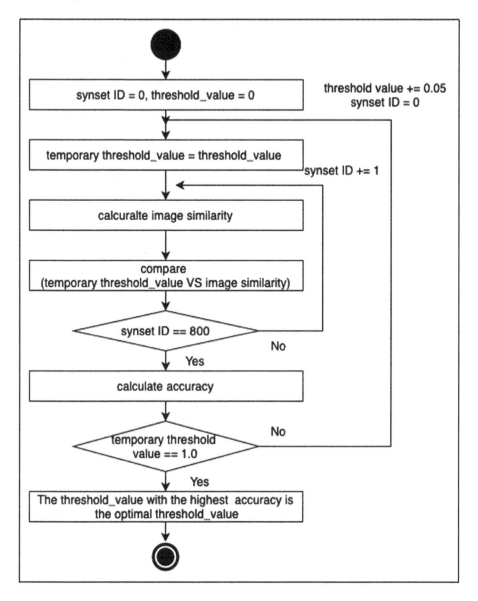

Fig. 3. Threshold value optimization procedure

4.3   Cultural Difference Judgement by Human

When the presence or absence of cultural differences is judged manually, different people are likely to make different judgements about what constitutes a cultural difference. Five Japanese judges were asked to judge the existence of a cultural difference for each concept. The final judgement taken to be the majority judgements.

Figure 4 shows a typical question sheet show to the people manually judging cultural differences. The question is:

Look at the keywords and choose whether "A" and "B" images match the keyword. If both match, select "Both". If neither match, select "Not applicable". **Numbers in () are question numbers.

Questionnaire1~25

Look at the keywords and choose which of "A" and "B" images are more associated.If you can associate both, select "両方(Both)'". If you can't associate both, select "該当なし(Not applicable)". **Numbers in () are question numbers.

A   (1)   *

B   (1)

keyword:wall

○ A   ✕

○ B   ✕

○ Both   ✕

○ Not applicable   ✕

Fig. 4. Questionnaire

Each sheet contained three pieces of information, the keyword, 10 group-A images and 10 group-B images. As shown only one of four choices were possible: "A",

"B", "Both", or "Not applicable", making it impossible to select multiple answers. Unknown to the respondents, the group-A images were taken from Japanese language sources while group-B images were taken from English language sources.

If "Both" was selected by a majority of examiners, it was taken to mean that there was no cultural difference. On the other hands, if "A" or "B" is selected, it means that only images located by either word are seen as appropriate by the examiners (all Japanese), so it is judged that there is a cultural difference. If the number of "Not applicable" answer is the highest, it may be considered that the image search results were inappropriate.

4.4 Optimal Threshold Value Verification

To validate the proposed threshold value optimization method, we conducted 5-fold cross validation using 1000 concepts chosen from the Japanese WordNet. Figure 5 shows the accuracy of the proposed method according to temporary threshold values.

The horizontal axis and vertical axis represent the temporary threshold and accuracy, respectively. As a result, it achieved the highest accuracy at the threshold value of 0.4. Therefore, we regarded 0.4 as the optimal threshold value.

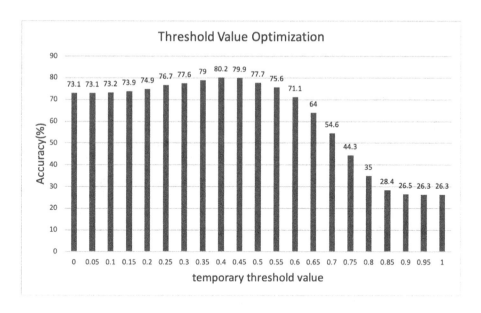

Fig. 5. Accuracy at each threshold value

Figure 6 shows the average of 5 test results among 5 folds. This matched to the average accuracy of validation tests in Fig. 5, 80.4%, when the threshold value was 0.4.

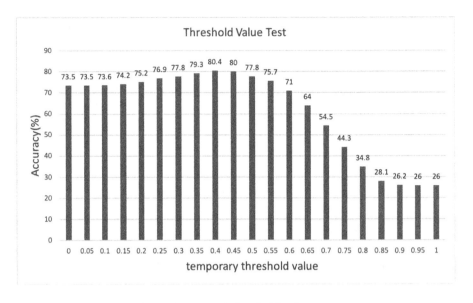

Fig. 6. Optimized threshold value test

5   Discussion

This section discusses the proposed method from the results obtained by threshold value optimization and testing.

5.1   Causes of Low Similarity

Since concepts with low similarity could lead to misunderstanding, we categorized below the causes of low similarity related to cultural difference.

Cause: 1. When a word does not exist in another language, a different word with different meaning is chosen as its translation. In some cases, words with close or similar meaning are used. For example, "sepulcher" in English is translation to "墓 (haka)" in Japanese. "Sepulcher" is a small room or monument, cut in rock or built of stone, in which a dead person is laid or buried, while "墓 (haka)" is not a room but more similar to graves in the graveyard. In another case, words with the same function are used. To illustrate, "mud pie" in English is linked to "土団子 (tutidango)" in Japanese by the concept dictionary. While both are made by children as an activity or in play, they differ in term of material and shape. Mud pie is made of mud and shaped like a pie, while 土団子 (tutidango) is made of soil and has round shape like the Japanese food called 団子 (dango).

Cause: 2. When a word exists in both languages with the same meanings but their nuance may be different based on culture. For example, coffins are usually influenced by religion and they look different in western and eastern countries.

Cause: 3. A word is a loan word but used differently from the original language. This cause also includes Pattern 1 in Table 3. An example is the word "mansion" in English; its translation in Japanese "マンション (*mansyon*)". "マンション (*mansyon*)" is a loan word which has similar pronunciation to the original word. However, the meaning is different. "マンション (*mansyon*)" is much smaller than mansion and is closer to the English concept of "apartment".

Cause: 4. One word can be used in broader area than its translation in another language. For example, "drain" in English is translated to "流出 (*ryusyutu*)" in Japanese but "流出 (*ryusyutu*)" covers a much broader context. While the meaning of both words is associated with the flow of fluid, "流出 (*ryusyutu*)" also includes the leak of information.

Cause: 5. One or both words have homonym(s). When a word has various meaning in one culture but the same word only has one meaning in another culture, the image search result could also be different. For instance, "ゴシキドリ亜科 (*goshikidoriaka*)" is a kind of bird but its translation "Barbet" is not only a kind of bird, but is also a breed of dog. Barbet dog is more popular and appears in the search result more often then the Barbet bird.

5.2 Misdetected Concept

Here, we introduce four characteristic patterns that were misdetected.

- (pattern 1) The automated detection judged that cultural difference presence existed, whereas human judgement showed no cultural difference
- (pattern 2) The automated detection judged that no cultural difference existed, while human judgement showed that cultural difference did exist
- (pattern 3) Cases with the highest number of "Not applicable" (No association for both sets of images) in the questionnaire
- (pattern 4) Cases with the highest number of "B" (With images from English keywords) in the questionnaire

Pattern 1: The Automated Detection Judged that Cultural Difference Existed, Whereas Human Judgement Showed No Cultural Difference
The fact that the automated method determined that there is a cultural difference means that the image similarity was low. Actually, one of the concepts that has such a pattern is that Japanese is "ウオーター (*uo-ta-*) ウォーター (*wo-ta-*) 水 (*mizu*)" and English is "water". The result of those image searches yields pattern 1 in Table 3.

The image search results for "water" were mostly images of water and water drops, whereas the image search results for "ウオーター (*uo-ta-*) ウォーター (*wo-ta-*) 水 (*mizu*)" were images of drinking water such as mineral water and bottled water. Therefore, it is expected that the image similarity would be low. Also, the reason why the image search results are so different is that images of mineral

Table 3. 4 pattern examples

Pattern	10 Images(Japanese)	10 Images(English)	Similarity
Pattern 1	"ウォーター ウォーター 水"	"water"	0.27
Pattern 2	"タピオカ"	"tapioca"	0.69
Pattern 3	"進化 進歩 プログレス 発展 成長 発達 発育"	"growth"	0.25
Pattern 4	"舞踏会 ボール"	"ball formal"	0.37

water were often yielded by the Japanese keyword "ウォーター (wo-ta-)". In Japanese, katakana is often used for product names and proper nouns of things, it is considered that the more specific drinking water image was acquired from the abstract water by including katakana[4] in the keyword.

Pattern 2: The Automated Detection Judged that No Cultural Difference Existed, While Human Judgement Showed that Cultural Difference Did Exist

In Table 3 "タピオカ (tapioka)" and "tapioca" are easy discerned examples of this pattern. The result of the image searches is shown in the second row of Table 3.

As for the result of "タピオカ (tapioka)" image search, there were many images of tapioca drink, known as bubble tea or pearl milk tea. On the other hands, the result of "tapioca" image search yielded images of tapioca in cups and glasses but most of the tapioca was in the form of jelly. The reason for the high similarity is the shape of the container. However, the results of the questionnaire showed cultural differences. In the questionnaire, 4 out of 5 people found that the image of "タピオカ (tapioka)" was more to recall. In recent years, drinks containing tapioca balls in Japan have become popular, so it is often recalled that tapioca should be included in drinks, and jellylike "tapioca" or pudding

---

[4] katakana, one of the Japanese character types, is used for mimetic words, foreign words, and slang.

is not a major food product, hence the human judgement found a cultural difference. In addition, it is difficult to generate feature vectors if the object in question occupies only a small proportion of the image; the feature vector is likely to be generated something other than tapioca, such as a container, so the determination may not be performed correctly.

Pattern 3: Cases with the Highest Number of "Not Applicable" in the Questionnaire

The concepts that were marked as "Not applicable" were dropped from the evaluation data. After the questionnaire session, we interviewed the respondents. Because the respondents did not know much about the concept, the concepts were marked as "Not applicable". In addition, the abstract concept, for example "進化 (*shinka*) 進歩 (*shinpo*) プログレス (*purosesu*) 発展 (*hatten*) 成長 (*seityo*) 発達 (*hattatu*) 発育 (*hatuiku*)" of pattern 3 in the Table 3, also yielded high rates of "Not applicable" because the image search returned results that were not specific to abstract concepts, such as emotion.

Pattern 4: Cases with the Highest Number of "B" in the Questionnaire

Because, all the examines were Japanese, we considered the pattern in which the image retrieved via the English words were selected. It was often seen in this pattern that the keywords corresponded to proper nouns or specific ones, and the image search results were the images of proper nouns in many cases. For example, with the keyword "舞踏会 (*butokai*) ボール (*bo-ru*)", the images of the ball were correctly acquired by the image search than "ball formal", but the images acquired via "舞踏会 (*butokai*) ボール (*bo-ru*)" were more often related to ball gowns and costumes. Since the words used as keywords corresponded to other specific words in this way, there were many cases where images search results that different from the original concept were acquired.

With the method proposed in this research, it is possible to judge cultural differences by using images, considering information and images that cannot be conveyed by just words, and the size of the concept. On the other hands, if there are keywords, product names, and proper nouns as in pattern 1 and pattern 3, images that are far from the meaning of the concept are acquired, so it may not be possible to accurately determine cultural differences. In addition, as can be seen from pattern 3, when the concepts that have no concrete shape are judged by this method, it may not be possible to make an accurate judgement.

From the problems mentioned above, we need to tackle those two problems in order to detect cultural differences more accurately.

Image Acquisition Method

As mentioned in the case of pattern 1, Katakana is often used for proper nouns based on foreign words in Japanese. In addition, an abstract image is likely to be acquired for the concept representing a shapeless object, as in the case of pattern 3. Therefore, it is necessary to improve performance by removing Katakana words derived from the English notation prior to searching for images, or by limiting the objects to those that have distinctive shapes.

Category-Specific Threshold Values
As in the case of pattern 2, it is not always possible to generate a useful feature vector from the images returned. Therefore, the similarity may change depending on the characteristics of nonessential parts of the image. For example, it is difficult to extract useful features for food that comes in containers, concepts in this category may need a different threshold value. It is also possible to divide the concepts into categories and create an optimum threshold value for each category by applying our proposed method.

6 Conclusions

In order to detect cultural differences in multilingual communication, this research has described a detection method based on image similarity and proposed a threshold value calculation method that yields a criterion for judging cultural differences. The contributions of this research are as follows:

- Identification of threshold value that serves as a basis for confirming cultural differences
    The automatic detection of cultural differences was evaluated by comparing judgements. The result indicated the threshold value of 0.4 achieved the highest accuracy of 80.2%.
- Verification of cultural difference detection accuracy using optimal threshold value
    The threshold value of 0.4 yielded the highest accuracy of 80.4%. This confirms that the optimal threshold value of similarity, which is the criterion of the cultural difference judgement for detecting the cultural difference, is 0.4.

The optimization of the threshold value enables us detect the cultural differences. It is important to divide into any genres according to the shape of the object and to find the optimal threshold value for each genre to improve accuracy. In addition, need to embed the cultural difference detection functionally into a multilingual communication tool to avoid miscommunication and misunderstanding caused by the cultural differences.

Acknowledgements. This research was partially supported by a Grant-in-Aid for Scientific Research (B) (18H03341, 2018–2020) and a Grant-in-Aid Young Scientists (A) (17H04706, 2017–2020) from Japan Society for the Promotion of Sciences (JSPS).

References

1. Deutscher, G.: Through the Language Glass: Why the World Looks Different in Other Languages. Metropolitan Books, New York (2010)
2. Yoshino, T., Miyabe, M., Suwa, T.: A proposed cultural difference detection method using data from Japanese and Chinese Wikipedia. In: 2015 International Conference on Culture and Computing (Culture Computing), pp. 159–166. IEEE (2015)

3. Pfeil, U., Zaphiris, P., Ang, C.S.: Cultural differences in collaborative authoring of Wikipedia. J. Comput. Mediat. Commun. **12**(1), 88–113 (2006)
4. Hofstede, G.H., Hofstede, G.J., Minkov, M.: Cultures and Organizations: Software of the Mind, vol. 2. Mcgraw-Hill, New York (2005)
5. Cho, H., Ishida, T., Yamashita, N., Inaba, R., Mori, Y., Koda, T.: Culturally-situated pictogram retrieval. In: Ishida, T., Fussell, S.R., Vossen, P.T.J.M. (eds.) IWIC 2007. LNCS, vol. 4568, pp. 221–235. Springer, Heidelberg (2007). https://doi.org/10.1007/978-3-540-74000-1_17
6. Koda, T.: Cross-cultural comparison of interpretation of avatars' facial expressions. In: IEEE/IPSJ Symposium on Applications and the Internet (SAINT-06) (2006)
7. Pituxcoosuvarn, M., Lin, D., Ishida, T.: A method for automated detection of cultural difference based on image similarity. In: Nakanishi, H., Egi, H., Chounta, I.-A., Takada, H., Ichimura, S., Hoppe, U. (eds.) CRIWG+CollabTech 2019. LNCS, vol. 11677, pp. 129–143. Springer, Cham (2019). https://doi.org/10.1007/978-3-030-28011-6_9
8. Fellbaum, C.: WordNet. In: The Encyclopedia of Applied Linguistics (2012)
9. Bond, F., Isahara, H., Fujita, S., Uchimoto, K., Kuribayashi, T., Kanzaki, K.: Enhancing the Japanese WordNet in the 7th Workshop on Asian Language Resources, in conjunction with ACL-IJCNLP 2009 (2009)

Creating Dialogue Between a Tutee Agent and a Tutor in a Lecture Video Improves Students' Attention

Ari Nugraha⬤, Izhar Almizan Wahono, Jianpeng Zhanghe, Tomoyuki Harada,
and Tomoo Inoue(✉)

University of Tsukuba, Tsukuba, Japan
{ari.nugraha,inoue}@slis.tsukuba.ac.jp, {s1826099,s1921659,
s1721687}@s.tsukuba.ac.jp

Abstract. One of the challenges found with learning using a lecture video is the short attention span of students due to high cognitive load when they are watching the video. Several methods have been proposed to increase students' attention, such as segmenting learning content into smaller pieces where each piece has short video duration. In this study we proposed an enhanced monologue lecture video with a tutee agent to mimic the dialogue between a tutor and a tutee to increase student attention to the lecture video. Based on lab evaluation including eye fixations data from an eye tracker, the videos enhanced with the tutee agent make the students' attention more frequent to the learning material presented in the lecture video and at the same time lowering their attention span to it.

Keywords: Tutee · Tutee agent · Pedagogical agent · Dialogue video · Lecture video · Student attention

1 Introduction

Delivering lecture in a form of video format becoming quite common nowadays as tools for creating a video already accessible where one can even produce just using their smartphone. While the Web video technology and standard getting more mature, in last decade we also saw the rise of massive open online courses (MOOC) and open courseware where its main way for learning content delivery is by the means of lecture video. MOOCs and open coursewares provided by several world' high ranking university such as the MIT, opening opportunity for everyone at their own time and their own pace. In this sense, MOOC and open courseware provide greater accessibility and time convenience for learners. However, even though learning through MOOC provides flexible way of learning for the enrolled students, problems such as high cognitive load caused by information overload is still faced by learners. High video dropout rates caused by too long videos duration, and boredom due to short attention spans are another problem in watching lecture video delivered in distance learning platform. In this study, we proposed an enhanced lecture video material with embedded tutee agent to make the lecture video more exciting to watch by the students and in the end increasing student focus with the learning content in the video.

A. Nolte et al. (Eds.): CollabTech 2020, LNCS 12324, pp. 96–111, 2020.
https://doi.org/10.1007/978-3-030-58157-2_7

2   Literature Review

2.1   Video as Learning Material

The emergence of MOOCs and Open Coursewares, brings thousands of online courses being offered in the Internet. Each of these online courses consists of several parts where most of the content is recorded lecture video as a learning material. One of the reason why video is still becoming the *de facto* format for delivering learning content in distance learning environment is that a video provides a rich and powerful medium and can present information in an attractive and consistent manner [1]. Another benefit of lecture video is that it can be well suited to visualize the abstract or hard-to-visualize phenomena that are important in many science classes such as biology [2]. Outside of MOOC's realm, the usage of lecture video as a learning material in traditional classroom are becoming popular as instructors are increasingly making use of flipped classrooms method, whereby students are encouraged to watch the recorded lecture video on their own time and engage in activities geared toward a more in-depth understanding of the subject matter in the classroom [3]. While videos on MOOCs are structured inside courses, popular video sharing application such as YouTube also offers unstructured educational video provided not only from professional tutor, but also from non-professional content creators.

One of important thing to be considered when delivering the learning material in a video format is how effective the video in maximizing student learning. In the literature review on principals of effective lecture video, Brame [2] suggests three elements for video design and implementation that can help instructors maximize video's utility: 1) cognitive load, 2) student engagement, and 3) active learning. The cognitive theory of multimedia learning defines two channels for information acquisition and processing: a visual channel and an auditory channel [4]. The use of these two channels can facilitate the integration of new information into existing cognitive structures and lecture videos are the perfect medium for this, as it provides both visual and auditory information at the same time.

2.2   Learning with Dialogue Video

Other factor that can affects student engagement in lecture video according to the study is how the tutor or teacher presented the learning material or lecture style inside the video. Several lecturing style in the video exists such as the Khan-style or the talking-head style. The talking-head style with the tutor's head appears in the video has positive impact to the student enjoyment and learning performance compared to paper book style [5]. Lecture video style which involves a dialogue between a tutee and student also proved to have positive impact to the students learning. In this case the student become an observer student who learning by watching the dialogue. Study found that the students who watched the dialogue video have better constructive and interactive behaviors compared to watching monologue-videos and they are benefited from the presence of the tutees as they pay more attention to what the tutees said than to what the tutors said [6]. The advantage of this method is that it even does not need to be conducted with professional tutors; a meta-analysis study found that people with untrained tutoring skills and had moderate domain knowledge could become tutor [7].

2.3 Role of Pedagogical Agent in Learning

A large body of research related to the pedagogical agent in learning environment exists. Regarding the student' focus and attention, pedagogical agent, which usually represented as a human-like character, can provides instructional support and motivational elements into multimedia learning [8]. Pedagogical agent's voice and representation will produce social signals that trigger social responses from students. Study on influence of learner's social skill in collaboration with pedagogical agent showed that learners with higher social skills performed better on the explanation task with the agent than those with lower social skills and this is an indication that learners perceived their interaction with the agent as same with human-human interaction, where learners with low social communication skills have difficulty in collaborative learning [9].

As the most studies on pedagogical agent define the role of an agent as a tutor to the student, an agent role as a tutee also have been explored. Students who overheard a dialogue between a virtual tutee and a virtual tutor, learned more, took more turns in mixed-initiative dialogue, and asked more questions than those in the monologue-like condition where only a virtual tutor exists [10]. In more recent study, researchers have proposed a virtual tutee system (VTS) to improve college students' reading engagement, where the students take on the role of tutor and teach a virtual tutee. The study found that the students in VTS group engaged in a deep level of cognitive processing and have higher reading performance than students in the non-VTS group [11].

One of the benefits of using animated pedagogical agent in multimedia learning is that it is possible to more accurately model the dialogs and interactions that occur during novice learning and one-on-one tutoring [12]. Based on these previous studies of pedagogical agent and combined with the benefits of dialogue between a tutee and a tutor in the lecture video, in this study proposed a prototype tool to add a tutee agent as a replacement for human tutee in monologue video.

3 Proposal

3.1 Tool Overview

To add a tutee agent inside the lecture video with our prototype tool, a teacher or course designer needs to make an annotation on the designed lecture video with our tutee agent annotation interface. The annotation texts created by the teacher serve as the tutee agent utterances inside the video and will be uttered by the tutee agent at specified time in the video. The tutee agent voice is created by utilizing text-to-speech cloud service. The steps to do this as illustrated in Fig. 1 are:

1. Upload the designated lecture video
2. Add important metadata to the uploaded lecture video
3. Create annotation texts to the uploaded lecture video by selecting specific time in the video using the Tutee Agent' Annotation interface.

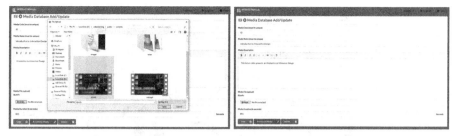

1) Choose and Upload Lecture Video   **2) Add Video' Metadata**

3) Create Tutee Agent Annotation

Fig. 1. Lecture video and Tutee Agent' Annotation workflow

3.2 Lecture Video Produced by the Tool

The result of the annotated lecture video is a lecture video with the tutee agent embedded into the lecture video. For the animated tutee agent itself, we created in animated PNG format as it provides high resolution image and can be embedded easily in Web environment. Using Web compatible format tutee agent also make customization of tutee agent easier for future development and study. When the tutee agent making a specific utterance at certain time in the video, the animated tutee agent animation is synchronized with the related voice generated from the cloud service while the lecture video is paused to mimic turn taking conversation between tutor and tutee agent. A text balloon containing the annotation text also showed up above the tutee agent while she is speaking.

4 Evaluation

4.1 Purpose

To evaluate the effect of lecture videos enhanced by our proposed tool, we have conducted a user study using within-subject experiment design by involving participants as an observer student. In this study, participants watched lecture videos using video user interface of our system in two conditions: 1) Monologue style (MON) where participants watch a monologue lecture video, where only a human tutor present inside the video and, 2) Dialogue style with tutee agent (DIA) where participants watch a monologue lecture video with a tutee agent added in the video. As a counterbalance for learning effect and bias from the learning style, we order the experiment condition differently for each participant. Before the experiment conducted, we have been granted an ethical approval from our university' IRB.

Fig. 2. The monologue lecture video as a learning material in this study delivered in talking head with presentation. In talking-head style, the tutor' head is appeared inside a lecture video explaining learning content.

4.2 Experiment Apparatus and Settings

In this experiment we used a personal computer (PC) connected to our tool and the tool was accessed via web browser. Participants watched the lecture video using the PC with 24-in. Full HD (1920 × 1080 resolution) monitor in our laboratory and listened to the learning material using headset. To collect data on user attention and eye fixation, we equipped participants with the open source Pupil eye-tracker [13] (see Fig. 3). While watching the lecture video, participants were seated in front of the PC's monitor and we asked participants to adjust their seat position as convenient as they want. Three video cameras in different angles are used in this experiment to record participant's behavior while watching the lecture video.

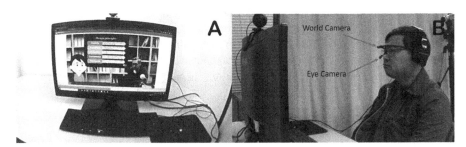

Fig. 3. A) Participant's world view from the Pupil's world camera represent what participant saw with their eye, B) Participant in our experiment seated in front of PC's monitor wearing the Pupil eye tracker and headset while watching the lecture videos.

Experiments with eye-tracker commonly restrict the head movement of participants using a chin rest to reduce head movements and ensure a constant viewing distance [14], we do not using this kind of tool in our experiment as it is not reflecting an ideal condition when student watching lecture video. We did not limit the movement of participants' head and body when they were watching the lecture video. The purpose for this was that we wanted our participants to be as convenient as possible while watching the lecture video and to reflect real world condition in watching lecture video.

4.3 Materials

4.3.1 Lecture Videos

For the learning materials used in our evaluation, we produced two lecture videos with different themes in a monologue style. These monologue style video then enhanced into dialogue style for the DIA condition, where the tutee agent presents inside the video and make questions and comments related to what the tutor explains in the video. The tutee agent utterances inside the video were scripted and annotated using our tutee agent annotation interface. The themes of the lecture videos produced are: 1) Introduction to Interaction Design (ID), and 2) Introduction to Metadata (MD). The learning content for ID theme video is taken from *The Interaction Design* textbook, while for the MD theme video is taken from the modified and simplified version of Metadata MOOC series videos from YouTube by Professor Jeffrey Pomerantz of School of Information and Library Science, The University of North Carolina of Chapel Hill (https://www.you tube.com/watch?v=fEGEJhJzrB0).

To investigate how the tutee agent could affect in variety type of video content, we designed The ID theme video presentation slides to contain more text than the MD theme video as it is known from limited capacity theory states that our short-term memory is quite small; therefore, offering too much information on the slides such as too many text could lead to a high cognitive load and split attention [15]. Both of these lecture materials was delivered using talking-head with presentation style (Fig. 2) as it is one of the popular learning content delivery style in lecture video [5]. To strike the balance between video duration and learning content, we designed both lecture videos to have duration up to 15 (fifteen) min.

4.3.2 Tutee Agent Utterances

Studies on pedagogical agent have shown that by employing strategic utterances in dialog, such as asking for an explanation, repeating learning content, or providing suggestions, could stimulate reflective thinking and the metacognition processes involved in understanding [9]. Based on this notion of strategic utterances of pedagogical agent, we annotated the tutee agent at specific time of video. As slide transition in presentation can be indicated as a transition to different learning topic, we were making our tutee agent to make utterances at the specific time on the lecture video where it is near the end of every slide or before the slide transition occurred.

By making the tutee agent to utters summary to the current slide content and tutor's explanation, we implemented the concept of repetition. Repetition can be one of the virtual tutee contribution in the dialog by uttering key concepts mentioned by the tutor in his previous conversational turn [16]. Example of this repetition can be seen on Table 1.

Table 1. Example of the tutee agent summarization in MD theme video

Tutor	*"... from library and librarian we learn how to describe something effectively. Effectively here means for the purpose of storage and later retrieval by the user of library. Information about the content of a thing or resource that aids in finding or understanding it, is referred to as descriptive metadata. If you are looking for a book, the most obvious thing you care as a reader are, first, what the book called or the title, second, who wrote it or the author and third what is the book about or the subject! Descriptive metadata describes the book using those three aspects"*
Tutee agent	*"I see, descriptive metadata describes the object that can help people to find it and understanding the content"*

Besides making repetition of the tutor explanation in the form of conclusion, we also designated our tutee agent to utter questions. The question from the tutee then answered by the tutor in the next turn of explanation. An example of question utterance from the tutee agent is: *"...Anything? what kind of things can be described?"*. This tutee' question is placed before the tutor changing his explanation about type of thing that can be described in metadata. Right after the tutee' utterance ended, the video playing again, and the tutor start to continue his explanation as can be seen on Table 2. This kind of interaction of the tutee agent is also form of virtual tutee contribution to the learning by making the observer students anticipated the next learning content explanation by the tutor [16].

Table 2. Example of the tutee agent utters question to the tutor

Tutee Agent	*"...Anything? what kind of things can be described?"*
Tutor	*"The thing being described maybe natural, or an artificial object, physical or digital object, whatever It also can be an information object, such as webpage, a book, an article, a historical manuscript, etc."*

4.4 Participants

In this experiment, we recruited twelve ($N = 12$) participants who were all undergraduate and graduate students. As our participants watching the dialog between a tutee agent and a tutor, they are becoming a dialog observer or an observer student.

4.5 Procedure

At the beginning of the experiment, we gave an explanation to the participants about the experiment and the consent paper. After the participant agreed with the experiment condition they read and filled the experiment consent form. Each participant experienced the two experiment conditions, DIA and MON, or MON and DIA, depends on the participant task order document we have made before. We equipped participants with the Pupil eye-tracker to collect data on their eye-fixation points. Our Pupil eye-tracker device is embedded with two cameras, first is the world camera which represent what participant saw with their eye and the second one is the eye-camera which detect participant's the eye movement.

Before participants start watching the lecture videos, we carried out the Pupil eye-tracker calibration procedure to make sure the eye-tracking process run accurately. Using the calibration feature provided by the Pupil' software suite, the Pupil eye-tracker calibration was done by asking a participant to follow five dots which are appeared on the screen without moving their head to make sure the Pupil' eye camera could detect the movement of participant' pupil correctly. We performed this procedure several times for each participant to make sure that the Pupil eye-tracker device has high confidence detection between 0.7 to 1.0 (maximum) value. Participants watched the lecture videos in one pass without re-watch and they were not allowed to control the pace of video by pause, seek backward, or forward the videos. After finished watching each video, the participant then filled a questionnaire related to their user experience and then answered free recall test related to the learning content in the last watched video.

5   Result

5.1   Analysis of the Data

Learning Gain
To measure learning gain particularly to short-term memory retention, we collected and calculated data from participants' free recall answer sheets. For each video theme, we created six deep questions related to learning content in the video. From these participant' answers sheet, we counted how many relevant, related, and irrelevant propositions. A relevant proposition can be a phrase or sentences which matched or has the same meaning with what tutor explained or tutee uttered in the video. A related proposition is a phrase or sentence which not too relevant to the question asked, but still have some relation with the right answer, and an irrelevant proposition is an answer which does not have any relevance with the question or incorrect answer.

Eye Fixation Frequency and Duration
To measure and analyze our participants attention to the lecture videos from the eye tracker video recordings and raw data, we followed four steps procedure for each video (Fig. 4).

Fig. 4. Workflow of eye fixation data collection and analysis

The procedure was as follow: 1) Collected eye fixation points raw data and videos recorded from the eye-tracker device using the Pupil Capture apps. 2) Each of these videos (in HD 1280 × 720 resolution) were then exported using Pupil Player apps into a rendered video which contain a yellow circle marker (generated automatically by the Pupil Player app based on the raw data). The yellow circle marker in the rendered video move based on the participant's eye fixation movements (Fig. 5A). 3) The rendered video then added into ELAN [17] annotation tool in which the eye-fixation periods of participant were annotated. 4) We then conducted statistical tests for the eye fixation occurrences frequency and the duration of eye fixation based on these annotations result.

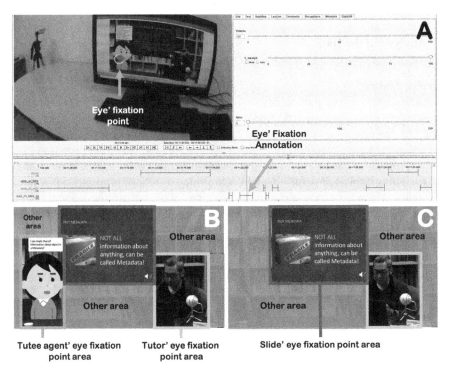

Fig. 5. A) Annotation of participant' eye fixation point (indicated by yellow circle) in the video using ELAN. B) Annotation's AOI where the eye fixation points landed on for the dialogue video. C) Annotation's AOI for the monologue video. (Color figure online)

The frequency of eye fixation was measured on how many times the eye of participant switch fixation to the one of AOI. For example, we counted one eye fixation to the tutor area after it is moved from the slide area to the tutor area. In doing the eye fixation points' video annotations, we defined three main areas of interest (AOI) on the video where the eye fixation landed on. These AOI are the tutee agent area, tutor area and the slide area as can be seen on Fig. 5B. If participants eye fixation landed on another area than these AOI, we annotated them as "other". We then counted how many times (the frequency) the eye fixation landed inside these areas and how long (the duration) the fixation points last.

Interview

To gain deeper understanding on the effect of the tutee agent in dialogue video which otherwise not reflected in learning gain or attention from eye-tracker, we conducted semi-structured interview at the end of each experiment session. The interview was audio recorded by the experimenter and then transcribed. When then making our analysis based on the transcript data.

5.2 Learning Gain

Based on the number of relevant, related, and irrelevant propositions from participants' answers, we measured the difference between DIA (dialogue) and MON (monologue) condition (Fig. 6).

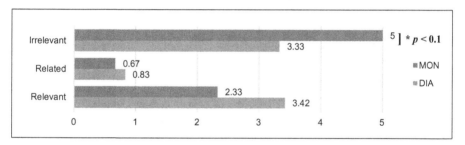

Fig. 6. The number of relevant, related, and irrelevant propositions

Our MANOVA test reported non-significant effect of video style/condition (DIA & MON) as the independent variable to all three independent variables (Relevant, Related & Irrelevant proposition) with $F (3, 20) = 1.40, p = .27$; Wilk's $\Lambda = .826$. Univariate test reported marginal effect of video style to the Irrelevant variable result where participants in the DIA condition were writing less irrelevant proposition compared to the MON condition, $F (1, 22) = 3.71, p = .06$.

5.3 Eye Fixation Frequency

The total eye fixation recording videos which we annotated were 20 videos from the total of 24 videos (each participant has two eye tracker video recordings). We excluded

4 videos from this analysis because of incomplete data from 2 participants. One video in the dialogue condition was not containing any eye-fixation marker because the eye-tracker failed to detect the participant eye' pupil in the middle of experiment, despite we already performed several calibration procedures. Another one in monologue condition resulted in incomplete eye fixation data because half of the eye tracker recording video was corrupted (Fig. 7).

Table 3. The average occurrence of eye fixations per minute

Fixation AOI	DIA (N = 10)		MON (N = 10)		MS	F	df	p
	M	SD	M	SD				
Slide	9.86	3.34	6.08	2.45	71.21	8.27	1	**.010
Tutor	8.73	4.23	5.89	3.27	40.38	2.81	1	.110
Other	2.36	1.74	3.47	1.36	6.11	2.48	1	.133
Agent	4.01	1.65	–	–		–	–	–

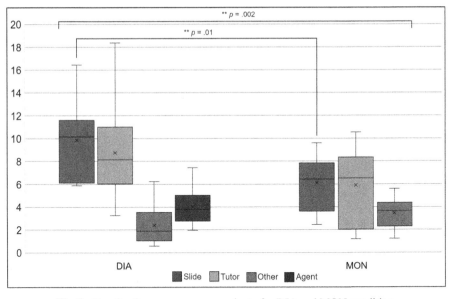

Fig. 7. Eye-fixation occurrence per minute for DIA and MON condition.

For the analysis to the eye fixation frequency, first we present the result on the eye fixation frequency to the three main AOI in both DIA and MON conditions. These numbers represent the number of eye fixation per minute (fpm) from the beginning until the end of the lecture video. We conducted ANOVA to compare the effect between video style (DIA and MON) for the three fixation AOI. The multivariate test reported a significant effect of video style with F (3, 16) = 8.03, p = .002; Wilk's Λ = .399. Furthermore, univariate tests showed there was a significant effect of video style where participants have higher frequency of eye fixations to the slide area in the DIA style than the MON style, F (1, 18) = 8.27, p = .010. However, as can be seen on Table 3, no significant differences were found in the tutor area (F (1, 18) = 2.81, p > .05) and the other area (F (1, 18) = 2.48, p > .05).

5.4 Eye Fixation Duration

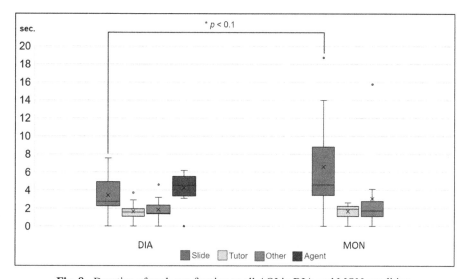

Fig. 8. Duration of each eye fixation to all AOI in DIA and MON condition.

Table 4. Duration of each eye fixation on AOIs (sec.)

Fixation AOI	DIA (N = 10)		MON (N = 10)		MS	F	df	p
	M	SD	M	SD				
Slide	3.78	1.86	7.25	5.17	60.06	3.96	1	*.062
Tutor	1.80	.88	1.86	.63	.01	.03	1	.861
Other	2.01	1.13	3.37	4.47	9.30	.87	1	.362
Agent	4.69	1.09	–	–		–	–	–

Beside from the number of times the participants fixated their eye to the three areas, we also try to look at the average duration of eye fixation between condition. Figure 8 illustrates the comparison of data spread between DIA and MON condition and all AOI. Our multivariate test reported non-significant effect of the video style to all fixation

AOIs. As can been seen on Table 4, univariate test reported marginal difference between video style where participants in MON have longer duration to the slide area, F (1, 18) = 3.96, p = .062. This result indicated that the attention of participants tended to more kept on the slide area in the monologue lecture video (Fig. 9).

5.5 Eye Fixation Rate

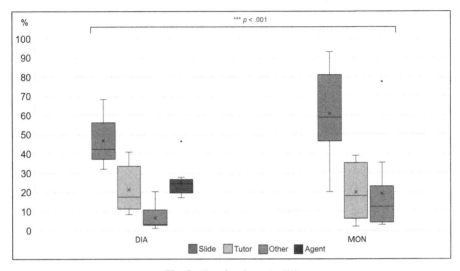

Fig. 9. Eye fixation rate (%)

Table 5. Eye fixation rate (%)

Fixation AOI	DIA (N = 10)			MON (N = 10)			*MS*	*F*	*df*	*p*
	M	*SD*	Rate (%)	*M*	*SD*	Rate (%)				
Slide	28.10	7.61	46.81	36.53	13.67	60.9	356.72	2.91	1	.105
Tutor	12.73	7.06	21.23	11.97	8.16	19.94	2.98	.05	1	.824
Other	4.01	3.61	6.69	11.50	13.61	19.16	280.05	2.82	1	.110
Agent	15.16	4.96	25.27	–	–	–	–	–	–	–
Total	60	–	100	60	–	100	–	–	–	–

To obtain the rate of eye fixation duration in each minute, we multiply the frequency of eye fixation per minute and the duration of each eye fixation. We normalized the data, so the total time is exactly 60 s for all AOI in each condition. Our MANOVA reported significant effect of video style, F (3, 16) = 29.05, p < .001; Wilk's Λ = .155. However univariate tests on each area as detailed on Table 5, did not reported any effect of video style on all AOIs.

6 Discussion

As we have described on the result part before, result from learning gain showed no significant difference in learning gain, particularly to the number of relevant propositions. This result might be caused by the tutee agent did not provide enough scaffolding to the memory retention of participants in watching the lecture videos. Study from Mayer on the presence effect of pedagogical agent found that students who learned with an agent on the screen did not get better results compared to students who study without agent on the screen [18].

From eye fixation data collected from the eye tracker, our data analysis found when participants watched the dialogue video with the tutee agent, they were tended to more frequently paid attention to the slide area. This might be an indication that the tutee agent utterances make participants to review the presentation slide inside the video more often than in the monologue video. However, result from the duration for each eye fixation in the monologue video revealed that the participants spent their attention longer to the slide area. In the dialogue video, the tutee agent took some attention from the slide. As the duration of attention could affect the cognitive load on working memory [19], with the tutee agent took some attention, it could be a positive way in lowering cognitive load of participants. Regarding the design of dialogue between tutor and the tutee agent, our participants gave their opinion. User6 commented on how the tutee agent can provides "break" from teacher/tutor:

> *Well there is several things, first one is that the animated tutee agent summarize the content by parts make it easier to follow. And then, it provides a dialog so it's not the same speakers all the time, probably it's like giving a little bit of a break from the teacher...".*

This particular comment is related to how we placed the tutee agent's utterances at certain time in the videos, specifically at the end of each slide explanation. Participant felt that the tutee agent can give them time to break from the tutor's explanation. As the participants cognitive load getting higher from long constant watch of the learning material presentation, we suggest that the tutee agent here can also help the students in decreasing their cognitive load as in learning segmentation [20]. Most of the participants who preferred the dialogue videos felt that the tutee agent's summarizations help them in understanding the tutor explanation. User7 expressed how the dialogue videos make the learning more enjoyable:

> *The dialogue version is more interesting and make me more enjoy to watch the video also. The animated person assistant also helps us to highlight what is the important content that the lecturer want to teach...".*

Similar with User7 expressed, User11 has similar opinion:

> *The animated agent help to summarize what the lecturer says, so I can memorize better about the key point in the lecture, each of the subtopics, or sub-lecture (subtopic) of the whole lecture...".*

Based on these subjective comments from our participants, the combination of the right timing for utterance and the scaffolding in term of summarization by the pedagogical agent can help student in learning while watching lecture video, particularly in giving back their focus to the learning materials and affording them in lowering cognitive load.

7   Conclusion

Previous studies have explored strategies to improve lecture video by adding reducing cognitive load of the students by means of learning segmentation and breaks, adding activities such as using in-video quizzes and making annotation, and by incorporating pedagogical agents such as virtual tutor and virtual tutee. Using our tool, a teacher or course designer can design an interaction between tutor and the tutee agent in the monologue video as if they are making a dialogue. In this study we proposed our novel method to increase student attention to the lecture video by adding a tutee agent inside lecture videos.

Our statistical test from learning gain reported no significant effect of the tutee agent presence in dialogue video. On the eye fixation data captured using eye-tracker we concluded that the tutee agent existence in the dialogue video has some effects to the attention of the student. Observation to the data spread visualization on the average eye fixation frequency revealed that participants have more frequent eye fixations and shorter duration to slide area when watching dialogue videos. These results suggest that the tutee agent has some effect in increasing participants attention to the learning material while at the same time make their eye fixation duration shorter to it. When we asked participants on their opinion to the dialogue video, they confirmed that the tutee agent had effect on their attention to the video and learning material itself. This study still has limitation as it need more data from other sources to reveal more on the effect of dialogue video with the tutee agent by triangulation, particularly to the learning gain which will be also a future direction for our next investigation with larger participants. Another limitation that we note based on our participants' comment is how the tutee agent's summarization affect them. Whether the presence of the tutee agent that utter the summary, or the summarization itself has more effect to the participants need to be investigated more. We believe that by utilizing our prototype tool, further study about an effective way to design the tutee agent interaction in a monologue video, and how to design a lecture video which can be delivered either way in monologue or dialogue style are interesting.

References

1. Zhang, D., Zhou, L., Briggs, R.O., Nunamaker, J.F.: Instructional video in e-learning: assessing the impact of interactive video on learning effectiveness. Inf. Manag. **43**, 15–27 (2006). https://doi.org/10.1016/j.im.2005.01.004
2. Brame, C.J.: Effective educational videos: principles and guidelines for maximizing student learning from video content. CBE Life Sci. Educ. (2016). https://doi.org/10.1187/cbe.16-03-0125

3. Jing, H.G., Szpunar, K.K., Schacter, D.L.: Interpolated testing influences focused attention and improves integration of information during a video-recorded lecture. J. Exp. Psychol. Appl. (2016). https://doi.org/10.1037/xap0000087
4. Mayer, R. (ed.): The Cambridge Handbook of Multimedia Learning. Cambridge University Press, Cambridge (2014)
5. Ilioudi, C., Giannakos, M.N., Chorianopoulos, K.: Investigating differences among the commonly used video lecture styles. In: CEUR Workshop Proceedings, vol. 983, pp. 21–26 (2013)
6. Chi, M.T.H., Kang, S., Yaghmourian, D.L.: Why students learn more from dialogue-than monologue-videos: analyses of peer interactions. J. Learn. Sci. **26**, 10–50 (2017). https://doi.org/10.1080/10508406.2016.1204546
7. Cohen, P.A., Kulik, J.A., Kulik, C.C., Cohen, P.A.: Educational outcomes of tutoring: a meta-analysis of findings. Am. Educ. Res. Assoc. **19**, 237–248 (1982)
8. Clark, R.E., Choi, S.: Five design principles for experiments on the effects of animated pedagogical agents. J. Educ. Comput. Res. **32**, 209–225 (2005). https://doi.org/10.2190/7LRM-3BR2-44GW-9QQY
9. Hayashi, Y.: Influence of social communication skills on collaborative learning with a pedagogical agent: Investigation based on the autism-spectrum quotient. In: HAI 2015 - Proceedings of the 3rd International Conference on Human-Agent Interaction, pp. 135–138 (2015). https://doi.org/10.1145/2814940.2814946
10. Craig, S.D., Gholson, B., Ventura, M., Graesser, A.C.: Overhearing dialogues and monologues in virtual tutoring sessions: effects on questioning and vicarious learning. Int. J. Artif. Intell. Educ. **11**, 242–253 (2000)
11. Park, S.W., Kim, C.: The effects of a virtual tutee system on academic reading engagement in a college classroom. Educ. Tech. Res. Dev. **64**(2), 195–218 (2015). https://doi.org/10.1007/s11423-015-9416-3
12. Shaw, E., Johnson, W.L., Ganeshan, R.: Pedagogical agents on the Web. In: Proceedings of the International Conference on Autonomous Agents, pp. 283–290 (1999). https://doi.org/10.1145/301136.301210
13. Kassner, M., Patera, W., Bulling, A.: Pupil: an open source platform for pervasive eye tracking and mobile gaze-based interaction (2014). https://doi.org/10.1145/2638728.2641695
14. Liu, H., Heynderickx, I.: Visual attention in objective image quality assessment: based on eye-tracking data. IEEE Trans. Circuits Syst. Video Technol. **21**, 971–982 (2011). https://doi.org/10.1109/TCSVT.2011.2133770
15. Blokzijl, W., Andeweg, B.: The effects of text slide format and presentational quality on learning in college lectures. In: IPCC 2005. Proceedings. International Professional Communication Conference, 2005, Limerick, Ireland, pp. 288–299. IEEE (2005)
16. Driscoll, D.M., Craig, S.D., Gholson, B., Ventura, M., Hu, X., Graesser, A.C.: Vicarious learning: effects of overhearing dialog and monologue-like discourse in a virtual tutoring session. J. Educ. Comput. Res. **29**, 431–450 (2005). https://doi.org/10.2190/q8cm-fh7l-6hju-dt9w
17. ELAN (Version 5.9). Nijmegen: Max Planck Institute for Psycholinguistics, The Language Archive (2020)
18. Mayer, R.E., Dow, G.T., Mayer, S.: Multimedia learning in an interactive self-explaining environment: what works in the design of agent-based microworlds? J. Educ. Psychol. **95**, 806–812 (2003)
19. Barrouillet, P., Bernardin, S., Portrat, S., Vergauwe, E., Camos, V.: Time and cognitive load in working memory. J. Exp. Psychol. Learn. Mem. Cogn. **33**, 570–585 (2007). https://doi.org/10.1037/0278-7393.33.3.570
20. Biard, N., Cojean, S., Jamet, E.: Effects of segmentation and pacing on procedural learning by video. Comput. Hum. Behav. (2018). https://doi.org/10.1016/j.chb.2017.12.002

Effect of Cultural Misunderstanding Warning in MT-Mediated Communication

Mondheera Pituxcoosuvarn[1]([⊠]) [iD], Yohei Murakami[1] [iD], Donghui Lin[2] [iD],
and Toru Ishida[3]

[1] Faculty of Information Science and Technology,
Ritsumeikan University, Shiga, Japan
{mond-p,yohei}@fc.ritsumei.ac.jp
[2] Department of Social Informatics, Kyoto University, Kyoto, Japan
lindh@i.kyoto-u.ac.jp
[3] School of Creative Science and Engineering, Waseda University, Tokyo, Japan
toru.ishida@aoni.waseda.jp

Abstract. Thanks to today's technologies, the world's borders have been fading away and intercultural collaboration has become easier and easier. Language and cultural differences are common problems in intercultural collaboration. Machine translation (MT) is now available to overcome the language barrier, so people can easily express and understand messages in different languages. However, misunderstandings often plague users from different cultures, especially in MT-mediated communication. To communicate productively, it is important to avoid such misunderstandings. One existing work proposed the idea of using automated cultural difference detection to warn the users of misunderstanding. However, no study has examined how such warnings affect the communication. To eliminate this gap, we conduct a controlled experiment on how users react to the warnings and what are the results in terms of communication. The results show that, with the data from cultural difference detection, warning the user of cultural misunderstanding can help reduce misunderstandings and increase awareness of cultural differences. The results of this experiment confirm the effectiveness of cultural misunderstanding alerts and suggest new directions in multilingual chat design.

Keywords: Intercultural collaboration · Machine translation · Cultural misunderstanding

1 Introduction

Given the advances in transportation and technology, we have more chance to communicate across cultures than before. Intercultural collaboration and cultural diversity provide societies with vast benefits [5]. Nevertheless, communication is challenged by many difficulties. In the past, people needed to learn

© Springer Nature Switzerland AG 2020
A. Nolte et al. (Eds.): CollabTech 2020, LNCS 12324, pp. 112–127, 2020.
https://doi.org/10.1007/978-3-030-58157-2_8

a foreign language or needed an interpreter to communicate smoothly across languages. Now, communication has been made easier through the support of machine translation (MT). There are various tools and services available to choose from. MT can be easily used by general users without any expert knowledge to translate documents, conversations, and messages. It has also been embedded in chat systems so that users without a shared language can communicate. Moreover, there are various web services that can be used by both general users with more technical knowledge to create their own resource [8].

However; MT is still not perfect and it can cause various difficulties, for example, misunderstanding due to mistranslation, conversation breakdown [13], and gaps in mutual comprehension [16].

Some difficulties, i.e. mistranslation, can be solved by improving MT quality. Even with improvements in quality, there are some situations where MT output hinders successful communication. For instance, a group of researchers [14] conducted a field study at a children's workshop where the children used an MT-embedded chat system communicate. They reported that communication became difficult when an adult facilitator showed a block of brown play dough to the children and asked "what does this looks like?". A Japanese participant answered it looks liked ' 餡子 *(Anko)*' which is can be translated as 'red bean paste'. The children from different cultures did not understand reference made by the Japanese participant. Later they used image browser to find pictures of *Anko* and they came to understand that it is a block of stiff red bean paste. Even with perfect MT quality, this kind of cultural problem still occurs and creates a barrier to achieving mutual understanding. For effective collaboration, it is important to establish mutual understanding but the current MT-embedded chat systems sometimes fail and actually cause cultural-based misunderstanding. Based on this field study, one study proposed automated cultural difference detection [15]. Their method detects cultural difference by comparing images in databases linked to each language. They also suggested that the result of cultural difference detection be used to warn the users of possible cultural differences. However, the impact of warning the users of these differences was not confirmed.

To fill this gap, we conduct a controlled experiment based on our research question: *how warning the user of possible cultural differences and cultural misunderstandings can affect MT-based communication?*. Our hypothesis is that warning the user of cultural misunderstanding will significantly help the user in reducing misunderstanding and thus support mutual understanding. We designed a collaborative task and asked our participants to complete the task together by chatting on an MT embedded chat system with cultural misunderstanding warnings for the experimental group and without warning for the controlled group. We interviewed the participants to find out if each participant understand correctly or not, then conduct a t-test to examine if there is a significant difference between the experimental group's understanding and the controlled group's understanding.

In the next section, we introduce studies related to our work. Section 3 reviews a key component of our experiment, a key method to detect cultural differences. Next, Sect. 4 details our experiment. The results of the experiment are shown in Sect. 5 and discussed in Sect. 6, which is followed by our conclusion of this paper.

2   Related Work

2.1   Misunderstanding in Intercultural Collaboration

Because people with different language backgrounds sometimes perceive things differently [3], misunderstanding can readily occur in intercultural collaboration. Because of this, many studies have tackled cultural misunderstanding.

Grounding a conversation or establishing mutual understanding is difficult, especially when communication is carried out via a chat system or MT. Yamashita et al. [16] studied why and how conversation grounding is problematic in MT-mediated communication. Their experiment found three problems. First, the users were not aware of which conversation content was or was not being shared. Second, the users were not aware which concepts they could or could not share with others. Third, users faced difficulties in constructing efficient utterances when using MT-mediated communication because of the first problem.

2.2   Cultural Difference Identification and Detection

In order to prevent misunderstanding, it is necessary to be able to detect it. Various works have tackled detecting and identifying cultural differences. Most studies collected and analyzed data from cross-national surveys. One of the most well-known works is Hofstede's cultural dimension [6]. He identified cultural differences in different regions. Yoshino et al. [17] also conducted a cross-national survey but compared some aspects of culture, such as social values and ways of thinking. The results from surveys are interesting, however, it is difficult to apply them to computer-mediated communication.

Other researchers have worked on cultural differences related to computer-mediated communication. In 2007, Cho et al. [2] published a study on the cultural differences found in pictogram interpretations. They conducted a web survey to understand the differences in pictogram interpretations between Japanese and Americans. Their report found that 19 of 120 pictograms were judged to have cultural differences.

Later, Yoshino et al. [18] proposed a method for cultural difference detection in Wikipedia. Japanese students and Chinese students were asked to examine words and phrases with different meanings and the results were used to create an initial dataset. Based on the dataset, they proposed a process for judging whether cultural differences existed or not in certain words or phrases.

Yet, the cultural difference detection methods mentioned above cover only specific areas and usages, i.e. pictograms, Wikipedia and all require human intervention. In 2019, a group of researchers [15] proposed a method to automatically detect cultural differences in words when they were translated into another language. This method can be applied to various languages and can cover broad area, as long as there lexical databases and image libraries are available. The authors also proposed that detection results can be used to warn the users of potential cultural differences. Base on this automated detection, Nishimura et al. [12] proposed a method and conducted an experiment to find the threshold that serves as a basis for confirming cultural difference.

3 Cultural Difference Detection (CDD)

To prevent and warn users of cultural misunderstanding in MT-mediated communication, it is important to detect possible misunderstandings. This work adopts a method from our previous work [15] that can automatically detect the words that might cause misunderstanding when they are used and translated into another language. This section briefly reviews how cultural difference detection (CDD) works.

To investigate if using a word W in language L_1 could cause misunderstanding due to cultural difference when it is translated into language L_2, the following procedure should be performed.

1. Translate word WL_1 (language L_1) into WL_2 (language L_2).
2. Search for images using WL_1 and WL_2 as *keywords*.
3. Extract image vector features of each image.
4. Compare the two images by computing their vector features.
5. If the similarity is low, the possibility of misunderstanding is high.

To apply this CDD concept, several variables must be considered, including, language (word) resource, number of images for each keyword, tools for feature extraction and comparison.

Here is an example of finding a list of words that have high possibility of causing misunderstanding when they are used in multilingual communication between Japanese and English.

Base on Fig. 1, first, from Japanese WordNet [7] which is a Japanese-English lexical database created from the original English WordNet [11], a *synset* is selected. A *synset* in Japanese Wordnet is a set of synonym containing words in English and Japanese under the same concept with similar meaning. Here, in Fig. 1 the *synset* randomly selected is the synset that contains *william_cowper* and *cowper* in English and クーパー *(Kuupaa)* in Japanese. Then search for 30 images for each language: 15 images for *william_cowper*, 15 images for *cowper* and 30 images for クーパー *(Kuupaa)*. Next the vector features of the images are extracted. Both the original paper and our paper used VGG16[1] from Keras. The feature values of each language are averaged. Next, averaged vector features of each language are compared, (here we use Cosine similarity).

A list of words that might cause misunderstanding can be made by repeating this process a few thousand times or more. Words whose similarity is lower than

---

[1] https://keras.io/applications/#vgg16.

a threshold, the original work suggested 0.6, are entered in a list and the user is warned when they use a word present in the list.

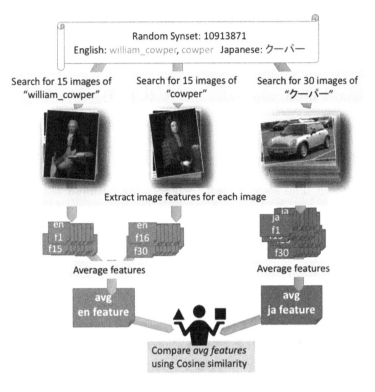

Fig. 1. An example of a process based on CDD

4   Experiment

To study how cultural misunderstanding warnings might impact communication we conducted an controlled experiment. Our hypothesis is that users who are warned of cultural-misunderstanding achieve better communication when using MT-mediated communication.

4.1   Participant

We asked 18 volunteers with various language and cultural back-grounds to participate in MT-mediated conversations. The participants were in their 20s and 30s. They were separated into six groups of three people. Details are as follows:

- A native Japanese or a person with native-level Japanese who has been educated in Japan or currently lives in Japan.
- A native Chinese or a person with native-level Chinese who has been educated in China or currently lives in China or a Chinese speaking environment.
- A native English speaker or a person with native-level English who has been educated in England or currently lives in an English speaking environment.

The six groups of participants were divided into three experimental groups ($E1$, $E2$, and $E3$) and three control groups ($C1$, $C2$, and $C3$).

4.2 Communication Tool

The tool used in this experiment was a web application developed around translation services from the Language Grid [8]. This application is an MT-embedded chat system that allows users to communicate in their preferred language. When a user logs-in to the application using a given link, he/she can select her/his preferred language on the right-top of the page. If a user chooses to chat in English, all the message from the other users, who might be accessing the system in different languages, are shown in English. When he/she enters and sends messages in English, the other users will see those message in their selected languages.

4.3 Task Design

Designing the task given the participants was challenging. In normal chat conversation or normal collaborative tasks, there is no guarantee that a cultural-misunderstanding will occur. To test our hypothesis, we designed a game that led the users to communicate using words that might cause misunderstanding. Because this game was designed only to create and lead the conversation, there is no evaluation of the game result nor the correct answer.

Our game was inspired by the Desert Survival Problem (DSP) [10]. DSP is widely used in team building and collaboration practice. The conventional DSP asks the players to collaboratively rank items by its important to their survival in the desert. Many variations of the game can be created by giving different situations and items. We create our variation and indirectly force the user to talk about things that might easily be misunderstood by adding words in the CCD-derived list to the item choices. To encourage participation in the conversation, the choices given to each group member were different, so everybody had to speak up and share. Every group member was given three choices; they were instructed to share and collaboratively select one of the most important choices from each list. Only three of the nine choices could be chosen. The collaboration ended when all members agreed on the three choices.

Examples of the lists given to the participants are shown in Fig. 2. Words that could cause misunderstanding were emphasized (red underlined) for clarity. For the control group, the lists given to them did not contain any text emphasis.

The list in Japanese translated into English reads

You found a train container that has not been destroyed yet. You can take one of the listed items.

Chinese Choices	Japanese Choices	English Choices
后来在车祸中，你们找到了另外三个乘客活了下里。在他们3人中，你只可以帮一个。剩下的两个会跟着另外一组，向南去试一试。这3个人当中，你不懂他们的工作或拿手的之术。你唯一的方法是看着他们穿着的衣服和形象。 1. 修行者 2. 青少年 3. 电气技师	あなたはまだ壊れていない電車のコンテナを見つけた。以下の中から一つだけ手に入れることができる。 1. 2台のママチャリ 2. 2つの花冠 3. 一本の刀	While you are walking, you found a cute plastic box with the following items in it, you can use one from the list. 1. A mud pie 2. Three cans of pop 3. One pack of family size crackers

Translation (Chinese):
1. A religious practitioner
2. A teenager
3. An electrician

Translation (Japanese):
1. Two bicycles
2. Two corollas
3. A sword

Fig. 2. Lists given to participants in each language. (Color figure online)

1. Two bicycles (ママチャリ - Mamachari)
2. Two corollas (花冠 - Kakan)
3. A sword

The list in Chinese can be translated into English as
You found the other three people who took the same train. They are alive but wounded by the wreck. You can choose to help one person and take that person with you. The rest will be helped and carried by the other group who are heading to the south. You don't know them, but you can guess who they are from how they look and dress.

1. A religious practitioner (修行者 -Xiuxing Zhe)
2. A young teenager
3. An electrician

The underlined choices are expected to cause cultural misunderstanding. Most underlined words were taken from the list of cultural differences made using CDD; some words were added manually to create difficulties, including ママチャリ *(Mamachari - Bicycle)* and 修行者 *(Xiuxing Zhe - Religious practitioner)*. The word 修行者 *(Xiuxing Zhe)* was detected when the CDD was run using Japanese Wordnet, as a Japanese word with Chinese character (Kanji); this word also exists in Chinese language but we did not run CDD on any Chinese resource.

4.4 Expectation

We expected that the participants would have communication difficulties when using the underlined words in Fig. 2 because of the cultural differences and translation problems, if not warned.[2]

---

[2] Note that the translation output is likely to change from time to time since MT is always developing and the output also depends on the services selected.

The choices exhibited significant cultural differences and thus problems in understanding. First of all, on the English list, mud pie is definitely problematic because there are two meanings. The original meaning is a pie made of mud by children. The other meaning emerged later as an edible pie that resembled a mud pie. People from different cultures might not sure if mud pie is edible or not, regardless of translation. The second choice on English list, *pop*, is a slang but well known for a carbonated drink. If MT does not know the content of conversation, it might translate pop into different word, such as "pop music".

On Japanese list, **ママチャリ** *(Mamachari)* is a word that not only means bicycle but also information about size and use. It is possible to carry children since it usually has space for luggage or child seats. The list choice was two bicycles since the team of three could fit onto 2 Japanese style bicycles. People who did not understand **ママチャリ** *(Mamachari)* would not know this fact.

For, **花冠** *(Kakan)*, the MT output was "corolla" which is a wreath. This usage is very archaic and rarely used nowadays. In many regions, corolla is recognized as a car since it is a famous car model.

We gave them two bicycle for the team of three which is enough to ride. People who does not understand **ママチャリ** *(Mamachari)* would not know this information. For **花冠** *(corolla)*, the translation in English is "corolla" which is a headgear, however not popularly used nowadays. In many regions, *corolla* is recognized as a car since it is a famous car model.

On Chinese list, **修行者** *(Xiuxing Zhe - Religious practitioner)* is the most difficult to explain. MT usually output the English word "practitioner" which most people understand to be a medical doctor. However, it actually means a religious practitioner or a monk who often goes on pilgrimages and so might be useful in helping the group to survive since he has experience in traveling.

4.5   Method

We conducted the experiment using the *Wizard of Oz* [9] technique which is often used in human-computer interaction studies. In our experiment on how communication is effected by the warning, the *Wizard* is a human who warns the participant instead of the computer system. The experiment group members were given the situation and their choices with the suspected words indicated by red underlining while the control group members were given the same situation and choices without any emphasis.

To evaluate the effect of warnings on communication, after the collaborative task, we asked each participant to explain the six choices the other participants had and recorded how many choices each participant actually understood. Then a t-test was conducted to examine the significance between two independent samples including the percentage of understanding from the experimental group and from the controlled group.

4.6 A Preliminary Experiment on Number of Languages Used in MT-Embedded Chat

Besides the main experiment, we also designed a preliminary experiment to study if number of languages used impacted the participants' understanding of the choices. To conduct this preliminary experiment, we instructed experimental group $E1$ to communicate using only two languages: English and Japanese. In this case, the Chinese speaker who was also fluent in English used English to communicate, but the given choices were written in Chinese, as in the main experiment.

5 Result

5.1 Cultural Misunderstanding

After asking the participants to explain the choices the others had been given, and quantitatively analyzing the chat log, we divided participant understanding of the six other items into three groups.

- U: The user understood right after the choice was first mentioned
- L: The user understood after the choice was introduced but before the game ended
- M: The user could not understand or misunderstood the choice

The results are shown in Table 1. Asterisk marks are used to indicate incomplete understanding of the detailed characteristics of the choice, for example, knowing pop is a drink but not that it is carbonated, and knowing that ママチャリ *(Mamachari)* is a bicycle but not that it is often used by mother so it often has enough space to carry things or has extra seat(s) for kid(s). In addition this table also displays the number of turns to show how many turns among three users were taken to complete the task. Time of interruption shows the number of times when the game flow was interrupted by questions about the choices the participants wanted to confirm or could not understand. However, in this experiment, there is no correlation between the time of interruption and understanding (t-test $p - value = 1$).

By the end of the game, all the experimental groups had successfully established mutual understanding. They successfully shared and understood all the given choices. On the other hand, none of control group successfully shared or understood those choices.

The experiment showed that when the being choice introduced did not cause misunderstanding, usually the other participants could easily understand it right away (tagged U). If the participant felt that the word was difficult to understand, usually someone would ask for an explanation which would allow the group members to finally understand the choice. The words from the CCD list were frequently misunderstood, especially by members of the control group.

Figure 3 shows the rate at which each choice was understood by each participant. The percentage is calculated by summing the choices tagged U and L

Table 1. Understanding result of each participant in each group

Group	Participant	English choice 1 (mud pie)	English choice 2 (pop)	English choice 3 (cracker)	Japanese choice 1 (bicycle)	Japanese choice 2 (corolla)	Japanese choice 3 (sword)	Chinese choice 1 (religious practitioner)	Chinese choice 2 (teenager)	Chinese choice 3 (electrician)	Number of turn	Time of interruption during the explanation	Mutual understanding established
Experiment E1**	English speaker	–	–	–	U	U	U	U	U	U	60	5	Yes
	Japanese speaker	U	U	U	–	–	–	U	U	U			
	Chinese speaker	U	U	U	U	U	U	–	–	–			
E2	English speaker	–	–	–	U*	L	U	L	U	U	43	5	Yes
	Japanese speaker	U	U	U	–	–	U	L	U	U			
	Chinese speaker	U	U	U	U	L	U	–	–	–			
E3	English speaker	–	–	–	U*	U	U	L	U	U	48	1	Yes
	Japanese speaker	U	U	U	–	–	U	L	U	U			
	Chinese speaker	U	U	U	U*	U	U	–	–	–			
Control C1	English speaker	–	–	–	U	M	U	M	U	U	33	3	No
C1	Japanese speaker	M	L	U	–	–	U	M	U	U			
C1	Chinese speaker	M	L	U	U	M	U	–	–	–			
C2	English speaker	–	–	–	L*	M	U	M	U	U	49	6	No
C2	Japanese speaker	L	L	U	–	–	U	M	U	U			
C2	Chinese speaker	L	L	U	L*	M	U	–	–	–			
C3	English speaker	–	–	–	U*	U	U	M	M	U	54	2	No
C3	Japanese speaker	M	U	U	–	–	U	M	M	U			
C3	Chinese speaker	M	U	U	U*	U	U	–	–	–			

Note

U The user understood right after the choice was introduced.

L The user understands later, after the choice was introduced but before the game ended.

M The user coud not understand or misunderstood the choice.

*The user understood but not completely. The detailed characteristic of the choice was missed.

**This group used 2 languages in the experiment.

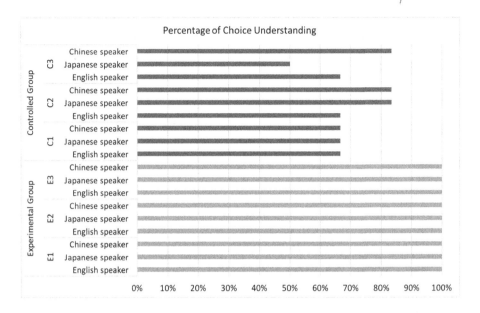

Fig. 3. Percentage of understanding of choice shared by the other group members

and dividing by six, the number of choices introduced by the other participants. The graph show that the experimental group had full understanding(100%) by the end of the game while the control group had less understanding (average of 70%). Warning the users of cultural misunderstanding significantly improved understanding in MT-mediated communication, especially when using words that might cause misunderstanding. We conducted a t-test with independent samples, including the percentage of the correct understanding of the experimental group and the percentage of the correct understanding of the controlled group. From the test, with $p-value$ equals to $5.54545E{-}07$, the null hypothesis is strongly rejected as $p < 0.001$ and we conclude that warning the user of cultural misunderstanding and cultural differences can improve understanding and reduce misunderstanding in MT-mediated communication.

5.2 User Behavior

The results detailed in Sect. 5 indicate that the experimental groups had better understanding than the control groups. To understand the reasons behind this, we qualitatively analyzed the chat log.

Explanation of Choices. Every participant in the experimental groups tried to explain the items in some detail when they were warned that those words might cause misunderstanding. Some examples are displayed in Fig. 4 and Fig. 5. The control group participants who were not warned seldom explained details of the items except when he/she was asked by their teammates, whereas the experimental group members were more careful in explaining the word being introduced or explained it soon after.

User	English (Original)	Japanese (Translation)	Chinese (Translation)
English Speaker [E1]	for me i have a mud pie, a pie made from mud. three can of soda and a 1 pack of family size cracker	私にとっては、泥のパイ、泥から作られたパイがあります。3缶のソーダと1パックのファミリーサイズのクラッカー	对我来说，我有一个泥饼，是用泥做的。三罐苏打水和一包家庭装饼干

Fig. 4. A chat message from English speaking user when is warned of cultural difference.

User	English (Translation)	Japanese (Original)	Chinese (Translation)
Japanese Speaker [E3]	Two corollas. It is a crown of flowers.	花冠がふたつ。花の冠です。	两个花冠。它是一朵花的冠冕。

Fig. 5. Chat messages from Japanese speaking user when is warned of cultural difference.

From the example in Fig. 4, the English speaker of the experimental group explained the word 'mud pie' and switched the word 'pop' to 'soda'.

In Fig. 5, the Japanese participant from another experimental group did not only introduce the word 花冠 (Kakan-Corolla), but also explained that are the corollas.

However, some experimental group members (very few) did not explain the choice. In the interview, a Chinese participant stated that "I just use it normally. I didn't think too deeply". He also commented that "I might be more careful if you add a warning message after the red letters". This opinion suggests that the warning was not obvious enough. Implementing the proposal in a real application would need stronger alerts.

Word Substitution. Sometimes a participant would use a word different from choice written in their documents. In the real world, especially when writing, we often use synonyms to provide variety and catch the reader's interest [1]. Synonyms are selected to best describe the matter being raised [4]. Thee experimental group members switched more words than the control group members as they were more aware of the cultural differences. We found that using alternate words could yield immediate understanding. For example, in the experiment, replacing the word *pop* with *soda* raised translation accuracy and allowed the other participants to understand more easily.

Skipping the Discussion of Incomprehensible Topic. Many times, the participants skipped the choices that were incomprehensible to them. For example, in control group $C1$, when the Japanese speaker introduced 花冠 *(Kakan-Corolla)*, the English speaker was presented with *corolla* which yielded uncertainty. Accordingly, the English speaker did not discuss the choice and followed the flow of the conversation, especially when the other two members agreed to settle on the two *bicycles* without further discussion of the other choices.

5.3   Preliminary Experiment Result

When we compare the understanding exhibited by the experimental groups from the data shown in Table 1, the experimental group that had two languages $(E1)$ understood all the choices right after they were introduced, while the other experimental groups, $E2$ and $E3$, understood 72.22% and 77.78% of the choices immediately upon introduction.

The reason for the sudden understanding of group $E1$ compared to groups $E2$ and $E3$ could be for the following reasons:

First, the message is only translated once in two-language communication but the message is translated twice in three-language communication. Moreover, the two translation outputs in three-language communication could be different. There is more chance of misunderstanding when the message is translated into many languages. In the case of using foreign language (i.e. the Chinese speaker using English), if the foreign language skill of the participant is good enough, the resulting communication is likely to be superior to that achieved when using MT.

Second, if fluency in the use of the foreign language is achieved (Chinese speaker using English), it is possible that the participant will be more aware of cultural differences. Since the participant had experience in using English, he instinctively tried to make his message understandable in English.

6   Discussion

This section discusses the pattern of failure to communicate via MT-embedded chat, the lost in translation, limitation, and the future direction of this work.

6.1   Pattern of Failure to Communicate

After the end experiment we analyzed the choices that yielded failures in establishing mutual understanding and found two patterns.

Surface Failure to Establish Mutual Understanding. Participants simply could not understand the words used. In this case, the participants acted in two different ways: ignoring the choice and trying to understand the choice. When the participants tried to understand the choice they would ask questions and they would often reach an understanding after some explanations. This does not negatively impact the understanding result but the questions and explanations might interrupt the conversation flow. However, when the participants chose to ignore what they did not understand, they would fail to establish mutual understanding. We categorized this problem as *surface failure* as it is obviously known to the participants themselves that they failed to understand and mutual understanding could not be established. However, the speaker would not know if the recipient understood the choice or not.

Underlying Misunderstanding. Sometimes, the discussion seems to be proceeding smoothly, without any problem; however, the participants actually misunderstood the conversation. We discovered this problem from the interview when we asked the participants about the choices shared by the other group members.

For example, **修行者** *(Xiuxing Zhe - Religious practitioner)* was translated as a practitioner. The groups that failed to understand this word thought they understood correctly, but they were wrong. In that situation, no questions were raised, and the conversation seemed to be simple and short. This problem is deeper than the surface failure and it is important that this kind of problem be detected and ameliorated.

6.2   Lost in Translation

Some misunderstanding occurred because of translation failures. A translated word could miss some or all of the full subtlety of meaning or significance. In the given list for Chinese speaker, **修行者** *(Xiuxing Zhe - Religious practitioner)* is translated as *practitioner* in English and **開業医** *(Kaigyoui - Medical practitioner)* in Japanese. But the term **修行者** *(Xiuxing Zhe)* actually means a practitioner of a religion, usually Buddhism, who often undertakes extensive pilgrimages. The English translation was too vague because practitioner has several meanings, and the translation in Japanese was wrong, as shown in Fig. 6.

User	English (Translation)	Japanese (Translation)	Chinese (Original)
Chinese Speaker [C2]	The first is a practitioner, the second is a teenager, and the third is an electrical technician	1人目は開業医、2人目は10代、3人目は電気技術者	第一个是修行者，第二个是青少年，第三个是电气技师

Fig. 6. Chat log of the control group when the word 'practitioner' was mentioned.

Here, people who do not understand Asian culture might not be able to draw on the knowledge of the extensive travels undertaken by monks who travel around and might instead recall their minister who often stays in her/his church.

The translation gaps are inherent across cultures, and it is difficult to deal with them.

6.3 Limitation and Future Work

Even though we found that the participants were more careful to explain the choices, it is also possible that the participants did so because they are told to be aware of potential misunderstandings. We would like to find this out in the future by conducting another experiment where the experimental groups are warned of the words with the potential to cause misunderstanding while the controlled group will be warned of the different words that have low potential to cause misunderstanding. In addition, the preliminary experiment to study the number of languages used here can be extended as a full experiment in the future.

7 Conclusion

Intercultural collaboration depends on establishing mutual understanding and minimizing as much misunderstanding as possible. MT can help with the language barrier but cultural misunderstanding still happens. To solve this misunderstanding problem, an existing work previously suggested warning the user of the possible cultural differences when using MT-mediated communication. The main contribution of this paper is the experiment conducted to validate the suggestion. Our research results are useful for multilingual chat tool design.

In this research, we designed and conducted an experiment comparing experimental groups that received the warnings and control groups that had no warning. We found that the experimental groups had successfully established mutual understanding, while the control group did not and encountered many misunderstandings. We conclude that warnings of cultural misunderstanding significantly improve understanding in MT-mediated communication.

In addition to our main experiment, we conducted a preliminary experiment to study if the number of languages used in multilingual chat affects the degree of understanding. The preliminary results showed that a group that used only two languages established mutual understanding earlier than the group that used three languages.

Acknowledgments. This research was partially supported by a Grant-in-Aid for Scientific Research (A) (17H00759, 2017–2020), a Grant-in-Aid for Scientific Research (B) (18H03341, 2018–2020), and a Grant-in-Aid Young Scientists (A) (17H04706, 2017–2020) from the Japan Society for the Promotion of Science (JSPS).

References

1. Bailey, S.: Academic Writing: A Handbook for International Students. Taylor & Francis (2003). https://books.google.co.jp/books?id=SUeRAgAAQBAJ
2. Cho, H., Ishida, T., Yamashita, N., Inaba, R., Mori, Y., Koda, T.: Culturally-situated pictogram retrieval. In: Ishida, T., Fussell, S.R., Vossen, P.T.J.M. (eds.) IWIC 2007. LNCS, vol. 4568, pp. 221–235. Springer, Heidelberg (2007). https://doi.org/10.1007/978-3-540-74000-1_17

3. Deutscher, G.: Through the Language Glass: Why the World Looks Different in Other Languages. Metropolitan Books, New York (2010)
4. Gookin, D.: Word 2013 For Dummies. For Dummies, Wiley (2013). https://books.google.co.jp/books?id=gxd6bMou76EC
5. Herring, C.: Does diversity pay?: race, gender, and the business case for diversity. Am. Sociol. Rev. **74**(2), 208–224 (2009)
6. Hofstede, G.: Cultural dimensions in management and planning. Asia Pac. J. Manage. **1**(2), 81–99 (1984)
7. Isahara, H., Bond, F., Uchimoto, K., Utiyama, M., Kanzaki, K.: Development of the Japanese wordnet. In: Sixth International Conference on Language Resources and Evaluation (2008)
8. Ishida, T., Murakami, Y., Lin, D., Nakaguchi, T., Otani, M.: Language service infrastructure on the web: the language grid. Computer **51**(6), 72–81 (2018)
9. Kelley, J.F.: An iterative design methodology for user-friendly natural language office information applications. ACM Trans. Inf. Syst. (TOIS) **2**(1), 26–41 (1984)
10. Lafferty, J.C., Pond, A.W.: The Desert Survival Situation: Problem: a Group Decision Making Experience for Examining and Increasing Individual and Team Effectiveness. Human Synergistics (1974)
11. Miller, G.: WordNet: An Electronic Lexical Database. MIT Press, Cambridge (1998)
12. Nishimura, I., Murakami, Y., Pituxcoosuvarn, M.: Image-based detection criteria for cultural differences in translation. In: International Conference on Collaboration and Technology. Springer (2020)
13. Pituxcoosuvarn, M., Ishida, T.: Multilingual communication via best-balanced machine translation. New Gener. Comput. **36**(4), 349–364 (2018)
14. Pituxcoosuvarn, M., Ishida, T., Yamashita, N., Takasaki, T., Mori, Y.: Machine translation usage in a children's workshop. In: Egi, H., Yuizono, T., Baloian, N., Yoshino, T., Ichimura, S., Rodrigues, A. (eds.) CollabTech 2018. LNCS, vol. 11000, pp. 59–73. Springer, Cham (2018). https://doi.org/10.1007/978-3-319-98743-9_5
15. Pituxcoosuvarn, M., Lin, D., Ishida, T.: A method for automated detection of cultural difference based on image similarity. In: Nakanishi, H., Egi, H., Chounta, I.-A., Takada, H., Ichimura, S., Hoppe, U. (eds.) CRIWG+CollabTech 2019. LNCS, vol. 11677, pp. 129–143. Springer, Cham (2019). https://doi.org/10.1007/978-3-030-28011-6_9
16. Yamashita, N., Inaba, R., Kuzuoka, H., Ishida, T.: Difficulties in establishing common ground in multiparty groups using machine translation. In: Proceedings of the SIGCHI Conference on Human Factors in Computing Systems, pp. 679–688. ACM (2009)
17. Yoshino, R., Hayashi, C.: An overview of cultural link analysis of national character. Behaviormetrika **29**(2), 125–141 (2002)
18. Yoshino, T., Miyabe, M., Suwa, T.: A proposed cultural difference detection method using data from Japanese and Chinese wikipedia. In: 2015 International Conference on Culture and Computing (Culture Computing), pp. 159–166. IEEE (2015)

Challenges for Distance Learning and Online Collaboration in the Time of COVID-19: Interviews with Science Teachers

Meeli Rannastu-Avalos$^{(\boxtimes)}$ and Leo Aleksander Siiman

University of Tartu, Ülikooli 18, 50090 Tartu, Estonia
`meeli.rannastu@ut.ee`

Abstract. Much of the research about distance learning and online collaboration comes from higher education or adult learner contexts. Less is known about the experiences and challenges of school teachers involved in instructing young teenagers remotely. In response to the coronavirus (Covid-19) pandemic, the government of Estonia ordered national school closures and established a temporary period of distance learning. This sudden move to online education was unexpected and required school teachers to quickly adjust. In this study, we interviewed five middle school science teachers about 5 weeks after the start of school closures. Prior research indicates that even during regular times, maintaining teenagers' interest for science studies is challenging. Our aim was to find out how science teachers had adapted their teaching at a time of unprecedented educational disruption, what challenges they encountered and to what extent they applied collaborative learning practices. All of the teachers reported using video conferencing tools to engage in synchronous communication with students. In addition, they all reported using school learning management systems to share information. However, none of the teachers felt that the distance learning situation was conducive to supporting collaborative learning. We discuss the main challenges mentioned by teachers and some of the implications for the design and development of online collaborative technologies and practices. Our findings highlight that establishing cognitive, social and teaching presence with young teenagers appears to be the main challenge for distance learning. Difficulty in establishing social presence was apparently a particularly serious barrier for school science teachers to promote collaboration at a distance.

Keywords: Distance learning · Collaborative learning · K-12 online learning · School teachers · Video conferencing · Social presence

1 Introduction

Distance education, for the purposes of this paper, will refer to a situation where educators and learners are physically separated from one another and digital technologies provide the means for them to interact. Research on various forms of distance learning has tended to focus on higher education or adult learning contexts [1–3], presumably because distance learning provides the flexibility demanded by many of the learners in

© Springer Nature Switzerland AG 2020
A. Nolte et al. (Eds.): CollabTech 2020, LNCS 12324, pp. 128–142, 2020.
https://doi.org/10.1007/978-3-030-58157-2_9

those contexts. In the kindergarten through grade 12 (K-12) context, there is a growing but narrow field of research related to K-12 online learning [4]. In the United States, it is estimated that the percentage of K-12 students in online schools is 2% or less [5]. However, it is unclear to what extent that estimate acknowledges some form of supplemental online learning that augments attending classes in a physical school or whether those students are being primarily schooled online. In any case, research on effective K-12 online learning practices and empirical evidence to guide K-12 online learning is noticeably lacking [6].

In late February 2020, the spread of the coronavirus disease reached Estonia. An emergency situation was established by the government on March 12th to prevent further spread of the virus, and subsequently, it was decided to close all educational institutions, except kindergartens, starting from March 16th. Additional physical distancing measures were later adopted by the government to further control the spread of the virus.

Schools in Estonia were directed to continue their educational mission via distance learning. Estonia has a relatively sophisticated digital educational landscape and has implemented modern digital technologies to be more efficient and effective in learning, teaching, and research contexts. All schools use e-school solutions and are required to implement a digital focus as described in the Estonian Lifelong Learning Strategy 2020 policy document [7]. The most popular school learning management systems are eKool (www.ekool.eu/index_en.html) and Stuudium (stuudium.com/en/). These technologies provide educators with digital platforms to organize various aspects of teaching such as marking attendance, commenting on student behavior, entering grades, posting assignments, setting deadlines, sharing digital learning resources and communicating via text messaging with students, parents or other teachers. Middle school students in Estonia predominantly own personal smartphones, but rarely use them for learning purposes at school [8].

In the transition from face-to-face science lessons to distance learning, teachers and students faced significant challenges in fulfilling the curricula requirements. Teachers had to prepare students to learn in a changing and non-traditional environment.

The purpose of this study is to explore the challenges science teachers faced in transitioning to distance learning during an unprecedented time and investigate to what extent teachers apply collaborative learning practices as part of distance education. More specifically, the research questions examined are: What learning activities do science teachers use for distance learning? (RQ1); What challenges do science teachers encounter with distance learning in general (RQ2) and with collaborative learning in particular? (RQ3); and how do science teachers try to support collaborative learning at a distance? (RQ4).

2   Related Work

Studies show that teenagers exhibit a low motivation towards learning science [9, 10]. Active learning approaches such as inquiry and collaborative learning are promising pedagogical methods to foster young people's interest in science studies. Moreover, collaboration is an important feature of contemporary scientific practice as scientists regularly share and discuss different representations of a problem with others when attempting to generate new knowledge. Kevin Dunbar studied the ways scientists work together in a social context and identified shared goals and the constructive exchange of different perspectives as two primary indicators associated with successful scientific collaboration [11]. Given the importance of collaboration skills in scientific practice and collaborative learning as a useful approach to motivate learning, it seems evident that science teachers should try to incorporate collaborative activities into instruction.

However, supporting collaboration in a time of distance learning due to Covid-19 is likely to face multiple challenges. School teachers require time to transition from face-to-face to distance learning and experiment with which instructional practices work best in the new situation. Students also need time to adjust to the new and changing expectations of their teachers. A challenge to implementing collaboration with online digital technologies may relate to establishing social presence, that is, the ability to communicate social cues using technology.

Social presence theory developed initially in the context of teleconferencing [12]. It posits that technologies vary according to how well socio-emotional cues are conveyed, which in turn are presumed to be critical in forming interpersonal connections. For example, visual communication technologies are assumed to offer a higher degree of social presence than alternatives like audio technology because nonverbal cues such as facial expression, body language, eye gaze, gestures, and proximity can be conveyed. The degree of social presence afforded by technology is seen as an important factor in determining the way people interact and communicate and is regarded as a central concept in distance learning [13].

The community of inquiry framework (CoI framework), which is an approach to online collaborative-constructivist learning, posits that meaningful distance learning consists of three types of presence: cognitive presence, social presence, and teaching presence [14]. Cognitive presence refers to a process whereby learners "construct meaning through sustained communication" (p. 89). In science education, cognitive presence can be understood as the construction of meaning by successful engagement in various phases of an inquiry cycle [15]. Social presence in the CoI framework is defined as "the ability of participants in a community of inquiry to project themselves socially and emotionally, as 'real' people (i.e., their full personality), through the medium of communication being used" (p. 94). Finally, teaching presence refers to designing, facilitating and directing learning experiences that serve to "support and enhance social and cognitive presence for the purpose of realizing educational outcomes" (p. 90). The three presences in the community of inquiry model are interconnected and provide a structure for a collaborative constructivist approach to distance learning.

3   Methodology

A qualitative research approach involving a structured interview was chosen to collect data to illustrate the experiences and perceptions of middle school science teachers who had transitioned to distance learning because of the Covid-19 situation. Participants were recruited using convenience sampling. Five science teachers, three from the same school, consented to giving interviews. Their age varied between 28 and 53 years old and they all had four or more years of teaching experience (see Table 1).

Table 1. Participant demographics

ID	Sex	Age	Years of teaching experience	Subjects taught (grade(s))[*]
T1	F	34	10	Biology (7–11), General Science (5–6)
T2	F	28	4	General Science (5–6), Biology (9), Human studies (7–8)
T3	F	53	30	General Science (6), Geography (7–9)
T4	F	28	4	Biology (7–9), Human studies (7–8)
T5	M	31	4	Physics (8–9), Biology (7), General Science (7)

[*]9th grade students in Estonia are on average 15 years old.

A structured interview protocol was developed to answer the research questions. The main questions asked were:

- In this emergency situation, what learning activities are you primarily using?
- What technologies are you primarily using?
- What difficulties have you encountered in using technology for distance learning?
- How have your tried to support collaboration?
- What difficulties have you encountered in supporting collaboration?

All of the interviews were video- and audio-recorded. The interviews took place between April 16th and 24th, about five weeks after the move to distance learning. The interviews were carried out by one interviewer, ranged in length from 54 to 75 min (on average 62 min long), and were all transcribed. One researcher read the transcripts and watched the recorded videos several times until a saturation point was reached and performed coding of the transcripts in MAXQDA 2020 [16]. Another researcher read in entirety all of the transcripts. Both researchers thematically analyzed the transcripts to identify features of interest relevant to answering the research questions and to develop themes from those features. The two researchers met to compare themes and formulate a common list of categories. For analysis related to answering RQ2 and RQ3, the three types of presence identified by the CoI framework [14] were used to organize themes as related to mostly cognitive, social or teaching presence.

4 Findings

The results of the interview analysis are organized into three main parts: (a) learning activities teachers mainly use; (b) challenges for distance learning; and (c) challenges for online collaboration.

4.1 Main Learning Activities Used by Teachers

At the start of the distance learning period, teachers were in a difficult situation where they did not have time to adapt and had to choose from a wide range of digital tools (either ones previously used in the classroom or online) that would suit their subject. One teacher who had used a large variety of digital tools in the past was in a privileged situation, and according to her, the prior use of these digital tools made for a smoother transition and prepared the students for distance learning:

I have practiced all the distance learning tools before with my students, so the change in my classes was not so big for them. (T1)

Initially, in many cases, learners were given independent assignments where they had to acquire study material themselves and provide the teacher with feedback on the knowledge they had learned. These independent learning tasks either involved reading texts, watching videos, studying textbook materials. Students had to work through the assignment and give a summary, answer questions or complete a test or task. The task could be solved in very different ways, such as in written form or by making a video. The teacher provided feedback on the students' submitted assignment. However, over time, it became clear that preparing learning activities and assessing students with worksheet assignments alone was very time-consuming:

I am saying that the time resource to have someone at home on their own to solve this thing, and now that it takes more time than someone to tell you about methods that are effective and provide more examples. It takes a certain amount of time to learn on your own. (T2)

Gradually, teachers started to also prepare and conduct video lessons. Video lessons, where the teacher is in live virtual contact with students in a digital room, and everyone can share his or her screen, audio and video seemed to teachers the most suitable way to re-create a regular classroom experience. For example, teachers mentioned the opportunity to play videos while sharing explanations at the same time; students could ask questions immediately; and the teacher could provide feedback immediately. Video lessons were conducted using either the video conferencing service Zoom or Google Meet. With video conferencing a teacher could give immediate oral feedback to students:

I have used different forms of learning activities: independent learning, video lessons where I can lead lessons through Zoom. Also, I have used video lessons where students have been able to do their presentations in different ways. (T4)

I have stayed on video lessons, and I see that this is best for my students: direct learning. (T4)

Video lessons give the most direct feedback, and the opportunity that now you can interact with students and teachers can interact with them. Synchronous communication is essential, as well. (T2)

Video lessons also allowed the teachers to develop collaboration between students: make joint presentations, presentations, group work, discussions and at the same time, give feedback to peers.

I use mostly these video lessons because there you can give instant feedback there is direct communication, you can communicate with the students, and they can communicate with the teacher. [...] they (students) have made presentations and presented to others. (T2)

I have also given them pair work tasks, again when creating presentations or when creating common document and presenting their work in a video lesson, so there are such things. (T1)

If I do interactive video lessons, there are several ways: we do it in Google Meets so that we can all chat, exchange pictures, we can share the screen, do something there [...] We create content together, and students can share the presentation [...] video, explanation and co-creation. (T5)

In interactive video lectures [...] they(students) are all together in a video lesson, and we can work together in a controlled place at a controlled time. (T5)

A forest quiz is one that takes into account the points of the whole class (right and wrong answers). I have done in such a way that they share and discuss with each other. That at first, they searched independently. And then in a video lesson. Then we discussed in video lesson together what these correct answers might be. (T3)

In the video lessons, the students have been able to present their presentations [...], And I have assessed the students [...] To some extent I have used pair work assignments [...] in collaboration one joint presentation have been made [...] On the topic, thematic. (T4)

4.2 Challenges for Distance Learning

Table 2 organizes the themes related to challenges for distance learning according to the three areas of presence identified by the CoI framework.

Table 2. Challenges for distance learning

Area	Themes
Cognitive presence	No time to adapt
	Lack of time management skills
	Lessons more concentrated in volume
	Learning difficulties
Social presence	Security issues
	Feeling of loneliness in a video lesson
	Low motivation
	Worries about cyberbullying
	Technical problems to connect
Teaching presence	Higher workload (preparation, implementation, feedback)
	Meaningful use of resources
	Difficult to observe all students
	Involving students is challenging
	Assessment issues

4.2.1 Cognitive Presence Challenges

Cognitive presence according to the CoI framework involves constructing meaning through constant communication. Cognitive presence is a necessary element of learning and of critical and higher-order thinking. We derived themes which negatively related to building cognitive presence. The two most mentioned themes were teachers concerns about the adjustment time needed to learn in a distance learning situation and meaningful use of resources:

> *Initially, everything was very new and, in general, the biggest obstacle was the transition to distance learning in the first week. There was a need to adapt quickly to the situation where you do not have the classroom anymore to teach the students directly. However, we have a lot of tools and digital tools, but now to distinguish what is useful and valuable, why this just is better than others that it is difficult to do. […] And in the same way, students need this time to get used to it. (T2)*

> *However, in the beginning, in the first half, when distance learning started, everything was new, and maybe I wanted to try different learning environments, but now I have been able to choose and use what I like and what students like. (T4)*

> *In the first week, I had the feeling that help me! What tools should I use now? (T2)*

Another theme mentioned by teachers affecting cognitive presence is a lack of time management skills by students. This category was often brought out from teachers in the context of keeping up with assignments:

Students may disappear for various reasons: they are too overwhelmed with their learning assignments, and they cannot keep up with all their subjects. They ask for an extension of the deadline. (T4)

Teachers faced difficulties in some cases where school management suggested shortening the lessons, which correspondingly requires them to be more intense and concentrated in volume:

The online lesson time should be more or less half of what we usually do in a classroom lesson. (T2)

Learning difficulties of students caused them to disappear from video lessons or from online contact:

Some students disappear for various reasons, and you have to write to them and ask what happened. Sometimes you have to wait for days for that answer when they dare to admit that they have learning difficulties. (T4)

4.2.2 Social Presence Challenges

Social presence according to the CoI framework is the ability of students to extend their functions to the community. The value of this element is to facilitate critical thinking in the learner community by supporting cognitive presence. We observed themes related to a lack of or negative social presence such as security issues, feeling of loneliness in a video lesson, low motivation and cyberbullying:

But Zoom I don't know, there has been such a thing that, for example, a link to a lesson has been passed on to other students [...] that usually in class, when someone comes to class, he asks permission to attend. But right now, you don't know who's in the class, because there are only black boxes [...]. I had one lesson, for example, one student who did not belong to my class was attending. (T4)

You feel alone, but fortunately, the smaller the class is, the more reliable they are to each other[...] where the class is larger, the more those students do not show their faces. (T4)

Motivation is crucial [...] Lack of motivation affects the result [...] If you are not interested in the results, then you are not a very good partner or teammate because you don't care. It takes others are less motivated; then it is more complicated for them to do collaborative tasks. (T5)

In our school, we do not require students to share their video in video lessons because there has been cyberbullying where students make memes with classmates' pictures. (T4)

Some technical problems were mentioned by teachers related to poor internet connections or lack of access to digital devices. The following were the only comments made related to technical problems:

Some students have bad internet. Maybe they are in the countryside on remote islands. (T3)

I always have to keep in mind that not all students have computers, some of them have only a phone, so I adapt assignments. (T1)

It depends on the number of siblings when they can study with classmates together. (T2)

So, there have been problems, maybe you cannot assume that all students have a computer option, then those who share with several sisters and brothers, maybe then and WiFi is in some homes is much weaker than in others. Well, because of that, they may not already go (to the online class) where I am leading them to go. (T2)

4.2.3   Teaching Presence Challenges

Teaching presence consists of two functions: shaping the educational learning experience and facilitating learning activities. This element reflects both cognitive and social existence and their creation, integration and facilitation. The management of online learning gives several possibilities to develop cognitive and social presence.

Analysis of the interviews brought out several challenges' teachers face in create teaching presence in online learning. Teachers frequently expressed concerns about higher workload. They brought out that preparation, implementation and giving feedback is more time consuming than before distance learning:

One challenge is that I have a considerable workload. More than before, and I'm still not able to do everything. I start in the early morning and finish late night to give students variance in learning. (T1)

Everything takes more time, learning by yourself at home takes more time for the student and also for the teacher. (T2)

To achieve curricula outcomes, teachers need to ensure that students understand the content to participate fully in learning activities. However, this is especially challenging in distance learning since the teacher is not always available to help all of the students at the same time to understand the content. Teachers find it challenging to observe and involve all of their students:

It probably takes more time than it usually would have taken. (T4)

I think that maybe this lack of a common platform /.../ from the students' feedback has come from the fact that the students would like it if these lessons took place in one environment and it would be easy to find everything necessary. (T2)

This (distance learning) is difficult for larger classes. When you have 26 students who should be in class, but the only thing is that they share a black screen for most of the class. It is difficult to observe their immediate emotion that students are having. [...] You put much effort into showing an experiment, but you have no clue what students are doing at the same time. (T2)

Nevertheless, the point is that if there are 26 students, it is complicated to reach all the students, so that those who are bold, so to speak, will emerge and, but perhaps some shy students would like to have more of an individual approach. Furthermore, this is difficult to solve in a distance learning situation. (T2)

I'm afraid that students who are difficult to engage are, even more, difficult to engage in distance learning. (T5)

One of the issues is that students collaborate when you give them individual assignments. They all give the right answers but later from the feedback, you see that stronger students have shared their replies with others, and you can't be sure 100% that they have done assignments by themselves. (T2)

4.3 Challenges for Online Collaboration

Table 3 summarizes themes related to the challenge's teachers face in implementing collaborative activities at a distance.

Table 3. Challenges for online collaboration.

Area	Themes
Social presence	Students do not contribute equally
	Finding a mutually suitable time to work together
	The teacher evaluates the content, not collaboration
	Students prefer to collaborate with their friends
Teaching presence	Lessons are more concentrated in volume
	Assessment of collaboration

4.3.1 Social Presence Challenges

Teachers brought out in interviews four themes what are challenging for students for online collaboration: students do not contribute equally, it is difficult to find a common time for collaboration with other students, teachers are more focused on the content, not collaboration and students prefer to collaborate with friends.

If students do not contribute equally, it is a continuous problem that negatively affects the benefits of collaboration. Thus, the benefits of collaboration may be dominated by students' negative experiences which are often related to the free riding.

Students have brought out in their feedback that it is more challenging to do group work because usually one takes charge and were pushing others to finalize work, then now they can't even get contact with their teammates, so the one makes all the work by himself. This is not happening in the classroom situation. (T4)

Some students are more passive and get lost for periods when they don't do anything. It is difficult to put other students in a situation where they are dependent on students who don't contribute. (T3)

As in a typical classroom situation, I believe that collaborative assignments should create a way that all students should contribute, and this is difficult in an online learning situation to create their equality. (T3)

Considering the collaborative learning there is a challenge for students to find a mutual time to work with fellow students. As distance learning is challenging for students, the collaboration would be easier for them if they could collaborate with their friends.

That it's a bit challenging here (distance learning). This collaboration should be like it has been in the classroom so that students can communicate with each other and do something real together. However, now it's more difficult for students to find a moment, where they can do something together, some students sleep longer, some students wake up in the morning earlier. Moreover, it's more difficult to find the moment for collaborative learning. (T4)

We have a schedule at school to plan lessons, but it also points out that not all students have the opportunity to use a computer at the same time, for example, that some people start their classes early in the morning or late in the evening. (T2)

If we think about collaborative online learning, I guess for students; it is more convenient to do these tasks with those with whom they are accustomed to do. However, if I put students together by myself to the groups, it could lead to the fact that these groups do not want to work with each other. (T4)

Another theme mentioned by teachers affecting social presence for online collaboration is that teachers are more focused to evaluate the content of assignments, not collaboration.

It is clear that we have priorities, the amount of time we can use in half from what it was, so I try to put more focus on most important topics instead of developing the general skills. (T5)

The lessons are almost half what they were, and we have to sacrifice some places to meet the requirements of the curricula. […] The collaborative learning has been aside in this period. (T2)

4.3.2 Teaching Presence Challenges

Teachers find it difficult to focus on collaboration; thus, most energy goes on orchestration the online classes, and as contact hours are more intense, the collaboration is not in the center now. Furthermore, at the same time, teachers agree, that especially in this distance learning situation, the need for collaborative learning is present, but they have to set priorities.

Unfortunately, (lectures) are the fastest way to get as much information as possible to students at once, and if there is a task at the end, you can see if it was accepted, and in the meantime, there is a change, you don't have to listen all the time. (T5)

For teachers, it was an issue in distance learning, that they do not see how students collaborate. When in classroom learning, they also observe the process of collaboration, they found it more challenging to assess the collaboration.

It is possible to use collaborative tasks where students have to do a common assignment at their own time, in their own agreed way. They can select the working environment by their-self, so you give them the task, but I'm avoiding them because I want to see how they collaborate, not just the result. (T5)

But in this situation, it's harder to grade because I don't follow them 24/7, and I do not see how they collaborate. (T4)

5 Discussion and Limitations

Overall, the science teachers we interviewed identified several challenges for distance learning and online collaboration during the coronavirus outbreak situation. Somewhat surprisingly, technical issues were relatively less mentioned than other issues. One reason why technical issues may have been relatively less mentioned is that the various distance education technologies chosen by teachers were already familiar to students or quickly adapted to, even though fully online learning was a new situation for teachers and students. Also, in the past, some schools have organized e-learning days where an entire school learns at a distance during that day. Such e-learning days might also be a contributing factor to why technical problems were not widely mentioned. The technical problems that were mentioned involved poor internet connection or lack of access to digital devices (e.g., a sibling already using the home computer for their own online school lesson).

An evolution from distributing weekly assignments and giving written feedback to organizing live-video lessons and/or consultations is evident from the findings. As social presence theory predicts, synchronous video technologies offer a higher degree of possibilities to convey socio-emotional cues and establish or maintain interpersonal connections. Nevertheless, video lessons lose some of their presumed advantages for establishing social presence when participants turn off their webcams or do not have webcams. Recall the comments of teachers: "…right now, you don't know who's in the class, because there are only black boxes"; "…where the class is larger, the more students do not show their faces". Also, issues of privacy and safety arise with sharing video, as was remarked by a teacher: "In our school, we do not require students to share their video in video lessons because there has been cyberbullying where students make memes with classmates' pictures." Thus, video conferencing with teenagers can be problematic with respect to privacy concerns.

Our findings revealed some positive examples of using distance learning technologies to support, in part, online collaboration. For example, students making presentations online during video lessons to their teacher and classmates. One teacher mentioned an example where the students planned to conduct a virtual school graduation ceremony for which they had a prepared a 3D virtual model in the software app Minecraft.

However, challenges for distance learning and online collaboration were evident, although we should keep in mind that effective collaboration in the *regular* classroom is itself a complex topic [17], and science teachers in general have expressed a need for additional support to integrate meaningful collaborative activities in the teaching of their subjects [18]. Thus, it is unsurprising that implementing effective collaborative strategies online was difficult or impractical for the teachers in the current situation. Successful strategies for promoting collaboration developed in the context adult education might be promising for school teachers in a similar situation in the future. Aragon [19] identifies several strategies to establish and maintain social presence, such as limiting class size, structuring collaborative learning activities, promptly and frequently providing feedback, sharing personal stories and experiences, using humor, using emoticons, etc. It remains to be seen whether they are also applicable with teenagers learning science at a distance. But in any case, developing collaboration technologies and online teaching strategies for young teenagers should specifically acknowledge and address the challenges related to establishing social presence.

The teacher interviews used in this study gave valuable insight into the complex issues facilitating collaboration of middle school students in a time of distance learning. However, it needs to be stressed that while teachers provided insights to advancing our understanding on this situation, the teachers do not represent a sample from a randomly selected population. As such, the conclusions drawn from this research should not be generalized to other, larger populations. Another limitation of this study is that the thematic analysis method used to derive themes from the transcripts is susceptible to inconsistency and is less precise when compared to more rigorous forms of qualitative analysis involving generation of codes and multiple iterations by two or more coders to extract thematic categories. An additional limitation is that teacher's perceptions of student online learning may differ from the actual perceptions of the students themselves. Finally, the data was collected using self-report methods, in which case responses may have been influenced by lapses in memory recall and potential social desirability bias. Overall, there is a need to investigate further these results with a more extensive, more diverse group of participants and varied techniques.

This study provides some insights into the use of technologies by middle school science teachers during an unprecedented time of mandatory distance learning. In general, teachers adapted by relying on school learning management systems for sharing information and by adopting video conferencing technologies to engage in synchronous audiovisual communication with students. However, the findings suggest that the technologies available to teachers for distance education, as well as current pedagogies for their use, are unsatisfactory in supporting the generation of social presence, and consequently unhelpful in facilitating collaborative activities at a distance. Social presence, along with teacher presence and cognitive presence, are essential elements of online collaborative-constructivist learning according to the CoI framework. Future work should focus on how K-12 teachers can best establish social presence with and among young people so that collaborative learning activities can be successfully implemented during times of physical distancing. Technology offers various means of generating social connection through virtual contact, and therefore, physical distancing rules should not be interpreted as social distancing. More research-based solutions are urgently needed to guide K-12 school teachers, especially those teaching subjects perceived as difficult or less interesting, on best practices for using technology effectively during distance learning and online collaboration situations.

Acknowledgements. This work was funded by the Estonian Research Council (ERC) through the institutional research funding project Smart technologies and digital literacy in promoting a change of learning (Grant Agreement No. IUT34-6).

References

1. Means, B., Toyama, Y., Murphy, R., Baki, M.: The effectiveness of online and blended learning: a meta-analysis of the empirical literature. Teachers Coll. Rec. **115**(3), 1–47 (2013)
2. Bernard, R.M., Borokhovski, E., Schmid, R.F., Tamim, R.M., Abrami, P.C.: A meta-analysis of blended learning and technology use in higher education: from the general to the applied. J. Comput. High. Educ. **26**(1), 87–122 (2014)
3. Zawacki-Richter, O., Alturki, U., Aldraiweesh, A.: Review and content analysis of the international review of research in open and distance/distributed learning (2000–2015). Int. Rev. Res. Open Distrib. Learn. **18**(2), 1–26 (2017)
4. Arnesen, K.T., Hveem, J., Short, C.R., West, R.E., Barbour, M.K.: K-12 online learning journal articles: trends from two decades of scholarship. Distance Educ. **40**(1), 32–53 (2019)
5. Digital Learning Collaborative: Snapshot 2019: A review of K-12 online, blended, and digital learning (2019). https://www.digitallearningcollab.com
6. Barbour, M.K.: The landscape of K-12 online learning: examining what is known. In: Moore, M.G., Dieh, W.C. (eds.) Handbook of Distance Education, 4th edn., pp. 521–542. Routledge, New York (2019)
7. Republic of Estonia Ministry of Education and Research The Estonian Lifelong Learning Strategy (2020). https://www.hm.ee/sites/default/files/estonian_lifelong_strategy.pdf
8. Siiman, L.A., et al.: An instrument for measuring students' perceived digital competence according to the DIGCOMP framework. In: Zaphiris, P., Ioannou, A. (eds.) LCT 2016. LNCS, vol. 9753, pp. 233–244. Springer, Cham (2016). https://doi.org/10.1007/978-3-319-39483-1_22
9. Sjøberg, S., Schreiner, C.: The ROSE project. An overview and key findings (2010). http://roseproject.no/network/countries/norway/eng/nor-Sjoberg-Schreiner-overview-2010.pdf
10. Teppo, M., Rannikmäe, M.: Paradigm shift for teachers: more relevant science teaching. In Holbrook, J., Rannikmäe, M., Reiska, P., Ilsley, P. (eds.) The Need for a Paradigm Shift in Science Education for Post-Soviet Societies: Research and Practice (Estonian Example), pp. 25–46. Peter Lang GmbH, Frankfurt (2008)

11. Dunbar, K.: How scientists think in the real world: implications for science education. J. Appl. Dev. Psychol. **1**, 49–58 (2000)
12. Short, J., Williams, E., Christie, B.: The Social Psychology of Telecommunications. Wiley, New York (1976)
13. Dunlap, J.C., Lowenthal, P.R.: The power of presence: our quest for the right mix of social presence in online courses. In: Mizell, A.P., Piña, A.A. (eds.) Real life distance education: Case studies in practice, pp. 41–66. Information Age Publishing, Charlotte (2014)
14. Garrison, D.R., Anderson, T., Archer, W.: Critical inquiry in a text-based environment: computer conferencing in higher education. Internet High. Educ. **2**, 87–105 (2000)
15. Pedaste, M., et al.: Phases of inquiry-based learning: definitions and the inquiry cycle. Educ. Res. Rev. **14**, 47–61 (2015)
16. Kuckartz, U., Rädiker, S.: Analyzing Qualitative Data with MAXQDA. Springer, Cham (2019). https://doi.org/10.1007/978-3-030-15671-8
17. Griffin, P., Care, E. (eds.): Assessment and Teaching of 21st Century Skills. EAIA. Springer, Dordrecht (2015). https://doi.org/10.1007/978-94-017-9395-7
18. Brown, R.E., Bogiages, C.A.: Professional development through STEM integration: how early career math and science teachers respond to experiencing integrated STEM tasks. Int. J. Sci. Math. Educ. **17**(1), 111–128 (2019)
19. Aragon, S.R.: Creating social presence in online environments. New Dir. Adult Contin. Educ. **100**, 57–68 (2003)

Learning Music and Math, Together as One: Towards a Collaborative Approach for Practicing Math Skills with Music

Eric Roldán Roa[1], Érika Roldán Roa[2], and Irene-Angelica Chounta[1(✉)]

[1] Institute of Education, University of Tartu, Tartu, Estonia
`pachoroldan@icloud.com, chounta@ut.ee`
[2] Department of Mathematics, Technische Universität München, Munich, Germany
`e.roldan.roa@gmail.com`

Abstract. In this paper we present a study that took place in an elementary school in Mexico. The study aimed to explore the use of a digital application for the design and orchestration of collaborative, game-based learning activities for STEAM and to study the impact of group formation with respect to students' background knowledge. In particular, our goal was to support students in practicing math skills using music in a series of workshops. The workshops took place in the form of a tournament where groups of students worked together to win sets of music and math rounds. We formed groups based on students' background knowledge in math and we explored the impact of group formation with respect to students' background knowledge on learning gains – as assessed in pre and post knowledge tests – and game score. The results indicate that homogeneous groups outperformed heterogeneous groups in terms of learning gains but heterogeneous groups achieved better results in terms of game score than homogeneous groups. The former does not confirm related research and it may suggest that the group formation impact on learning gains depends largely on the context. The latter may indicate the need for aligning the game objectives with learning goals in order to ensure that educational games indeed prioritize learning.

Keywords: Collaborative learning · STEAM · Group formation · Game-based learning · Math · Music

1 Introduction

The aim of this work is to explore how we can use music to support students in learning math. In particular, we focus on designing game-based, musical activities that engage K-12 (that is, from kindergarten to 12th grade) students in practicing basic math concepts, such as addition and subtraction.

Mathematics, along with science and reading, is one of the core knowledge domains periodically assessed by the Programme for International Student

A. Nolte et al. (Eds.): CollabTech 2020, LNCS 12324, pp. 143–156, 2020.
https://doi.org/10.1007/978-3-030-58157-2_10

Assessment (PISA)[1] pointing out the need to ensure that elementary students will develop key math skills and logical thinking in order to equip them to be able to solve practical and complex mathematical problems in the long term. Educational research argues that traditional teaching approaches and instructional methods for mathematics curricula do not have a positive impact on students [1,15]. On the contrary, learning experiences that are not based on traditional teaching approaches for mathematics curricula can contribute to bridging the achievement gap and to reducing mathematical anxiety [23]. For example, when arts are used as a vehicle for teaching we encounter several benefits such as: a) promoting communication among students, b) transforming learning environments, c) reaching out to students that otherwise may not be reachable, d) offering new challenges to students, e) decreasing curricula fragmentation, e) connecting in-school learning with real-world, among others [10,12].

A literature review on the relationship between music and math performance [25] showed that there was only a small positive association between the two topics and no solid evidence that music enhances math performance. However, this literature review mainly focused on whether musical performance relates to math performance rather than using music as an instructional tool for teaching math. On the other hand, [20] employed a game-based learning approach that engaged students in a mix of music and math activities. The results suggested that this approach encouraged students to draw conceptual relationships between mathematics and music, to critically think, analyze and solve problems and to be faster in carrying out learning tasks.

1.1 Research Objective

In this study, we follow up on the work of [20]. In particular, we study how we can support K-12 students in practicing basic math skills - such as addition and subtraction - by engaging them in game-based musical tasks. Furthermore, we explore how technology-enhanced collaboration can potentially support students' engagement and increase students' learning gains. To that end, we carried out a small-scale study in an elementary school in Mexico where we asked students to participate in a Music and Math Tournament for groups. During the tournament, a collaborative game-based learning app was used to orchestrate learning activities that engaged students in practicing collaboratively music and math skills. The results of this study suggest that students who participated in the activity along with team-mates of similar background knowledge achieved higher learning gains than students who participated in the activity with team-mates with different background knowledge. However, it was also shown that diverse student groups - in terms of students' background knowledge - were performing better in terms of game-play. The contribution of this work is twofold:

a. to contribute to research regarding the relationship between music and math in the context of Science, Technology, Engineering, Arts and Mathematics (STEAM) Education;

---

[1] https://www.oecd.org/pisa/.

b. to offer insight with respect to group formation for collaborative game-based learning contexts.

In the following sections we will provide a brief overview on related research regarding the combination of music and math in formal education and group formation for collaborative learning approaches. Then we will provide information about the methodological approach of this work and we will elaborate on the study set up. Next, we will present the analysis and results and finally we will conclude with a contextualized discussion on the findings, the limitations and the implications of this work.

2   Related Work

2.1   Music and Math in Formal Education

Research has indicated potential links between musical concepts such as melody, rhythm, intervals, scales, and harmony, with mathematical concepts such as integers, numerical relations, arithmetical operations and trigonometry [4,14]. Furthermore, research has been exploring the physical effects music has on the human body. For instance, music relates to very primal parts of the brain [16] and it affects cognitive processes such as attention and engagement [6,26]. Several studies have focused on different ways in which music can be used as an element to improve mathematical performance.

Vaughn [25] conducted a meta-analysis from published studies on the relationship between music and mathematics. The focus of the literature analysis was to explore three questions: 1) Do individuals who voluntarily choose to study music show higher mathematical achievement than those who do not choose? 2) Do individuals exposed to a music curriculum in school show higher mathematical achievement as a consequence of this music instruction? and 3) Does background music heard while thinking about math problems serve to enhance mathematical ability at least during the music listening time? The analysis suggested that there was a small positive association between the voluntary study of music and mathematics achievement, a minor causal relationship that music training enhances math performance and that there was no solid evidence that background music enhances math performance. It is important to note that the studies used for the analysis were exploring the relationship between music and math performance and not the use of music as a means for practicing math.

On the contrary, research that focuses on the use of music as a teaching means for math, suggests that there are positive effects. Geist, et al. [13] described the power of music as follows: "Music brings order to disorder. Teachers can demonstrate patterns without using any materials". They conducted a study with 3 and 4 year old children at the Ohio University Child Development Center in Athens, Ohio, which showed that children who engaged in music-related activities were able to explain mathematical concepts using their musical experience as a medium. Conversely, children not exposed to lessons with music along with mathematics, had trouble recalling the math concepts when asked. An, et al. [2]

investigated the effect of combining music with regular math courses on elementary students' performance. The results suggested that music and math courses had a positive impact on students' math skills. In a similar vein, Rajić [20] carried out a study to explore how a game-based approach that brought together music and math may affect students' motivation and engagement of work. The study was conducted with children aged from 8 to 12 years old from two schools of Belgrade, Serbia. By surveys as an instrument with three levels of answers (not at all, partially or completely) it was found that a high percentage of students (between 70% to 80%) confirmed that the game encouraged them to connect content in mathematics and music, to analyze and solve problems, to be faster in work and think critically. According to Rajić, this practice can also influence and scaffold the development of students' cognitive skills.

2.2 Collaborative Learning and Group Formation

Collaborative problem solving, collaborative learning, and teamwork, are terms that have been echoing for decades. Roschelle and Teasley [22] defined collaboration as the construction and maintenance of a shared conception of a problem resulting from a co-ordinated and synchronous activity. A growing emphasis in state and national education systems is that they are shaping curriculum and instruction around problem solving, critical thinking, self-management, and collaboration skills [8]. For collaboration to happen, we need to carefully craft the conditions that will enable it: learning scenarios that require students to work together, communication channels that facilitate information exchange and the space and time for social interactions between students to emerge. One critical aspect to accommodate these social interactions is the dynamics that come into play when people form teams to achieve a common goal.

A common approach for group formation is based on the students' knowledge complementarity. The rationale is that students with complementary knowledge will benefit from collaboration since they will have to exchange information knowledge in order to carry out the common task. This group formation approach is followed by the Jigsaw approach [3] that is also applied for orchestrating activities, distributing resources and learning materials in CSCL settings [9,19]. A step further, Erkens et al. [11] investigated how knowledge-complementary groups react upon receiving awareness support regarding knowledge exchange.

Existing research shows that heterogeneous groups usually achieve better results than homogeneous groups despite the fact that students prefer to group with students with similar characteristics [5,24]. For example, Manske et al. [18] found that heterogeneous groups regarding background knowledge would achieve higher learning gains than homogeneous learning groups when practicing with an online inquiry learning platform that engaged students in online labs activities. Furthermore, research has explored the formation of groups with respect to students' personality traits. For example, heterogeneous groups in terms of extraversion is considered to be beneficial [17]. This has been also confirmed by Bellhauser et al. [24] who investigated group formation with respect to extraversion and conscientiousness. Their findings suggest that heterogeneous extravert groups and homogeneous conscientious groups demonstrate positive effects on students' performance. However, it is not clear what happens in the case both personality traits are manipulated at the same time.

In this work, we aimed to explore the impact of group formation with respect to students' background knowledge in a collaborative game-based setting and whether heterogeneous groups would benefit more than homogeneous groups.

3   Methodology

3.1   Experimental Setup

For the purpose of this work, we conducted a study in collaboration with an elementary school in Zapopan, Mexico. During this study, we carried out a series of workshops that aimed to support students collaboratively practice around basic mathematics concepts along with music. The workshops were facilitated by a digital app (MusicalMonkeys) that delivered the learning activities to the students. In total, 14 students (9 female and 5 male) from 4th grade (approximately 9 years old) participated in the study. A workshop was organized each week for 7 weeks in total, resulting in 7 workshops overall. The duration of each workshop was about 45–50 min and during the workshops, students were working in groups on different learning activities, as provided by the app.

3.2   Musical Monkeys

Musical Monkeys Fig. 1 is an educational game application designed by Music-Math[2]. The game app allows connecting client iPads (that is, iPads operated by student groups) to a server iPad which is controlled by the teacher. The potential of using one mobile device to support the student group – instead of providing one device to each member of the group – has been previously studied is a similar context for scaffolding collaboration [7]. The rationale is that students will coordinate, define roles, distribute responsibilities and plan their action around the device. Thus, the one device will enable them to work together. The game allows teachers to organize students in groups and play two different types of "rounds" or challenges to combine math and music concepts. This game-based collaborative activity can be related to the following characteristics of a STEAM approach[3]:

1. Students are active in the learning process by doing (in this case, playing);
2. Cooperation, collaboration, communication and creativity are promoted during the gameplay, since children are challenged to think collectively in order to solve puzzles and trivias that connect math problems to music rhythms and vice versa;
3. This game aims to promote students creativity to find, evaluate and try their own processes for answering the math and music rounds.

---

[2] www.musicmath.mx.
[3] https://www.edweek.org/tm/articles/2014/11/18/ctq-jolly-stem-vs-steam.html.

Fig. 1. Two screenshots from the Musical Monkeys interface: The welcome screen (on the left) and an example of setting up a math round activity (on the right)

The first round is called the "math round". This round is designed to engage elementary students in thinking and practicing with arithmetic concepts as an introduction to algebraic thinking. The latter is being presented as trivia, for example "2+? = 10" instead of "2 + 8 = ?". The math round allows practicing with four topics or math arithmetic operands: addition, subtraction, multiplication and division. During this round, student groups are called to answer randomly generated trivia exercises without the support of additional material (for example, pen and paper). The teacher can choose the difficulty level for these exercises and also set a time limit for the round in order to make the activity more challenging.

The second round is called the "music round". In this round, the app plays a musical rhythm to the student group and the group has to represent the rhythm as a geometric figure. To establish this representation, the students have to associate the rhythm beats to figure vertices. In other words, a musical rhythm that has 4 beats can be represented as a square or rectangle (4 vertices). Similarly, a rhythm with 5 beats will be represented as a pentagon, and so on.

3.3   Method of the Study

The study was carried out in the format of a *"tournament"*. We adopted this game-based approach with tournament rounds because we assumed that students would become more engaged in playing a competitive game based on problem-solving math problems rather than repetitively practicing them alone or in the classroom. Each round of the tournament was one workshop and was associated with either math or music rounds. The tournament started with a welcome workshop. There, the students had the opportunity to play a math and a music round in order to familiarize with the app. In this study, we wanted to explore the impact of these workshops on students' performance regarding math.

After the welcome round, we followed up with a math round where we administered a pre-knowledge math test. The structure of the pretest consisted of students playing individually a math round of the Musical Monkeys app. The task was addition in mode A + B = C, where the students were asked to calculate the value of B when A and C were given. The pretest consisted of five items and the duration of the pretest was five minutes. Each pretest item was awarded 0.2 points. Thus, the pretest score range was [0, 1].

Similarly, the tournament ended with a math round, where we administered a post-knowledge math test. Each student took the knowledge tests individually. For the rest four workshops (between the pre and post tests), the students played both math and music rounds. That is, for each workshop the student groups played 4 math rounds and 4 music rounds. Based on their performance, the team was awarded with a score at the end of each workshop. In this study, all rounds were similar in terms of difficulty (including the pre and post tests) and the scores for all rounds (pretest, posttest and workshop scores) work range from 0 to 1. For pre and post tests, the students were assessed individually and for the workshop rounds (week1 to week 4) the students were assessed as a group.

In order to explore the impact group formation might have on students' activity and learning gains, we divided students into two conditions: students who participated in the tournament as members of homogeneous teams (control condition, HM) and students who participated in the tournament as members of heterogeneous teams (experimental condition, HT). To form student groups, we used the students' scores in the pre-knowledge test. In this context, homogeneity refers to the background knowledge of students as this is assessed by the pretest.

Overall, two homogeneous groups were formed, each consisting of 4 students of similar background knowledge and two heterogeneous groups were formed, each consisting of 4 students with different background knowledge. When grouping the students into heterogeneous groups our goal was that the standard deviation of the pretest score per group would be high - indicating that the background knowledge of students was different. On the contrary, for homogeneous groups the standard deviation of pretest scores should be low. Additionally, we aimed to have a similar median pretest score per condition - so that the learning gains would be comparable. The details about the groups' pretest scores and formation is presented in Table 1. Our research hypothesis was that students of the experimental condition would show higher learning gains that the students of the control condition. As learning gain (LG), we define the score's difference between the posttest and the pretest (LG = Posttest Score - Pretest Score). To study the research hypothesis, we carried out a two-way, non parametric t-test (Mann Whitney U test). Furthermore, we carried out a descriptive analysis over time to explore patterns in the progress of students over the duration of the tournament regarding their performance in terms of gameplay.

4   Results

4.1   Descriptive Analysis

Overall, the students achieved on average 0.22 points on the pre-knowledge test ($Median_{pretest} = 0.2$, $SD = 0.2$). On the post-knowledge test, the students received on average 0.65 points ($Median_{posttest} = 0.6$, $SD = 0.28$). This shows that on average, there was a learning gain of 0.43 ($Median_{LG} = 0.4$, $SD = 0.17$). The results on the group level – that is the average and median pre and post tests scores and the gameplay scores for every group per week – are presented in Table 1. Almost all of the student groups improved their scores while playing the game rounds over time. Group 1 (HT) achieved the biggest improvement in terms of game score from week 1 to week 4 while group 4 (HM) showed no improvement in terms of the game score.

Table 1. Groups mean and median pretest and posttest scores and group scores during weekly gameplay reflecting groups' formation into heterogeneous and homogeneous with respect to their background knowledge

	Group 1 HT	Group 2 HT	Group 3 HM	Group 4 HM
Mean pretest score (SD)	0.47 (0.46)	0.47 (0.46)	0.20 (0.16)	0.25 (0.25)
Median pretest score	0.20	0.20	0.20	0.20
Week 1	0.5	0.75	0.6	0.7
Week 2	0.65	0.65	0.7	0.6
Week 3	0.65	0.55	0.6	0.7
Week 4	0.8	0.85	0.7	0.6
Mean posttest score (SD)	0.47 (0.31)	0.53 (0.42)	0.65 (0.34)	0.65 (0.25)
Median posttest score	0.4	0.4	0.7	0.6

4.2   Conditions Comparison

In order to be able to compare the two conditions with respect to the students' learning gains, we compared the students' prior knowledge as it was assessed by the pre-knowledge test. As aforementioned, the pretest, posttest and workshop scores ranged between 0 and 1. The average pretest score for students who formed homogeneous teams was 0.22 (sd = 0.2) and the average pretest score for students who formed heterogeneous teams was 0.47 (sd = 0.41). Heterogeneous teams marked 0.27 more than homogeneous teams (approximately double). This difference is mainly attributed to the high performers who were assigned to these teams in order to make them heterogeneous. This is also evident from the large standard deviation in the student groups' average pretest scores. Next, we compared the two conditions with respect to the median pretest score. The median pretest score for both students who formed homogeneous and heterogeneous teams was 0.2. A Mann-Whitney U test further indicated that there was no statistically significant difference between the pretest scores of the two conditions (at the p = 0.05 level). This finding suggests that the students of the control and the experimental condition had a similar background knowledge. Therefore, the two conditions can be compared in terms of learning gain.

Regarding the posttest, the average posttest score for students who formed homogeneous teams was 0.65 (sd = 0.28) and the average pretest score for students who formed heterogeneous teams was 0.5 (sd = 0.3). Similarly, the median posttest score for students who formed homogeneous teams was 0.6 and the median pretest score for students who formed heterogeneous teams was 0.4. However, a Mann-Whitney U test indicated that there was no statistically significant difference between the posttest scores of the two conditions (at the $p = 0.05$ level).

Then, we calculated the average learning gain, per condition. The average learning gain for students who formed homogeneous teams (control condition) was 0.43 (sd = 0.17) and the average learning gain for students who formed heterogeneous teams (experimental condition) was 0.03 (sd = 0.15). Similarly, the median learning gain for students who formed homogeneous teams was 0.4 and the median learning gain for students who formed heterogeneous teams was 0. A Mann-Whitney U test indicated that the learning gain was significantly greater for the students who participated in homogeneous teams (Median = 0.4) that for students who participated in heterogeneous teams (Median = 0) at the $p = 0.05$ level (U = 1, $p = 0.037$). These results are presented in Table 2.

Table 2. Individual student's results on the pre and post knowledge tests and learning gains

Student ID	Condition	Group	Pretest score	Posttest score	Learning gain
s7	HT	Group 1	0.2	0.2	0
s12	HT	Group 1	1	0.8	−0.2
s13	HT	Group 1	0.2	0.4	0.2
s1	HT	Group 2	1	1	0
s5	HT	Group 2	0.2	0.2	0
s14	HT	Group 2	0.2	0.4	0.2
s2	HM	Group 3	0.2	1	0.8
s4	HM	Group 3	0.4	0.8	0.4
s8	HM	Group 3	0.2	0.6	0.4
s10	HM	Group 3	0	0.2	0.2
s3	HM	Group 4	0.6	1	0.4
s6	HM	Group 4	0	0.4	0.4
s9	HM	Group 4	0.2	0.6	0.4
s11	HM	Group 4	0.2	0.6	0.4

4.3   Analysis of the Collaborative Activity over Time

Overall, we cannot identify a particular pattern in groups' gameplay scores over time (Fig. 2). It seems that heterogeneous groups managed to improve their scores over time while homogeneous groups scored the same points during the tournament. At the same time, even though heterogeneous groups achieved better scores for the tournament's final gameplay week (Week 4), they also had ups and downs in their game scores while homogeneous groups had a steady performance. The uneven performance over time could be an indication of the groups' heterogeneity and a result of in-group dynamics: one could hypothesize that when the high-performers take over the activity then the group achieves higher scores. However, in order to investigate deeper into this we would need to observe the groups' practice for long periods of time and in detail.

From the analysis, it is also evident that the gameplay scores do not reflect the performance of students in terms of learning gains. For example, Group 1 that achieved the highest gameplay score on Week 4 and the biggest improvement over time regarding gameplay, also demonstrated no learning gain (on average) regarding the pre and post knowledge tests. Similarly, Group3 scored similarly on every week of gameplay but demonstrated the highest learning gain regarding the knowledge test.

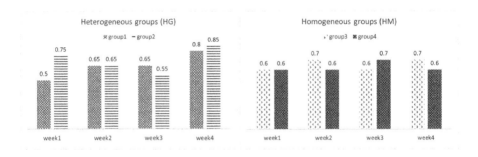

Fig. 2. Weekly game score over the duration of the tournament for heterogeneous (left) and homogeneous (right) groups

5   Discussion

The results of this work suggest that students who participated in the tournament as members of heterogeneous groups had lower learning gains than students who participated in the tournament as members of homogeneous groups. However, heterogeneous groups outperformed homogeneous groups with respect to game score during gameplay. Heterogeneous groups scored higher during the tournament rounds than homogeneous groups and they improved their performance from the first to the last round of the tournament to a greater extent.

On the one hand, this does not confirm related research findings that show that students from heterogeneous teams tend to demonstrate higher learning gains than students from homogeneous teams as demonstrated by Manske, et al. [18]. However, Manske, et al. studied the impact of groups' homogeneity for collaborative learning activities in the context of online labs. Our findings could suggest that the dynamics of collaboration have a different impact on learning gain depending on the collaborative context. For collaborative game-based learning activities, students' coordination is more important than communication and information flow. In collaborative problem solving, students have to establish a common ground and build knowledge in order to carry out the learning activity. In our study, students had to coordinate and use their background knowledge in order to achieve the game's objective. Therefore, it might have been easier for students with similar background knowledge to coordinate and craft a plan of action based on their existing domain knowledge. On the contrary, heterogeneous groups would not prioritize bridging the knowledge gap and establishing common ground but instead, they might have relied on the high-performing members to lead the activity in time in order to beat the game. This would consequently mean that the low-performing members of heterogeneous groups would neither gain new knowledge nor practice their math skills.

Another potential interpretation of the results may be that the game activities are not well aligned with the pre and post knowledge test items or that the game rewards points for game strategies the students' develop instead of actual knowledge. Therefore, achieving a high score in the game, does not indicate that the students also achieved the learning goals.

5.1   Theoretical and Practical Implications

We envision that this work has two main implications. On the one hand, it provides insight with respect to group formation for collaborative game-based learning for STEAM Education. Our findings suggest that the learning setting may potentially affect the criteria we use when forming student groups. Therefore, we may need to establish alternative criteria for group formation depending on the context.

On the other hand, our study emphasizes the importance of the design of the game activity regarding learning objectives. Educational games are considered a fun way to deliver learning experiences and to instigate children's interest, enthusiasm and curiosity [21]. Nonetheless, it is critical to prioritize learning when designing game-based learning activities and to ensure that carrying out the game's objective presupposes that the students have achieved the learning goals.

Finally, this work provides a practical example on the use of technology for orchestrating collaborative learning activities for STEAM. In this case, we used technology - in the form of a game application for tablets - to set up a music and math tournament. The teacher was able to have full control of the activities in terms of timing and difficulty while the students would engage with music and math activities in a fun and challenging way. Overall, the teachers and students who participated in the tournament were positive regarding this experience and they expressed their willingness in repeating the activity.

6   Conclusions

One of the challenges of modern education is to provide technology-enhanced learning experiences that can improve students' performance and to scaffold the acquisition of high-order skills such as creativity, critical thinking, problem solving and collaborative skills along with curriculum-based knowledge. The aim of this work was to explore the use of a game-based application for the orchestration of collaborative STEAM activities. In particular, we used Musical Monkeys to organize a tournament with music and math activities for groups of elementary (4th grade) students. Student groups were characterized as heterogeneous and homogeneous with respect to students' background knowledge, as assessed by pre-knowledge tests. The findings suggest that homogeneous groups demonstrated higher learning gains regarding domain knowledge (math) than heterogeneous groups. However, heterogeneous groups outperformed homogeneous groups in terms of game score. This points out the need for careful design of game-based learning activities in order to ensure on the hand hand that game-play achievement relates to learning gains and on the other hand the meaningful collaboration and knowledge exchange between students.

We acknowledge that this research has some limitations such as the small number of participants and the lack of qualitative information, for example information regarding students' satisfaction. Another limitation is that students' collaboration is happening "offline", meaning that we cannot track the practice of individual members of groups through the application but we would need to rely on observations during gameplay. Furthermore, in this work we did not consider teachers' perspectives. In the future, we plan to expand our research towards two directions: on the one hand we aim to engage teachers into creating music and math learning activities in order to ensure that practicing skills using the game-based apps leads to learning gains. Additionally, we plan to integrate an intelligent virtual agent that will track students' progress and modify gameplay accordingly. On the other hand, we want to organize music and math workshops in the form of tournaments in a systematic way in order to be able to track the impact of these workshops on a wider scale and over time.

Acknowledgments. The authors want to thank the elementary school "Colegio Anderson School" and Misael Hernández Leal (Lead programmer of MusicMath).

This project received funding from the European Union's Horizon 2020 research and innovation program under the Marie Sklodowska-Curie grant agreement No. 754462.

References

1. An, S.: The effects of music-mathematics integrated curriculum and instruction on elementary students' mathematics achievement and dispositions. Texas A&M University (2012)
2. An, S., Capraro, M.M., Tillman, D.A.: Elementary teachers integrate music activities into regular mathematics lessons: effects on students' mathematical abilities. J. Learn. through Arts **9**(1), n1 (2013)

3. Aronson, E., et al.: The Jigsaw Classroom. Sage, Beverly Hills (1978)
4. Beer, M.: How do mathematics and music relate to each other. East Coast College of English, Brisbane, Queensland, Australia (1998)
5. Bell, S.T.: Deep-level composition variables as predictors of team performance: a meta-analysis. J. Appl. Psychol. **92**(3), 595 (2007)
6. Bengtsson, S.L., et al.: Listening to rhythms activates motor and premotor cortices. Cortex **45**(1), 62–71 (2009)
7. Chounta, I.-A., Giemza, A., Hoppe, H.U.: Multilevel analysis of collaborative activities based on a mobile learning scenario for real classrooms. In: Yuizono, T., Zurita, G., Baloian, N., Inoue, T., Ogata, H. (eds.) CollabTech 2014. CCIS, vol. 460, pp. 127–142. Springer, Heidelberg (2014). https://doi.org/10.1007/978-3-662-44651-5_12
8. Darling-Hammond, L.: Surpassing Shanghai: An Agenda for American Education Built on the World's Leading Systems. Harvard Education Press, Cambridge (2011)
9. Dillenbourg, P., Jermann, P.: Designing integrative scripts. In: Fischer, F., Kollar, I., Mandl, H., Haake, J.M. (eds.) Scripting Computer-supported Collaborative Learning, vol. 6, pp. 275–301. Springer, Boston (2007). https://doi.org/10.1007/978-0-387-36949-5_16
10. Erickson, H.L.: Concept-Based Curriculum and Instruction: Teaching Beyond the Facts. Corwin Press, Thousand Oaks (2002)
11. Erkens, M., Manske, S., Hoppe, H.U., Bodemer, D.: Awareness of complementary knowledge in CSCL: impact on learners' knowledge exchange in small groups. In: Nakanishi, H., Egi, H., Chounta, I.-A., Takada, H., Ichimura, S., Hoppe, U. (eds.) CRIWG+CollabTech 2019. LNCS, vol. 11677, pp. 3–16. Springer, Cham (2019). https://doi.org/10.1007/978-3-030-28011-6_1
12. Fiske, E.B.: Champions of Change: The Impact of the Arts on Learning. Arts Education Partnership (1999)
13. Geist, K., Geist, E.A., Kuznik, K.: The patterns of music. Young Child. **2**, 74–79 (2012)
14. Harkleroad, L.: The math behind the music. Cambridge University Press, Cambridge (2006)
15. Hiebert, J.: Relationships between research and the NCTM standards. J. Res. Math. Educ. **30**(1), 3–19 (1999)
16. Hudson, N.J.: Musical beauty and information compression: complex to the ear but simple to the mind? BMC Res. Notes **4**(1), 9 (2011)
17. Kramer, A., Bhave, D.P., Johnson, T.D.: Personality and group performance: the importance of personality composition and work tasks. Personality Individ. Differ. **58**, 132–137 (2014)
18. Manske, S., Hecking, T., Chounta, I.A., Werneburg, S., Hoppe, H.U.: Using differences to make a difference: a study on heterogeneity of learning groups. International Society of the Learning Sciences, Inc.[ISLS] (2015)
19. Pozzi, F.: Using jigsaw and case study for supporting online collaborative learning. Comput. Educ. **55**(1), 67–75 (2010)
20. Rajić, S.: Mathematics and music game in the function of child's cognitive development, motivation and activity. Early Child Dev. Care, 1–13 (2019)
21. Rajić, S.B., Tasevska, A.: The Role of Digital Games in Children's Life (2019)
22. Roschelle, J., Teasley, S.D.: The construction of shared knowledge in collaborative problem solving. In: O'Malley C. (eds.) Computer Supported Collaborative Learning, vol. 128, pp. 69–97. Springer (1995)
23. Tobias, S., Weissbrod, C.: Anxiety and mathematics: an update. Harvard Educ. Rev. **50**(1), 63–70 (1980)

24. Tsovaltzi, D., et al.: Group formation in the digital age: Relevant characteristics, their diagnosis, and combination for productive collaboration (2019)
25. Vaughn, K.: Music and mathematics: Modest support for the oft-claimed relationship. J. Aesthetic Educ. **34**(3/4), 149–166 (2000)
26. Zentner, M., Eerola, T.: Rhythmic engagement with music in infancy. Proc. Natl. Acad. Sci. **107**(13), 5768–5773 (2010)

Work-in-Progress Papers

Quantifying Collaboration Quality in Face-to-Face Classroom Settings Using MMLA

Pankaj Chejara[1]([✉]), Luis P. Prieto[1], Adolfo Ruiz-Calleja[2],
María Jesús Rodríguez-Triana[1], Shashi Kant Shankar[1], and Reet Kasepalu[1]

[1] Tallinn University, Tallinn, Estonia
{pankajch,lprisan,mjrt,shashik,reetkase}@tlu.ee
[2] GSIC-EMIC Group, University of Valladolid, Valladolid, Spain
adolfo@gsic.uva.es

Abstract. The estimation of collaboration quality using manual observation and coding is a tedious and difficult task. Researchers have proposed the automation of this process by estimation into few categories (e.g., high vs. low collaboration). However, such categorical estimation lacks in depth and actionability, which can be critical for practitioners. We present a case study that evaluates the feasibility of quantifying collaboration quality and its multiple sub-dimensions (e.g., collaboration flow) in an authentic classroom setting. We collected multimodal data (audio and logs) from two groups collaborating face-to-face and in a collaborative writing task. The paper describes our exploration of different machine learning models and compares their performance with that of human coders, in the task of estimating collaboration quality along a continuum. Our results show that it is feasible to quantitatively estimate collaboration quality and its sub-dimensions, even from simple features of audio and log data, using machine learning. These findings open possibilities for in-depth automated quantification of collaboration quality, and the use of more advanced features and algorithms to get their performance closer to that of human coders.

Keywords: Computer-Supported Collaborative Learning ·
Multimodal Learning Analytics · Collaboration quality

1 Introduction

Collaboration has been traditionally studied using observation, interviews and ethnographic methods [10]. Although these methods offer in-detailed information, they also demand a lot of human effort and time, which are difficult to scale up [10]. The use of technology to mediate collaboration has provided researchers with large amounts of learner activity data (in the form of logs), offering an alternative to traditional analyses of collaboration. Researchers have used a variety

© Springer Nature Switzerland AG 2020
A. Nolte et al. (Eds.): CollabTech 2020, LNCS 12324, pp. 159–166, 2020.
https://doi.org/10.1007/978-3-030-58157-2_11

of data (e.g., system logs, chats, discussion forums) to understand the underlying process of collaboration using Learning Analytics (LA) methods like content analysis, and interaction analysis [3]. The results of these analyses have been employed to develop various kinds of feedback systems, from mirroring to guiding support [6]. While Computer-Supported Collaborative Learning (CSCL) often involves face-to-face and computer-mediated interactions, collaborative LA support often relies on just digital logs, thus offering only a partial picture of the interactions. Aware of this limitation, the field of Multimodal Learning Analytics (MMLA) [2] emerged with the goal of understanding learning through multimodal data from digital and physical spaces. Recent MMLA studies showed that it is feasible to estimate collaboration aspects categorically (e.g., high vs. low collaboration) in face-to-face settings by combining physical and digital activity traces [12,13]. In addition, researchers have found verbal interactions and speaking activity features as an important indicator for collaboration behavior [1,7]. However, most of these studies are conducted in laboratory settings, so their results might not hold under authentic classroom constraints (e.g., noisy data). Moreover, the qualitative estimation of collaboration quality into a few classes provides end users (e.g., a teacher) with little information about what might be the underlying problem or reason why collaboration quality is high/low.

In order to estimate quality of collaboration in a more fine-grained fashion, this paper explores regression analysis models to quantitatively estimate collaboration quality in a classroom setting from audio and log data. To reach that goal, we carried out a case-study where we collected data from two groups (each with four participants) in an authentic classroom setting. The learning activity involved face-to-face discussion and collaborative writing using digital means. We applied various regression models and compared their performance with that of human coders, in the task of coding collaboration quality and its sub-dimensions along a continuum.

2   Related Work

Researchers have investigated the problem of estimating collaboration into a limited set of categories, in various settings: pair-programming [4], project-based learning [12], and tabletop-based collaborative learning [8]. These studies collected data through different means (audio [1,13], Kinect sensors [4], system logs [7,13], and video [13]) and extracted a wide variety of features from them, e.g.: non-verbal features like MFCC features, energy [1]; or spatial and dynamic features like hand movement or distance between learners [12]. These features were in turn used to estimate different aspects of the collaboration process: collaboration quality [1,8,13], or success in collaboration [12]. Certain studies [4,8,13] have included data from *both* physical and digital spaces to investigate collaboration behavior.

While most of these studies devised their own coding schemes to annotate or classify collaboration quality, others [8] have used collaboration rating schemes that are widely used in the collaborative learning sciences (e.g., [9]).

Although these rating schemes often output quantitative scores (e.g., collaboration quality [8], grading of collaboration work [12]), such scores have often been mapped into two or three categories (e.g., high vs. low collaboration), as binary classification is an easier problem (from an information theory point of view) and often results in better performance when using machine learning models [12,13]. However, this "flattening" of the scores also takes away much of the nuance and the different aspects that contribute to high-quality collaboration. In terms of performance, classification accuracy has been reported from above average (48% [4]) to moderate (69% [7]) and high level (80% [12], 96% [13]).

A number of gaps emerge from the aforementioned state of the art. First, that MMLA researchers have mostly built models to estimate collaboration quality categorically, which offers limited information about the reasons or underlying structure of that judgement (i.e., limited explainability and actionability). In consequence, there is still a lack of understanding regarding whether we can estimate collaboration quality along a continuum (or to what extent). Third, that MMLA studies often report their results without frames of reference that can help the community understand how far (or how close) we are to developing solutions of practical relevance to our classrooms (e.g., how they compare with human-level classification or quantification of collaboration quality).

3 Methodology

To address the gaps identified in previous section, we setup a study to explore the following research questions: **RQ1.** How well can we estimate collaboration quality using machine learning, using audio and log data from an authentic classroom setting in upper secondary school? **RQ2.** How well can we estimate the various sub-dimensions of collaboration quality with machine learning, using audio and log data from an authentic classroom setting?

To start addressing these questions, we have conducted a first case study [14] in an authentic classroom setting, where learners performed collaborative discussion and writing tasks, as part of their normal classes. Such case study methodology allowed us to understand the situation in depth, and explore multiple aspects of the research questions (e.g., data fusion and regression models).

A 30 min collaboration activity was co-designed by a researcher and a teacher in which the students had to discuss and fill in a worksheet regarding genetic mutations[1]. The activity was enacted in a secondary education biology course with 10 students in autumn 2019. During the enactment, two researchers were present in the classroom for data collection purposes and technical support. A brief introduction was given to the students about the aim of study and their consent for data collection was taken in written form before the activity. In the case study, the data from two groups (four students each) are analyzed.

---

[1] Given learning activity is available at: https://bit.ly/collabtech-LD.

3.1 Data Collection

The students used an audio-capturing prototype -CoTrack- with an omni-directional microphone placed in the center of the group's table, and Etherpad[2] for the collaborative writing. CoTrack detects presence of voice and provides the direction from which voice is detected. CoTrack then maps the direction to a particular learner and extracts various features (e.g., speaking time, number of characters added or deleted) from the audio and Etherpad logs. Our analyses below use a total of 12 features: three features (speaking time, number of characters added, and number of characters deleted) for each of the four students in the groups, for every 30-s window of time (see below).

Table 1. Inter-rater agreement of human coders in each collaboration quality sub-dimension (Cohen's kappa)

SMU	CF	KE	ARG	SPST	CO	ITO-1	ITO-2	ITO-3	ITO-4
0.71	0.91	0.74	0.80	0.65	0.68	0.72	0.76	0.75	0.78

3.2 Data Annotation

We used Rummel et al. [11] collaboration quality rating scheme (itself adapted from [9]), assigning a collaboration quality score along seven dimensions[3]. We decided to use the adaptable version instead of the original scheme due to its applicability to a variety of CSCL settings. Two raters coded the dimensions at the group level (except the ITO, which is coded at an individual level and averaged to get the group-level feature). Following the recommendations by Martínez et al. [7], we used time windows of 30 seconds, in which each of the aforementioned sub-dimensions was assigned a score between -2 (very bad) and $+2$ (very good). The sub-dimension scores at the group level were then added up to get the overall collaboration quality score of the group for that time window (which can theoretically range from -14 to $+14$). This overall score was used as dependent variable in the regression analysis. The annotation phase resulted in a dataset with 121 data points from the collaboration of two learner groups. Two raters went through four iterations of coding before reaching substantial agreement on each sub-dimension in terms of Cohen's kappa (Table 1).

3.3 Data Analysis

To map the individual student audio and log features to group-level features, we explored three different approaches[4]: simple averaging of individual scores,

---

[2] An open source real-time collaborative text editor, see https://etherpad.org.

[3] Sustaining Mutual Understanding (SMU), Collaboration Flow (CF), Knowledge Exchange (KE), Cooperative Orientation (CO), Argumentation (ARG), Structuring Problem Solving Process and Time Management (SPST), and Individual Task Orientation (ITO).

[4] Data analysis source code available at: https://bit.ly/collabtech-code.

using dimensionality reduction, and entropy-based fusion. In the dimensionality reduction approach we applied principal component analysis (PCA) on all individual-level features and extracted the four components that explained most variance. The entropy-based approach has been used to map individual features to group-level features in previous research [1] using Shannon's Entropy.

For the training and evaluation of the machine learning models, we used Python's Scikit-learn library[5]. We randomly divided our dataset into training and test sets, using a ratio of 70:30. We trained regression models of different kinds on our training set and investigated their performance on the test set. Concretely, machine learning model families explored included K-Nearest Neighbors, Random forest, Adaboost, Gradient boost, XGboost, Support vector regressors (SVR), Neural networks, and ensemble (voting) regression models (using SVR, Random forest and Adaboost). We used GridSearchCV (from Scikit-learn) with 3-fold cross validation to tune the model's parameters.

3.4   Results

We used RMSE (Root Mean Square Error) as the performance metric to compare the different regression models. As frames of reference, we computed the RMSE that the human coders had achieved in their last round of manual collaboration quality scoring. We also computed the RMSE of two "no-information" regressors, one that just estimates random values within the range of possible quality scores, and one that provides an estimation equal to the average value of the collaboration quality (quality = 1.93, for this dataset).

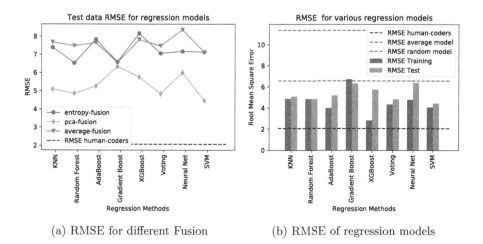

(a) RMSE for different Fusion   (b) RMSE of regression models

Fig. 1. Performance scores of regression models

---

[5] https://scikit-learn.org/stable/.

From our analysis of the three fusion approaches, we found PCA-based fusion as a better option than entropy and average, in terms of the performance of the different regression models on test data. Figure 1(a) shows that PCA-fusion based regression models achieved lower RMSE on test data than entropy-fusion and average-fusion based regression models.

For the comparative analysis among regression models, we used PCA-based fusion and trained different kinds of regression models, computing RMSE for both the training and test data. All regression models (except Gradient Boost) performed better than the average estimation model (Fig. 1(b)). XG Boost and Neural Network regression models reported the highest variation between training and testing errors, which can probably be explained by the models overfitting the small dataset available. The support vector regression (SVR) model performed better than the other models, both in terms of lower RMSE, and lower difference between training and test error. Comparing the performance of this SVR model (which, let's remember, used only very basic audio and log features) with that of the no-information models (average and random) and the human coders' own RMSE values, we find that SVR covered about 50% of the gap between the best no-information predictors and human-level performance.

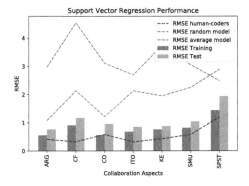

Fig. 2. SVR performance on various sub-dimensions of collaboration quality

We also applied similar regression models to estimate the seven subdimensions of collaboration quality. Again, support vector regression models performed better than other models in estimating the majority of the subdimensions. Figure 2 shows the RMSE scores of support vector regression model, compared with the no-information and human-level frames of reference. For these dimensions, SVR covered 50% or more of the gap between no-information and human-level performance.

4   Conclusions and Future Work

This paper investigated the feasibility of estimating the quality of collaboration in face-to-face classroom settings using simple features from audio and log data, and machine learning regression models. These results suggest that it *is* feasible to quantitatively estimate collaboration quality along a continuum, and even open the door to more in-depth estimation of the different collaboration sub-dimensions (e.g., collaboration flow, knowledge exchange), which can be of greater value to practitioners. We also provided three frames of reference (average and random no-information estimators, as well as human coders' performance) with the aim to offer a more interpretable view on their performance. We suggest future MMLA researchers to analyze their models' performance using such frames of reference, to help our research community in better understanding how far our models and solutions have to go to achieve human-level performance.

This work is not without limitations. The small size of our dataset is probably the main weakness of our results so far, limiting greatly the generalizability of the particular models and performance claims made. This issue can explain the discrepancy between training and test errors of some of the regression models (e.g., Gradient Boost, AdaBoost, Neural Networks) due to over-fitting. The expansion of this dataset with data from groupwork performed in different kinds of authentic classroom settings, is one of our most important avenues of future work. Thus, we plan to assess the generalizability of the results in terms of effectiveness of the approach.

Moreover, in the current case study we only used simple audio and log features, and a limited set of machine learning models, considering all dataset samples independently (i.e., not looking at their sequence). The use of more complex features (e.g., intensity, pitch, MFCC for audio data, or conversion of voice to text and subsequent analyses of content), consideration of final document quality (in terms of matrices e.g., error rate, redundancy, keywords [5]), different data fusion models, impact of task duration, and the exploration of time-dependent machine learning models (e.g., Hidden Markov Models, sequence analysis) will be considered as strategies to expand our work towards automated estimation of collaboration quality that is close to human-level performance.

Acknowledgement. This research has been partially funded by the European Union via the European Regional Development Fund and in the context of CEITER and Next-Lab (Horizon 2020 Research and Innovation Programme, grant agreements no. 669074 and 731685). It was also partially funded by the European Regional Development Fund and the Regional Council of Education of Castile and León under grant VA257P18 and the National Research Agency of the Spanish Ministry of Science, Innovation and Universities, under project grant TIN2017-85179-C3-2-R.

References

1. Bassiou, N., et al.: Privacy-preserving speech analytics for automatic assessment of student collaboration. In: Proceedings of the Annual Conference of the International Speech Communication Association, INTERSPEECH, pp. 888–892 (2016)
2. Blikstein, P., Worsley, M.: Multimodal learning analytics and education data mining: using computational technologies to measure complex learning tasks. J. Learn. Anal. **3**(2), 220–238 (2016)

3. Dillenbourg, P., Järvelä, S., Fischer, F.: The evolution of research on computer-supported collaborative learning. In: Balacheff, N., Ludvigsen, S., de Jong, T., Lazonder, A., Barnes, S. (eds.) Technology-Enhanced Learning: Principles and Products, pp. 3–19. Springer, Dordrecht (2009). https://doi.org/10.1007/978-1-4020-9827-7_1

4. Grover, S., Bienkowski, M., Tamrakar, A., Siddiquie, B., Salter, D., Divakaran, A.: Multimodal analytics to study collaborative problem solving in pair programming. In: Proceedings of the Sixth International Conference on Learning Analytics & Knowledge, LAK 2016, NY, USA, pp. 516–517. ACM (2016)

5. Ignat, C.-L., Oster, G., Fox, O., Shalin, V.L., Charoy, F.: How do user groups cope with delay in real-time collaborative note taking. In: Boulus-Rødje, N., Ellingsen, G., Bratteteig, T., Aanestad, M., Bjørn, P. (eds.) ECSCW 2015: Proceedings of the 14th European Conference on Computer Supported Cooperative Work, 19-23 September 2015, Oslo, Norway, pp. 223–242. Springer, Cham (2015). https://doi.org/10.1007/978-3-319-20499-4_12

6. Jermann, P., Soller, A., Muehlenbrock, M.: From mirroring to guiding: A review of the state of art technology for supporting collaborative learning. Int. J. Artif. Intell. Educ. (IJAIED) **15**, 261–290 (2005)

7. Martinez, R., Wallace, J.R., Kay, J., Yacef, K.: Modelling and identifying collaborative situations in a collocated multi-display groupware setting. In: Biswas, G., Bull, S., Kay, J., Mitrovic, A. (eds.) AIED 2011. LNCS (LNAI), vol. 6738, pp. 196–204. Springer, Heidelberg (2011). https://doi.org/10.1007/978-3-642-21869-9_27

8. Martinez-Maldonado, R., Dimitriadis, Y., Martinez-Monés, A., Kay, J., Yacef, K.: Capturing and analyzing verbal and physical collaborative learning interactions at an enriched interactive tabletop. Int. J. Comput. Support. Collab. Learn. **8**(4), 455–485 (2013). https://doi.org/10.1007/s11412-013-9184-1

9. Meier, A., Spada, H., Rummel, N.: A rating scheme for assessing the quality of computer-supported collaboration processes. Int. J. Comput. Support. Collab. Learn. **2**(1), 63–86 (2007)

10. Mercer, N., Littleton, K., Wegerif, R.: Methods for studying the processes of interaction and collaborative activity in computer-based educational activities. Technol. Pedagog. Educ. **13**(2), 195–212 (2004)

11. Rummel, N., Deiglmayr, A., Spada, H., Kahrimanis, G., Avouris, N.: Analyzing collaborative interactions across domains and settings: an adaptable rating scheme. In: Puntambekar, S., Erkens, G., Hmelo-Silver, C. (eds.) Analyzing Interactions in CSCL: Methods, Approaches and Issues. Computer-Supported Collaborative Learning Series, vol. 12, pp. 367–390. Springer, Boston (2011). https://doi.org/10.1007/978-1-4419-7710-6_17

12. Spikol, D., Ruffaldi, E., Dabisias, G., Cukurova, M.: Supervised machine learning in multimodal learning analytics for estimating success in project-based learning. J. Comput. Assist. Learn. **34**(4), 366–377 (2018)

13. Viswanathan, S.A., VanLehn, K.: Using the tablet gestures and speech of pairs of students to classify their collaboration. IEEE Trans. Learn. Technol. **11**(2), 230–242 (2018)

14. Yin, R.K.: Case study methods. APA handbooks in psychology®. American Psychological Association, Washington, DC, US (2012)

Showing-Displays-Together: A Co-located Web Search Support Exploiting the Terminal Orientation

Naoki Furuie, Tomoki Yabuuchi, Takatsugu Yamamoto,
and Hideyuki Takada(✉) 🆔

Ritsumeikan University, Kusatsu, Shiga 525-8577, Japan
htakada@cs.ritsumei.ac.jp
http://www.cm.is.ritsumei.ac.jp/~htakada/e.html

Abstract. Today, people perform web search tasks with smartphones on a daily basis, forming a group of several users to achieve a common goal, such as finding a good restaurant and deciding a product to buy. During such a task, they naturally show the smartphone screen to share the displayed information, Showing-Displays-Together, after personally performing a web search. If the functions of a tool to support the collaborative web search could be automatically switched, users would be able perform their task more smoothly. In this paper, we propose a function to compare shared web pages among users, which is automatically invoked by exploiting the terminal orientation. We have developed a collaborative web search support tool which has three functions switched each other according to the terminal orientation, searching personally in portrait mode, browsing a shared favorites list in landscape mode, and comparing web pages in horizontal mode. The result of evaluation shows that user satisfaction, communication, and easiness in making a decision had a good impact on the tasks, but usability needed to be improved to avoid unintentional switching of the functions to users.

Keywords: Collaborative web search · Co-located collaboration · Information sharing

1 Introduction

Today, smartphones are the most popular terminal on which to use the web. People perform search tasks not only personally, but also collaboratively, forming a group to achieve a common goal while searching and sharing websites. This collaborative form of web search is called "Collaborative Web Search" [4,5], and a collaborative web search task is performed both in a co-located setting and in a remote environment.

In a co-located setting, users gathering in proximity often show their display to others to share the content of web pages of their interest. If three or more users are working together, each of them holds their terminal horizontally to

© Springer Nature Switzerland AG 2020
A. Nolte et al. (Eds.): CollabTech 2020, LNCS 12324, pp. 167–174, 2020.
https://doi.org/10.1007/978-3-030-58157-2_12

the ground to *show the display together* and compare web pages, after personally performing the web search to find pages to share by vertically holding the terminal. If the user interface could reflect a characteristic that users naturally change the orientation of the terminal depending on what they are doing, users would be able to perform their collaborative web search task more smoothly.

In this paper, we propose to automatically invoke a function to compare shared web pages according to how the terminal is held by a user, specifically to the situation where users show the display of their terminal together. We also report a user study to evaluate the effectiveness of this function, in terms of user satisfaction, communication, usability and easiness in making a decision.

2   Related Works and Our Approach

Many of research works on collaborative web search focus on the remote environment [2,6]. These systems typically support sharing queries and web pages synchronously or asynchronously, also allowing users to send messages each other.

Research works to support co-located collaborative web search have been also conducted. CoSearch [1] uses a shared large display which is incorporated with mobile devices for each user. A content comparison function [3] provides users with an interface on mobile devices to effectively share web pages collected by group members and add reviews to compare such pages, considering that a collaborative web search task is performed in three phases, personal search phase, opinion exchange phase and comparison phase. O-SNAP [7] uses device orientation (portrait and landscape) to change the functions between personal mode and collaborative mode in web search. The specific feature of O-SNAP is that users can physically signal collaboration intent to others around them by using their phone's orientation. In the portrait mode users can perform traditional search, but when users rotate the device into landscape orientation, the device snaps into a collaboration mode in which users can share their search results.

Our approach is to add the third mode to O-SNAP, the horizontal mode. When people search in a group, they naturally show the display of their device to other members in order to exchange opinions and compare web pages. O-SNAP assumes that users see only their own display even though they are facing each other, so web contents which can be seen by individual users are limited. Showing multiple web pages on a screen of each of users' devices would make it easy to compare the content of pages collected by group members.

3   Proposed System

3.1   Functions

Figure 1 shows the transition among functional states when users are conducting collaborative web search using our system. Functions given by the system are automatically switched to each other depending on the following three states of how the user holds the terminal.

Portrait mode: Google's search site is displayed at the beginning, and users can perform a usual web search. If the user finds a page to share with others, the page can be added by tapping a button on the screen to the favorites list which is shared by all users.

Landscape mode: The shared favorites list with titles of web pages is shown at the left side of the screen, and users can see the content of the web page by tapping one of the titles on the list.

Horizontal mode: Web pages in the favorites list are displayed at the terminals, each of which shows one of the web pages in the list. Users can navigate through the web pages stored in the list and compare them at a glance.

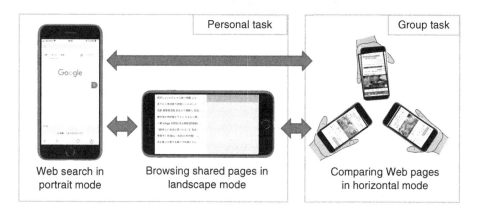

Fig. 1. Transition among functional states in co-located collaborative web search

As described in the previous section, users search the web personally at beginning of a collaborative web search task. While searching personally, they keep several web pages to share with others for later reference. This activity is performed in the portrait mode in our system. During their personal activity, they also want to know what pages are found by other users to get some hints for their further search. This activity is performed in the landscape mode. After the users finish collecting web pages of interest, they compare the collected pages for discussion. This activity is performed in the horizontal mode.

The favorites list stores the references to web pages with a timestamp representing when the page is added by the user. An item which has the latest timestamp in the list is displayed in the terminal of the user, who changes the terminal orientation to the horizontal mode first. If another user changes the terminal orientation to the horizontal mode next, an item which has the second latest timestamp in the list is displayed in the terminal of this user. In the tab bar of the horizontal mode screen, there is a button labeled "Discard" which enables users to remove the corresponding web page from the list. There is also a button labeled "Defer" with which users can move the corresponding web page at the end of the favorites list.

3.2   Implementation

Detection of the Terminal Orientation. We use Apple's iPhone as an implementation platform. The terminal orientation is detected by using the internal accelerometer equipped with iPhone. Detection of the orientation is performed every 0.2 s, based on the conditions shown in Fig. 2.

```
if the slant is within 15 degrees from the initial status
    mode = horizontal
else if X-acceleration > Y-acceleration
    mode = landscape
else
    mode = portrait
```

Fig. 2. Detection of the terminal orientation

Management of Shared Web Pages. This system uses the service offered by Firebase Realtime Database to share the content of the favorites list among terminals. All terminals access a common database built on this service. The database contains the following fields for each of the shared web pages.

Title: Title of the web page
URL: URL of the web page
Timestamp: A timestamp when shared
Switch: A Boolean value to indicate whether the web page is already shown on the terminal in the horizontal mode (true: shown, false: not shown).

In this prototypical implementation, how to make a group with multiple terminals is not considered, and all terminals running at the same time are grouped together.

When the terminal is changed to the horizontal mode, it looks up the favorites list and finds an item which has the latest timestamp in those with the false value in the "Switch" field. If such an item is found, the terminal changes the value of the "Switch" field to true and shows a web page according to the URL stored.

When the "Discard" button is tapped, the terminal deletes an item corresponding to the currently shown web page from the favorites list. When the "Defer" button is tapped, the "Switch" field is changed to false and the timestamp field is assigned to a negated value of the current time to make it the oldest time.

4 Evaluation

In this section, we evaluate the system in terms of what effect is obtained for communication between users. We also verify the usability of the system.

4.1 Experiment Settings

The purpose of this experiment is to investigate whether the proposed system has an advantage compared to an existing system in terms of promoting communication among users and the system usability in a co-located collaborative web search environment.

For this experiment, 18 student participants were recruited, forming six groups of three participants. They sat in a circle where they could show their iPhone's display each other.

This experiment was conducted in a way that our system which has the "showing-displays-together" function was compared with the pre-installed web browser, Safari, used with Apple's AirDrop which enables users to exchange a web page with other users. When using Safari, the participants were not forced to use AirDrop.

The task for participants to perform in collaborative web search was to choose a party place near a specified train station. They achieved two tasks of this nature by using each of the two systems, the proposed system and Safari with AirDrop. They were given 10 min for each of the two tasks. Considering the order effect, three groups used Safari with AirDrop first while the other three groups used the proposed system first.

After completing the tasks, participants answered the questionnaire in Table 1. They answered in the 5-point scale and were requested to leave comments for each of the questions.

Table 1. Questionnaire

Q1	In which task do you feel that you could get a satisfactory result also for the group members?
Q2	In which task could you make communication with the group members?
Q3	Which system could you use without feeling stress?
Q4	With which system could you easily make a final decision?

Q1 is to evaluate the satisfaction level of users. Higher points would mean that participants felt a sense of fulfillment in performing their task, led by more collaborative activity. Q2 is to evaluate the communication among users, in terms of how showing the displays together affects their communication. Q3 is to evaluate the usability of the system. The proposed system might interfere their task if automatically switching the function did not work well. Q4 is to evaluate the easiness of making a decision. Higher points would mean that showing the displays together had a positive effect in their decision.

4.2   Results and Discussion

Figure 3 shows the questionnaire result for Q1 to Q4. Each number in the result represents how many participants rated their preference ranging in five points from the existing system (Safari with AirDrop) to the proposed system (Showing-Displays-Together) for each question. As an overall tendency, we can see that the proposed system is rated high in terms of satisfaction, communication and easiness in decision, while it is weak in usability.

We validate this result by referring to participants' comments on each of the questions.

– Satisfaction
  One of the participants commented that each person had an equal opportunity to say something by having at least one piece of information to share. Being given a chance to naturally recommend their own candidate would increase the collaboration level, leading to higher satisfaction on the result of a task. Others commented that they could make a decision from multiple choices, and they could easily show their own candidates on the display and compare them with each other. Enabling users to compare several candidates on multiple smartphones at a glance in the horizontal mode would also increase the collaboration level.
– Communication
  Participants commented that they could examine each of the candidates one by one through all of their intentions, they could explain in the horizontal mode why they chose their candidate, they could make a discussion while looking at all of the terminals, and they naturally felt the necessity of discussion on each of the candidates collected by the participants. Showing the displays together would offer an opportunity to explain their candidates on the displays and make a discussion by comparing them, leading to a rich communication among users.

	Existing system		Neutral		Proposed system
Q1 (Satisfaction)	0	1	5	6	6
Q2 (Communication)	0	3	5	4	6
Q3 (Usability)	7	4	0	3	4
Q4 (Easiness in decision)	0	0	5	10	3

Fig. 3. Questionnaire result

- Usability

  The proposed system was rated low by the participants. They commented that the function was switched unintentionally depending on the terminal orientation, and the detection of the horizontal mode was not accurate. Five groups out of six pointed out the incorrectness of switching the function. Another possibility to switch the function is to let users press a button on the screen, but this might lose the advantage of using the terminal orientation which enables users to physically signal collaboration intent to others, as emphasized for O-SNAP. In order to improve the accuracy of automatically switching the function, the conditions to detect the terminal orientation illustrated in Fig. 2 have to be elaborated by changing the threshold value of the slant degree.

- Easiness in decision

  Participants commented that comparing the candidates on multiple displays was comprehensive, and showing different websites on multiple displays led to reducing time. Showing the displays together would allow users to easily compare the candidates while discarding or deferring them, leading to easiness in making a decision.

5   Conclusion

In this paper, we have proposed a function called "Showing-Displays-Together" which automatically switches the functions of a tool for supporting the collaborative web search by exploiting the terminal orientation. Using this function, users can easily move across the phases which are taken during a search task. We also have described the result of evaluation on the effectiveness of the tool, showing that user satisfaction, communication, and easiness in decision had a good impact on the tasks, but usability had a problem of switching the functions unintentionally to users.

As a future work, we will elaborate the mechanism to detect the terminal orientation to improve the usability. Comparative evaluation with other collaborative web search systems would also be necessary to reveal the user awareness and engagement in tasks as well as the effectiveness of using the terminal orientation.

References

1. Amershi, S., Morris, M.R.: CoSearch: a system for co-located collaborative web search. In: Proceedings of the SIGCHI Conference on Human Factors in Computing Systems, pp. 1647–1656 (2008)
2. Bentley, F.R., Peesapati, S.T.: SearchMessenger: Exploring the use of search and card sharing in a messaging application. In: Proceedings of the 2017 ACM Conference on Computer Supported Cooperative Work and Social Computing, pp. 1946–1956 (2017)
3. Komaki, D., et al.: Content comparison functions for mobile co-located collaborative web search. J. Ambient Intell. Humaniz. Comput. **2**(3), 239–248 (2011)

4. Morris, M.R.: A survey of collaborative web search practices. In: Proceedings of the SIGCHI Conference on Human Factors in Computing Systems, pp. 1657–1660 (2008)
5. Morris, M.R.: Collaborative search revisited. In: Proceedings of the 2013 Conference on Computer Supported Cooperative Work, pp. 1181–1192 (2013)
6. Morris, M.R., Horvitz, E.: SearchTogether: an interface for collaborative web search. In: Proceedings of the 20th Annual ACM Symposium on User Interface Software and Technology, pp. 3–12 (2007)
7. Teevan, J., Morris, M.R., Azenkot, S.: Supporting interpersonal interaction during collaborative mobile search. Computer **47**(3), 54–57 (2014)

Travel Plan Recommendation Based on Review Analysis and Preference Diagnosis

Satoshi Ichimura[(✉)]

Information Design Course, School of Social Information Studies, Otsuma Women's University, Sanbancho 12, Chiyoda-ku, Tokyo 102-8357, Japan
ichimura@otsuma.ac.jp

Abstract. When making a travel plan, we often use travel sites. However, there is a problem that it is difficult to decide a travel destination because the amount of information including users' reviews is too large. Also, usually, travel information is separately registered for each destination (e.g. sightseeing place), which is difficult to use for those who have not yet decided the destination they want to go to. Therefore, the authors set a research goal to make it possible to choose a travel destination without having to browse a lot of travel information when making a travel plan, and developed a web service for recommending travel plans, called Tabi-gator (Travel navigator in English). Tabi-gator automatically creates several questions to diagnose user preferences with machine-learning technology, and then recommends a travel plan that is suitable for the user's preference.

Keywords: Travel plan recommendation · Machine learning · NLP

1 Introduction

It is common to make travel plans using travel sites on the Internet. It is reported that about 85% of respondents said they would use travel sites first when planning a trip [1].

When using travel sites, a user not only searches the sites for travel information, but also, often reads users' reviews written by others about the searched destinations (e.g. sightseeing places). The reviews written by those who have actually visited are very useful, and you can find a lot of information other than photos and text provided by travel agencies.

However, the number of sightseeing places registered on travel sites is very large, and the volume of the reviews written for each place is usually large. It is reported that approximately 70% of respondents who answered the questionaire had found it difficult to make a travel plan [1]. The top two reasons are, "because there are so many information and options (66.7%)", and "because it is necessary to examine many destinations to find necessary information (52%)".

Focusing on the above problems, we set a research goal to make it easy to choose a travel destination without having to browse a lot of travel information

© Springer Nature Switzerland AG 2020
A. Nolte et al. (Eds.): CollabTech 2020, LNCS 12324, pp. 175–182, 2020.
https://doi.org/10.1007/978-3-030-58157-2_13

when making a travel plan, and developed a travel recommendation web service "Tabi-gator" (Travel navigator in English).

Tabi-gator automatically creates several questions to diagnose user preferences with machine-learning technology, and then travel plans suitable for the user's preference are recommended based on how the user answered each question. The user only has to answer a few questions from the system, and the travel destination that suits him is recommended.

2   Related Work

There is a large amount of travel information stored on travel sites, so that it takes time to get to the necessary information. Similar problems have occurred with other services on the Internet, and related work on these problems is described below.

Ahn et al. [2] use Word2Vec technology [9] to analyze a large amount of review text registered on a game review site, and classify popular games and unpopular games. Word2Vec is a method to vectorize each words in the sentence. Once words are converted to vectors, the distance between each vector can be measured and the distance (similarity) between each word can be calculated. For example, you can easily get a similar word with high similarity by using Word2Vec. Generally, Word2Vec is composed of a neural network consisting of two layers, a hidden layer and an output layer.

Kurihara et al. [3] use Doc2Vec [7,8] to analyze a large amount of review text registered on movie review sites. While Word2Vec converts each word into a vector, Doc2Vec converts each sentence of any length into a vector. Doc2Vec calculates the similarity between review text of each movie. Movie reviews that are semantically similar to the query can be found even when the words described in the query are not included in the review text. Doc2Vec is also composed of a neural network consisting of two layers, a hidden layer and an output layer.

On the other hand, there are studies that try to shorten reading time by summarizing long sentences into short sentences.

ERKAN [4] et al. proposed LexRank, that is a method that summarizes sentences based on the relationships between sentences and words in the sentences. In the method, sentences similar to many sentences are regarded as important sentences, and also the sentences similar to the important sentences are considered important. This method is a general-purpose text summarization method that can be used for general sentences other than review text, however, it is likely that the desired summarization will not be obtained compared to the summarization method specialized to review text.

3   Proposal

The goal of the research is to make it easy to decide a travel destination without having to browse a lot of information when planning a trip. Based on this goal, we developed a travel recommendation web service "Tabi-gator". The system automatically creates several questions, to diagnose the user's preference, by analysing review text in advance with machine-learning technology, and proposes a destination suitable for the user's preference based on how the user answered each question. When answering a question, the user only needs to pick one from keyword selections presented by the system, so that the user can quickly and easily find the desired destination.

When you access the Tabi-gator web page, a set of keywords (buttons) are displayed. When you choose one and press the button, then the next keywords appear. After repeating this operation several times, the system shows the recommended travel destination and the review texts about the place, at the end.

The Fig. 1 shows a usage scenario. When the Tabi-gator web page is accessed, the questionnaire with several choices is displayed on the web browser as shown in Fig. 1(1). If a user selects "pool", the following questionnaire shown in Fig. 1(2) is displayed. The selection history is displayed in "Your favorites:". If the user selects "waikiki" in Fig. 1(2), and then chooses "beach" in Fig. 1(3), the system finally answers that the recommended travel destination is "Outrigger Waikiki on the Beach Hotel" as shown in Fig. 1(4), and returns to the first questionnaire. The screens like Fig. 1(2) and 1(3) are repeatedly displayed until the recommended travel destination is determined.

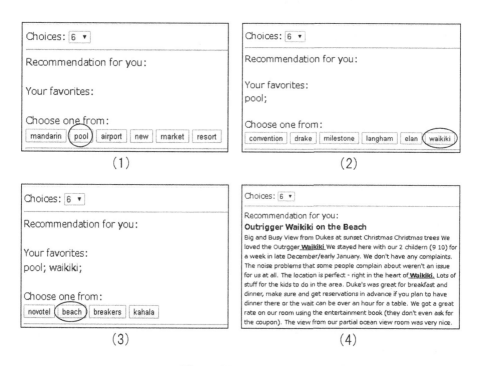

Fig. 1. Usage scenario

4 Implementations

We implemented two prototype systems for Japanese and English speaking users.

Japanese version was for 70 famous sightseeing places at the Kanto region in Japan. Review texts for each place (the average number of reviews for each place was seven) were obtained from "4travel.jp." All of the reviews were written in Japanese. On the other hand, English version was for 77 hotels located in North America, Canada, United Kingdom, Australia and Hong Kong. Review texts for each hotel (the average number of reviews for each hotel was ten) were collected from "TripAdvisor.com." All of the reviews were written in English.

The system consisted of a server program implemented in Python [11] and a client program implemented in JavaScript.

4.1 Description of the Main Features

The main features of the prototype are (1) Vectorization of review text, (2) Clustering of review text, (3) Extraction of an important word from each cluster, and (4) Recursive subdivision of selected clusters.

(1) **Vectorization of review text:** All review texts of all travel destinations are entered into Doc2Vec and converted to the vector representation (the sentence vector).

A large number of users' reviews for one travel destination are combined into one sentence, and a unique sentence ID (equivalent to travel destination ID) is assigned to it. Then, all review texts of all travel destinations and all sentence IDs are entered into Doc2Vec, and converted to the vector representation.

In this implementation, Doc2Vec included in the Python library gensim [10] was used, the model of Doc2Vec was PV-DM (Paragraph Vector with Distributed Memory), the vector was 100 dimensions, and the length of the word window was 5.

Any input text to be input to Doc2Vec has to be in the form of word-separation, so that, in the case of Japanese version, MeCab (a morphological analyzer) [5] was used for word separation because Japanese language has no term separation.

(2) **Clustering of review text:** The sentence vector created in (1) is divided into a predetermined number of clusters by the K-means method. The K-means method is one of the non-hierarchical clustering methods, in which vectors with high similarity are gathered and classified into a specified number of clusters. We used the implementation of K-Means included in the gensim library. The system allows users to choose the number of clusters (the number of choices).

(3) **Extraction of an important word from each cluster:** The important word for each cluster created in (2) is extracted by TF-IDF method. The TF value is the frequency of occurrence of the word in a document. The value increases as the number of occurrences of the word increases, and decreases

as the number of occurrences decreases. The IDF value is the reciprocal of the percentage of the number of the documents that contain the word. The more the word appears in other documents, the smaller the IDF value, and the less the word appears in other documents the value increases. TF-IDF value can be obtained by multiplying the TF and IDF. A word with a larger TF-IDF value can be regarded as an important word in a cluster.

The TF-IDF module included in the gensim library is used to calculate TF-IDF. A set of important words, each of which is extracted from each cluster, are shown to the user as choices. Specifically, they are displayed as choice buttons on the Web browser.

In addition, in this implementation, an important word from each cluster is always a noun. To extract a noun from a review sentence, the morphological analysis function provided by NLTK (Natural Language Toolkit) is used in English version, and the morphological analysis function provided by MeCab is used in Japanese version.

(4) **Recursive subdivision of selected clusters:** If any of the choices displayed on the screen is selected by the user in (3), it is considered that the cluster corresponding to the choice has been selected, and the process goes back to (2). Then, the selected cluster is subdivided into a predetermined number of clusters again by the K-means method, and (3) and (4) are similarly applied to each cluster. Finally, when the user selects a cluster containing only one destination, the system finally shows the recommended travel destination on the Web browser.

Although the same noun may be repeatedly shown as an important noun representing a cluster in (3) during recursive processing, it is considered inappropriate to repeatedly show the same noun because the noun has already been selected by the user. Therefore, if the noun with the highest TF-IDF value is one of the displayed nouns, the system shows the noun with the second highest TF-IDF value (or the noun with the third highest TF-IDF value if it is also displayed) instead.

5 Evaluations

We evaluated Japanese version in our University. Japanese version contained 70 sightseeing places at the Kanto region in Japan. A total of 509 review sentences stored in the dataset were all written in Japanese.

In the experiment, the subjects (eight university students) were instructed by the following written text.

"Please select one of the displayed choices. You can change the number of choices displayed on the screen yourself. Repeat the selection until a recommended travel destination appears."

In order to compare the case where the system was used and the case where it was not used, we prepared a paper document having all review texts of all sightseeing places. We asked the subjects to measure the time (in seconds) that was needed to decide a travel destination. When using the system, we also asked them to try to change the number of choices to 3, 5, 7, and 9.

Here are the results. The time needed to decide a travel destination was 18 s in average when using the system, while 149 s in average when using the document, so that the required time was reduced to about 1/8 by the system. We also asked two of the subjects to read the entire document, and measure the time. As a result, it took 695 s in average. 149 s was approximately 1/5 of 695 s, so that it is assumed that the subjects were likely to give up reading when they read only 1/5 of the document.

About the number of choices, there were users' comments "Sometimes there was no favorite places among three choices, but there was at least one among five choices." and "Five-choice was just right. Choosing one from many choices was tedious." We asked the subjects how many choices they felt most useful. As a result, one subject said 3-choice was the best, five said 5-choice was the best, one said 7-choice was the best, one said 9-choice was the best. The required times were 22, 22, 17, 17 and 16 s in average when the number of choices was 3, 5, 7, and 9, respectively. Therefore, the default number of choices of Tabi-gator system was set to 5.

Next, we asked them some questionnaires in a five-point scale (1: not applicable to 5: applicable) about their impressions for each case with and without the system.

The result of a five-point scale is shown in Table 1.

Table 1. Results of questionnaires

Question	Tabi-gator	Paper document
It was easy	4.4	1.9
It was fun	4.0	1.8
Favorite place was found	4.3	2.9

Table 2. Users' comments when using the system

Recommended destinations were places I did not know and wanted to go to
I found it useful because my favorite places were recommended
I found it useful especially when I was in a hurry
The system sometimes recommended a place I have already been, so that I wanted more than one recommendations
Five-choice was just right. Choosing one from many choices was tedious
Sometimes there was no favorite places among three choices, but there was at least one among five choices

Table 3. Users' comments when reading the document

It was too long, so that I stopped reading on the way
I felt tired to read it
There was so much information hard to understand
Even when some candidates were found, it took time to choose one from them

As a result of Wilcoxon's signed rank sum test, there was a significant difference in the significance level of 5% on both sides for "It was easy" and "It was fun." No statistically significant difference was found for "Favorite place was found", but despite the fact that it took only about 1/8 of the time, it turned out that the subjects were satisfied with the destination proposed by the system.

The comments from the subjects when using the system are shown in Table 2, and when reading the document are shown in Table 3.

6   Summary

We have proposed a travel recommendation web service called "Tabi-gator." which allows users to choose a travel destination without having to browse a lot of information. Tabi-gator automatically creates a series of questions to diagnose user preferences with machine-learning technology, and recommends travel plans suitable for the user's preference based on how the user answered each question.

As the results of the evaluation experiment, Tabi-gator got better scores than a traditional method, from the view point of "It was easy", "It was fun." and "Favorite place was found."

Acknowledgment. This work was supported by JSPS KAKENHI Number 16K00506.

References

1. Survey on Travel in Japan - 70% worry about planning-fatigue (2018). https://www.tabikobo.com/company/news/press/2018/06/180605. (in Japanese)
2. Ahn, S., Kang, J., Park, S.: What makes the difference between popular games and unpopular games? ICIC Express Lett. **11**(12), 1729–1737 (2017)
3. Kurihara, K., Shoji, Y., Fujita, S., Durst, J.: Target-Topic Aware Doc2Vec for Short Sentence Retrieval from User Generated Content (2019). http://shoji-lab.jp/research_paper/iiWAS2019_shoji_TTA-D2V.pdf
4. Erkan G., Radev, D.R.: LexRank - Graph-based Lexical Centrality as Salience in Text Summarization (2004). http://www.cs.cmu.edu/afs/cs/project/jair/pub/volume22/erkan04a-html/erkan04a.html
5. Kudo, T. FMeCab - Yet Another Part-of-Speech and Morphological Analyzer (2019).https://taku910.github.io/mecab/
6. mecab-ipadic-NEologd: Neologism dictionary for MeCab (2019). https://github.com/neologd/mecab-ipadic-NEologd/blob/master/README.ja.md

7. Lau, J.H. and Baldwin, T.: An Empirical Evaluation of Doc2Vec with Practical Insights into Document Embedding Generation (2016). https://arxiv.org/abs/1607.05368
8. models.doc2vec - Doc2vec paragraph embeddings (2019). https://radimrehurek.com/gensim/models/doc2vec.html
9. models.word2vec - Word2vec embeddings (2019). https://radimrehurek.com/gensim/models/word2vec.html
10. gensim, Free Python Library (2020). https://radimrehurek.com/gensim/
11. https://www.python.org/ (2019)

Parents' Reflection with a Digital Family Calendar: A Case of Using Scrapbook Calendars in Japanese Families

Akihiro Maehigashi[1][✉] and Sumaru Niida[2]

[1] Shizuoka University, Ohya, Shizuoka, Japan
maehigashi.akihiro@shizuoka.ac.jp
[2] KDDI Research Inc., Fujimino, Saitama, Japan
niida@kddi-research.jp

Abstract. HCI research is increasingly focused on how technologies can help parents understand children's needs and state by enabling them to reflect on their children's activities. Use of a digital family calendar could have great potential in helping facilitate this process. However, relatively few studies have been carried out on this topic. This study investigated (1) how parents reflect on children's activities with a digital family calendar, (2) how parent-child interaction is like at the time of the reflection, and (3) how the parents' reflection and the parent-child interaction change over time. A three-month research study was conducted involving nine Japanese families using a digital family scrapbook calendar to share past, current and future events. Based on the results, we have proposed several design suggestions for reflective use of family calendars.

Keywords: Parents' reflection · Parental awareness · Digital family calendar · Parents · Children · Multiple user interaction

1 Introduction

Parents have an important role to play in children's psychological, social and educational development [1]. Parents need to adjust their behaviors to their children's current developmental, emotional, or mental states and needs in order to provide effective support and help them to engage in healthy social and educational activities [1]. This requires parents to be aware of and reflect on their children's behaviors [2]. However, how parents become aware of and reflect on their children's behavior depends on each parent's cognitive ability to envision the child's mental state [3], and the amount of time and energy they have for family activities [4]. Therefore, supporting parental awareness and facilitating reflection is a very important topic in the field of HCI [5].

The digital family calendar is a popular tool for facilitating parental awareness [2]. It is especially helpful for parents to be aware of each family member's daily activities in order to help coordinate the family schedule [2]. Use of the digital family calendar could, therefore, have great potential for facilitating reflection. However, prior work has

© Springer Nature Switzerland AG 2020
A. Nolte et al. (Eds.): CollabTech 2020, LNCS 12324, pp. 183–190, 2020.
https://doi.org/10.1007/978-3-030-58157-2_14

rarely focused on how effectively parents can actually reflect on children's activities by means of a digital family calendar, and how best to use a digital family calendar for this purpose.

In this project, we conducted a three-month research study involving the use of a scrapbook calendar (Fig. 1). The objective of this research study was to investigate (1) how parents reflect on their children's activities when using a scrapbook calendar, (2) how parent-child interaction is like at the time of the reflection, and (3) how the parents' reflection and the parent-child interaction change over time. Based on the results, we provided several design suggestions and proposals for more reflective use of family calendars in the future.

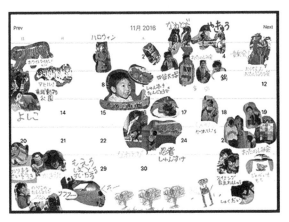

Fig. 1. Scrapbook calendar

2 Research Methods

2.1 Participants and Procedure

Nine families participated in this research. Table 1 shows the family members and their respective ages. One parent and child pair from each family, shown underlined in Table 1, participated in a workshop before the actual research trial began.

Four workshops were held from the end of April 2019 to the beginning of May 2019. Each parent and child pair participated in one of these workshops. In the workshop, an iPad was provided to each pair, the scrapbook calendar was introduced. An operating manual was also given to the parents. The parents, shown underlined in Table 1, answered the questionnaires provided and were interviewed twice over the three-month trial period. The first questionnaire and interview took place six weeks after the workshop, in the middle of June 2019, and the second one was conducted three months after the workshop, at the beginning of August 2019. The interview used a semi-structured interview style in which the interviewer and the interviewee were able to converse freely, based on a predetermined set of open-ended questions [6]. Each interview took about two hours to complete, including answering the questionnaire.

Table 1. Summary of the families. The letters, "F", "M", "S", and "D" indicate father, mother, son and daughter, respectively. The numbers in parentheses indicate their ages. Those parents underlined were interviewed and answered questionnaires throughout the research trial. Those children underlined participated in the first workshop.

No.	Family member (age)				
	Parents		Children		
1	F (55)	M (51)	S 22)	D (20)	S (11)
2	M (43)		S (11)		
3	F (41)	M (41)	S (12)	D (10)	D (6)
4	F (40)	M (39)	D (9)	D (6)	S (4)
5	M (37)		D (12)	S (7)	
6	F (42)	M (41)	S (17)	S (13)	S (11)
7	F (41)	M (40)	S (13)	S (11)	D (8)	D (8)
8	F (41)	M (43)	S (9)	D (6)	
9	F (41)	M (36)	S (7)	S (5)	

2.2 Materials

The scrapbook calendar allows users to decorate it with pictures and typed words or emojis (Fig. 1). It was developed to help families share details and impressions of past, current and future events and activities [7].

In this research, in order to evaluate parents' reflection on their children's activities, in keeping with the procedures outlined by Kocielnik et al. [8]: stage 1 (noticing—building awareness of events and behavior patterns), stage 2 (understanding—analysis of the situation from different perspectives, formulating explanations and observations about the reasons for the things noticed), and stage 3 (future actions—development of a new perspective, learning a lesson, or gaining new insights for the future). In accordance with the definition of each reflection stage described above, we developed a questionnaire to assess parents' reflection (Table 2). We also asked all participants about the amounts of family conversation that occurred when the scrapbook calendar was used (How much conversation does the family engage in when the scrapbook calendar is used?) and when it was not used (How much conversation does the family engage in when the scrapbook calendar is not used?). All the questions were answered using a 7-point scale (1: never - 7: very often/very much).

3 Results

3.1 The First Interview Results

The first interview was held six weeks after beginning to use the scrapbook calendar. In all the families interviewed, children actively edited the calendar and some parents

Table 2. Questions in the questionnaire used to assess parents' reflection

Reflection stage	Questions in the questionnaire
1	How often do you find out about your children's activities by looking at what your children have edited with the scrapbook calendar?
2	How often do you discuss what your children have edited on scrapbook calendar with them?
3	How often do you change your mind or behavior by looking at or talking about something your children have edited with the scrapbook calendar?

reported reflection at stages 2 and 3. The following sections show the types of reflection reported by parents.

At stage 2, parents and children discussed children's events or activities added on the calendar, along with some additional information. P4 described how she talked about the past events added by her daughter:

P4: I can easily come up with detailed questions about the added events. Therefore, I can understand the details of her daily activities.

P4 realized that the scrapbook calendar had helped them come up with detailed questions about activities added by their children. The overall quality of parent-child conversation became deeper as parents asked questions, received additional information, and gained a better understanding of their children's activities by means of reflection.

At stage 3, parents gained new insights about their children's interests or characteristics. P7 explained what he discovered when he saw the calendar edited by his children:

P7: I understand which events my children are interested in and how much they look forward to them, and I can clearly understand their preferences.

In the case of P7, he gained new insights simply through observing the calendar edited by his children. In contrast, P6 gained new insights through having a conversation with his son.

There was no parent who reported reflection stage 1 at which they noticed children's events with scrapbook calendar. One reason why this happened is because the most families, except F3 and 7, had paper family calendars at home to share individual events and coordinate family schedules. Parents fully understood children's future activities, as usual in Japan. Another reason is because in the most families, there is a daily habit in which family members talk about their daily activities. Therefore, parents knew children's past activities through their daily conversation habits without scrapbook calendar. Because of these reasons, reflection stage 1 was considered not to be mentioned in the interview.

3.2 The Second Interview Results

The second interview was held 3 months after beginning to use scrapbook calendar. Some parents mentioned the same kinds of reflection as in the first interview. At stage 2, parents and children discussed children's events or activities added on the calendar with some additional information. P4 reported that scrapbook calendar facilitates asking her child detailed questions as in the first interview. Also, P7 told us that they gained new insights about their children's interests or characteristics:

P4: I ask my daughter about the added activities. Therefore, I can understand the details of her daily activities.

P7: By seeing the calendar edited by my children, I understand which events they are attracted by.

Some parents mentioned reflection at stage 3 not observed in the first interview. They newly found their children's characteristics over a certain amount of time. Figure 2 shows the edited calendars by P3 and C3. P3 mentioned that he found his daughter well-organized and patient. P5 also told us that she newly found her son's preference because of his sustained activities with scrapbook calendar. Figure 3 shows the edited calendars by C5.

Fig. 2. Edited calendars by P3 and C3 for June and July. The orange letters were added by P3, and other letters, pictures, and emojis were added by C3. Some pictures and letters are obscured by a mosaic effect for privacy protection.

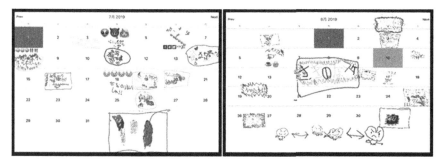

Fig. 3. Edited calendars by C5 for July and August. All the letters and pictures were edited by C5.

P3: My daughter decorates the calendar in a very specific way, and she has kept doing it this way for months. She seems to like to do it. I did not know that she was so well-organized and patient.

P5: My son keeps drawing decorations and pictures on the calendar even though most of the pictures are unrelated to any actual events. I did not know that he liked to draw pictures so much.

As in the first interview, no parents reported about reflection stage 1. As a specific feature of the second interview, there were families, F1, 2, and 9, who stopped using scrapbook calendar by the second interview. P1 explained that her son lost his motivation to use it because of the undesirable behavior of the system. P2 told us that she and her son could not find compelling reasons for using it because she and her son continued with the same routine. Also, P9 also described that it was difficult for his family to use digital family calendar as a new family habit.

3.3 Questionnaire Results

In order to investigate the relationship trends between parents' reflection and family activities, we performed correlational analyses based on the questionnaire and log data achieved in the first and second interviews. From the log data, we calculated the average numbers of times the calendar was edited per day for each family from the first workshop to the first interview and from the first to the second interview. The data of 3 families, F1, 2, and 9, in the second interview were excluded from the analyses because they stopped using scrapbook calendar before the second interview. The correlational relationships among the evaluated scores and calculated log data are shown in Table 3a for the first interview and Table 3b for the second interview. The average score of each reflection stage in the first interview was 4.25 ($SD = 1.41$), 3.42 ($SD = 2.15$), and 3.58 ($SD = 1.69$) for stage 1, 2, and 3 respectively. Also, that in the second interview was 5.00 ($SD = 1.10$), 4.33 ($SD = 1.21$), and 3.83 ($SD = 0.75$) for stage 1, 2, and 3 respectively.

In the first interview, the amount of family conversation without scrapbook calendar was positively related to reflection stage 1. On the other hand, in the second interview, it was negatively related to all the stages of reflection. The novel tools are initially incorporated into daily life and, later on, used meaningfully in various situations [9]. Scrapbook calendar was assumed to be used in pre-existing habitual family conversation in the first interview. Therefore, families accustomed to have a lot of family conversations had more opportunities to talk with scrapbook calendar and facilitate parents' reflection.

Moreover, in the first interview, reflection stage 1 and 2 were positively related to the amount of family conversation without scrapbook calendar and negatively related to the average number of times the calendar was edited per day. When users start to use novel digital tools, the learnability of the tools is important, and the functionality of the tools becomes more important than the initial learnability over time [9]. As the initial stage of using scrapbook calendar, there were more opportunities for the parents and children to talk about how to use scrapbook calendar. Such opportunities seemed to facilitate talking about the edited events and parents' reflection. In the second interview, such conversation and opportunities for parents' reflection seemed to disappear because of parents' and children's expertise in using scrapbook calendar.

Table 3. Correlational relationships in (a) the first interview and (b) the second interview. The numbers show the correlation coefficients. "Conv. w/o SC" indicates the amount of family conversation without scrapbook calendar, "Conv. w/ SC" indicates the amount of family conversation with scrapbook calendar, and "Ave. No. of add" indicates the average number of times the calendar was edited per day. S1, 2, and 3 indicates reflection stage 1, 2, and 3 respectively. The grayed out correlational coefficients indicate significant or marginally significant correlations. ^+p < .10, $^*p$ < .05, $^{**}p$ < .01.

(a) Correlational relationships in the first interview

	Conv. w/o SC	Conv. w/ SC	Ave. No. of add	S1	S2	S3
Conv. w/o SC	1					
Conv. w/ SC	.18	1				
Ave. No. of add	-.06	-.91**	1			
S1	.73*	.64$^+$	-.58$^+$	1		
S2	.24	.73*	-.75*	.60$^+$	1	
S3	.17	.03	-.22	.44	.40	1

(b) Correlational relationships in the second interview

	Conv. w/o SC	Conv. w/ SC	Ave. No. of add	S1	S2	S3
Conv. w/o SC	1					
Conv. w/ SC	-.22	1				
Ave. No. of add	.27	.51	1			
S1	-.87*	0	-.63	1		
S2	-.78$^+$	-.37	-.30	.75$^+$	1	
S3	-.84*	-.15	-.24	.73	.95**	1

4   Discussion and Conclusion

We discussed in the Related Work that digital family calendar can be a tool to help parents deepen their reflection on children's activities. Based on the results of this research, we found that parents experienced various levels of reflection on children's activities with scrapbook calendar. Several conclusions regarding how to design digital family calendar for facilitating parents' reflection can be drawn from the results of this study.

First, digital family calendar should be considered for children to add activities and events. Children's active use of digital family calendar is a critical factor to cause parents' reflection. In this study, scrapbook calendar allowed children to use with simple operations. As a result, children in all the families actively used it, all the parents' reflection was triggered by the activities added by children.

Second, digital family calendar should be supportive for children's sustained use. In this study, we found that children's sustained use of scrapbook calendar caused parents' deep reflection. Children's sustained use of digital family calendar could be supported by letting them use alternately with their parents or siblings, giving them cues for taking turns as an example, or play with it, such as drawing pictures.

Third, digital family calendar should be designed with a consideration of parent-child conversation based on edited contents. In this research, we found that parent-child conversation based on children's edited contents caused parents' reflection. Moreover, the quality of questions from parents influenced the type of the reflection. Parents can ask questions for additional information or finding out children's feelings or thoughts.

References

1. Lamborn, S.D., Mounts, N.S., Steinberg, L., Dornbusch, S.M.: Patterns of competence and adjustment among adolescents from authoritative, authoritarian, indulgent, and neglectful families. Child Dev. **62**(5), 1049–1065 (1991)
2. Neustaedter, C., Brush, A.J.B.: "LINC-ing" the family: the participatory design of an inkable family calendar. In: Grinter, R., Rodden, T., Aoki, P., Cutrell, E., Jeffries, R., Olson, G. (eds.) CHI 2006, Proceedings of the SIGCHI Conference on Human Factors in Computing Systems, pp. 141–150. ACM Press, New York (2006)
3. Slade, A.: Parental reflective functioning: an introduction. Attach. Hum. Dev. **7**(3), 269–281 (2005)
4. Khan, V.-J., Markopoulos, P.: Busy families awareness needs. Int. J. Hum. Comput. Stud. **67**(2), 139–153 (2009)
5. Pina, L.R., et al.: From personal informatics to family informatics: understanding family practices around health monitoring. In: Lee, C.P., Poltrock, S., Barkhuus, L., Borges, M., Kellogg, W. (eds.) CSCW 2017, Proceedings of the 2017 ACM Conference on Computer Supported Cooperative Work, pp. 2300–2315. ACM Press, New York (2017)
6. Bernard, H.R.: Social Research Methods: Qualitative and Quantitative Approaches, 2nd edn. Sage Publications, Thousand Oaks (2012)
7. Tojo, N., Ishizaki, H., Nagai, Y., Niida, S.: Tool for enhancing family communication through planning, sharing experiences, and retrospection. In: Silva, H.P., Ramirez, A.J., Holzinger, A., Constantine, L., Helfert, M. (eds.) CHIRA 2019. Proceedings of the International Conference on Computer-Human Interaction Research and Applications, pp. 34–44. Science and Technology Publication, Setubal (2019)
8. Kocielnik, R., Xiao, L., Avrahami, D., Hsieh, G.: Reflection companion: a conversational system for engaging users in reflection on physical activity. In: Kay, J., Kientz, J.A., Kostakos, V., Santini, S., Scott, J., Yatani, K. (eds.) IMWUT 2018, Proceedings of the ACM on Interactive, Mobile, Wearable and Ubiquitous Technologies, vol. 2, no. 2, article no. 70. ACM Press, New York (2018)
9. Karapanos, E., Zimmerman, J., Forlizzi, J., Martens, J-B.: User experience over time: an initial framework. In: Greenberg, S., Hudson, S.E., Hinckley, K., Morris, M.R., Olsen, D.R. (eds.) CHI 2009, Proceedings of the SIGCHI Conference on Human Factors in Computing Systems, pp. 729–738. ACM Press, New York (2009)

Four Approaches to Developing Autonomous Facilitator Agent for Online and Face-to-Face Public Debate

Shun Shiramatsu$^{(\boxtimes)}$ (ORCID), Ko Kitagawa, Shota Naito, Hiroaki Koura, and Chao Cai

Graduate School of Engineering, Nagoya Institute of Technology, Nagoya, Japan
`siramatu@nitech.ac.jp`

Abstract. Recently, the importance of public debate is increasing both globally and locally for addressing sustainability problems such as pandemics, climate change, and economic crisis. To support such public debate, software agents need to be developed to facilitate discussions, for example, to recommend relevant information by detecting stagnation and flaming in online public debate, to invite debate participants from SNS, or to record face-to-face public debates. In this study, we prototyped four software agents for facilitation: (1) an agent for detecting stagnation and flaming while quantifying the degree of discussion progress in a Web-based debate, (2) an agent for providing relevant information in accordance with the preceding context of a Web-based debate, (3) an agent for finding people who are interested in the content of the discussion and inviting them to a public debate from Twitter, and (4) an agent for recording a face-to-face public debate and supporting users' reviewing of the debate. In this paper, we overview these four agents and evaluation experiments and present the feedback from the participants in an event organized by Facilitation Association of Japan.

Keywords: Discussion facilitation · BERT · Public debate · Civic tech

1 Introduction

Societies worldwide are currently facing various threats to their sustainability, e.g., rapid climate change, the COVID-19 pandemic, natural disasters. Local societies in Japan are also facing sustainability problems such as low birth rate and aging population. In tackling these problems, people need to actively participate in public debate and collaboration.

However, it is not so easy for people to participate in such collaborations because they do not always have enough background knowledge. For example, since hackathons for civic tech activities require diverse participants who has various skills [11], there should be participants who have less background knowledge about the focused on social issues such as IT engineers. Discussion facilitation is

© Springer Nature Switzerland AG 2020
A. Nolte et al. (Eds.): CollabTech 2020, LNCS 12324, pp. 191–200, 2020.
https://doi.org/10.1007/978-3-030-58157-2_15

thus important for enabling people to constructively participate in public debates on sustainability issues.

We aim to develop software agents for helping facilitation of online and face-to-face public debates. In this paper, we introduce the following four prototype software agents for facilitating public debate in Japanese.

1. An agent for detecting stagnation, flaming, and deviation from the topic while quantifying the degree of discussion progress in an online debate. To post the facilitator's questions at appropriate times, a facilitator agent needs to detect when the debate is not progressing.
2. An agent for providing relevant information in accordance with the preceding context of an online debate.
3. An agent for finding people who are interested in the content of an online debate and inviting them to a public debate from Twitter.
4. An agent for recording face-to-face debate and supporting users' reviewing of the debate.

The first three agents are for online debate and the last one is for face-to-face debate. This paper overviews the experimental results and presents the feedback from the participants in an event organized by Facilitation Association of Japan (FAJ).

2 Related Works

Online debate systems called COLLAGREE and D-Agree [6,10] are the basis of this study. Ikeda et al. [5] developed a facilitator agent with a rule-based question generation for online debates on COLLAGREE. However, the timing at which their agent posts the question was not carefully considered. Since their agent just periodically posts the questions, sometimes the agent's posts were excessive. Shibata et al. [10] developed an agent for automated questioning on D-Agree. This agent was used in a social experiment of public debate on the Nagoya City Next Comprehensive Plan in 2018. However, this agent did not consider appropriate timing for automated posts because it just periodically posts the questions.

We have proposed a method to quantify the degree of discussion progress on the basis of the structure of the issue-based information system (IBIS) for online debates in Japanese [8]. However, our previous method considers not the content of a post in the debate but only the node type of IBIS structure extracted from the post. We have also proposed a method to estimate Twitter users' interests and to invite online debate participants from Twitters [1]. However, our previous experiment did not investigate the versatility of the method because the experiment was conducted for only one particular topic of debate.

3 Four Software Agents for Discussion Facilitation

This section overviews the four facilitator agents we prototyped and results of evaluation experiments.

3.1   Agent Estimating the Degree of Discussion Progress

We aim to quantify the degree of discussion progress (DDP) toward the final goal of the debate in order to estimate appropriate timing the facilitator should intervene. To detect such appropriate timing, it is not enough to observe only the number of utterances because even if there are many remarks, they may be the result of flaming or deviate.

We improve our previous IBIS-based method [8] for quantifying the DDP. To consider the content of posts in online debate, we incorporate the bidirectional encoder representations from transformers (BERT) [2]. For the training data of BERT, we used 17 discussion threads in Japanese collected by a social experiment using COLLAGREE in 2013 [6], in which 13 subjects rated the argument progress of each post on a six-point Likert scale from 0 to 5. For each post, we evaluated two types of the DDP: one for the divergence phase of a debate and the other for the convergence phase. Since three annotators evaluated one discussion thread, we averaged them together and normalized the range of the DDP to be $[0, 1]$. These average values are used as reference data for training and testing. This training dataset is used both for IBIS-based calculation [8] and our BERT-based one.

The IBIS-based DDP d_{ibis} is a summation of the weights of IBIS nodes extracted from the preceding debate content. The weight of a node, which is determined only by the IBIS node types (task, idea, merit, and demerit), is optimized by the genetic algorithm [8]. The BERT-based DDP d_{bert} is calculated by regression using BERT. This regression is anomalously implemented on the basis of a BERT model fine-tuned for classifying 6-point Likert scale. Before the fine-tuning, the BERT model is pre-trained using Japanese Wikipedia with SentencePiece [7].

To complementarily use these two calculations of DDP, we define the DDP d as the weighted summation of d_{ibis} and d_{bert} as follows:

$$d = \alpha d_{\text{ibis}} + (1 - \alpha) d_{\text{bert}},$$

where $0 \leq \alpha \leq 1$.

As the evaluation experiment, we calculate the correlation coefficient between the estimated DDP and the reference data. As the result showed in Table 1, the DDP for the divergence phase is accurately estimated by d and d_{bert}. Especially, d with $\alpha = 0.5$ indicates strong positive correlation since $r = +0.69$.

Table 1. Correlation coefficient between the estimated DDP and the reference data (the average of three experiment participants' subjectively evaluated DDP)

Method	Corr (divergence)	Corr (convergence)
IBIS note type	+0.47	+0.30
BERT	+0.62	+0.44
Weighted sum	+0.69 ($\alpha = 0.5$)	+0.42 ($\alpha = 0.1$)

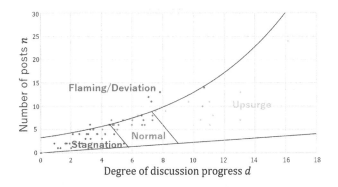

Fig. 1. Classification model for four types of discussion state

Here, we examined how reliable each experimental participant was, since the value of progression in the training data was the average of the three experimental participants. Specifically, we also calculated the correlation coefficients between the mean value of progression and the degree of progression assessed by each experimental participant. The mean correlation coefficient was $r = +0.67$ for the degree of progress in the divergence phase and $r = +0.74$ for the convergence phase. This indicates that the performance of DDP estimation for the divergence phase ($r = +0.69$) is comparable to that of the average human experiment participants. However, it was also suggested that the performance of the convergence phase was significantly inferior to that of humans. This could be attributed to the fact that most of the 17 discussion threads used in the training data did not actually converge towards consensus building.

Furthermore, using the DDP estimation of divergent phases, we prototype a classification model of discussion states shown in Fig. 1. In this figure, the horizontal axis represents the estimated DDP and the vertical one represents the number of recent posts. The plots in the figure represent 65 moments in Slack debates which the agent needs to determine whether it posts some questioning or not. On the basis of the assumption that the facilitator should intervene when the amount of change in DDP is low in relation to the number of posts, this model classifies Web-based debate into four discussion states: Stagnation, Normal, Upsurge, and Flaming/Deviation. The colors of plots in Fig. 1 represent the discussion state manually determined by a human annotator. The experimental results show a precision of 75% in an open test and 89% in a closed test. The model shown in Fig. 1 is obtained by the closed test.

3.2   Agent Providing Relevant Information

When a Web discussion is stagnant, providing information related to an online debate content may help participants to think about what they will post next. In this study, we implement a software agent recommending relevant information for this purpose. To provide relevant information, it is necessary to first determine the search query from the preceding context and then select the paragraphs and segments to be presented from the Web content obtained by search engines such as Google.

Fig. 2. An example of relevant information provision for a debate in Japanese on Slack (Color figure online)

To determine the search query, the agent calculates the score of the term frequency- inverse document frequency (TF-IDF) of the words appearing in each post by integrating the decay ratio γ and extracts the words with the highest score as the search query. In addition, we also tried to determine the search query by predicting the words that appear in the next statement with BERT. However, the search query determination method by BERT was not adopted because the words at the top of TF-IDF with the accumulated decay ratio γ were more similar to the search queries chosen by human experiment participants than the words predicted by BERT.

Using the extracted queries for Google search, the agent extracts segments as relevant information to provide in the online debate from the top 10 pages of the search result. In this case, we adopted the approach of finding and presenting segments close to the IBIS node type in the search results, assuming possible IBIS node types as a response to the previous statement. Specifically, using the training data also used in the Subsect. 3.1, we trained a classifier that predicts the relationship between the IBIS nodes included in the immediately preceding and subsequent utterances with BERT. The relationships we use are classified into five ones: advantages of the recent idea, disadvantages of recent idea, solutions to the recent issue, examples of the recent idea, and reasons for the recent idea. We use this classifier to predict the relationship between recent posts in online debates and segments consisting of four adjacent text sentences in the search results. The agent chooses the relationship with the most classified segments from the above five relationships, extracts the top three scored segments from the segments classified into the chosen relationship, and presents them as the relevant information (the red dotted frame in Fig. 2).

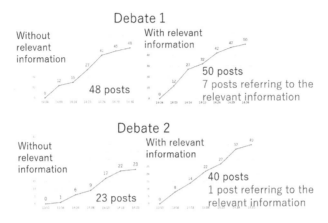

Fig. 3. Comparison of the number of posts between Slack debates with and without relevant information provision

Figure 3 compares the number of posts in online debates with and without the relevant information provision by our method. The theme of debate 1 was "Reduction of food loss," and the theme of debate 2 was "Ms. Greta Thunberg, a teenage climate change activist." As can be seen from the figure, there was no significant difference in the number of contributions with and without the presentation of relevant information. This suggests that the effect of providing relevant information has not been verified because the debate does not noticeably stagnate without a longer period of time. Qualitatively, the accuracy of segment selection presented as relevant information needs to be further improved because relevant information was found that was not necessarily in line with the content of the discussion.

3.3   Agent Inviting Participants from Twitter

When conducting an online debate on a social issue, the discussion sometimes stagnates if the number of interested participants is small. To attract more interested people to the Web discussion, we suppose that it is effective to invite them through social networking services (SNS). We have developed a software agent to find Twitter users who are interested in Web discussion topics and generate invitation messages for them [1]. This agent calculates the cosine similarity between tweets and a debate topic using BERT. There are two types of vectors for calculating the cosine similarity: the distributed representation output by the bert-as-service [12] and the output vector of a BERT model for predicting hashtags from text. The similarity between a tweet and a discussion topic is calculated as a weighted summation of the two kinds of similarities. A Twitter user's score is defined as a summation of the scores of the user's top three tweets of the user.

Our previous experiment [1] was conducted for only one particular public debate, i.e., the Nagoya City Next Comprehensive Plan in Japanese, which was conducted in 2018 on an online debate system called D-Agree [10]. For the hashtag estimation, 91 hashtags relevant to the debate topic were prepared. Experiment participants evaluate pairs of a Twitter user and a discussion thread from two aspects: "Is the target user interested in the agenda of the target online debate?" and "Is the target user likely to participate in the target online debate?" As a result, the agent could more accurately estimate first aspect on Twitter users' interests than the second one on users' participation possibility.

We conduct an additional experiment on Slack. The debate topic is changed to the privacy protection to investigate the versatility. As a result, we found that enough variety of hashtags is needed for estimating Twitter users' interests. Moreover, the tendency that the interests is more accurately estimated than the participation possibility was commonly observed. We found that this tendency was influenced by the subjective observation of "even if a Twitter user seems to be interested in the agenda, he/she seems less likely to participate in the debate when the user does behave seriously on Twitter" through interviewing the experiment participants. This finding indicates that the invitation agent should consider not only the target user's interest in the debate agenda but also the characteristics of the user's behavior on Twitter.

3.4 Agent Supporting Review of Debate

To promote collaboration and co-creation among a region's residents, it is important to discuss not only through the Web but also in face-to-face workshops. We aim to develop an agent facilitating face-to-face debate by combining Hylable Discussion [9] and Google Cloud Speech-to-Text [3]. However, Hylable Discussion currently specializes in post-discussion analysis, so it is not possible to obtain the results of analysis in real time during the discussion. For this reason, we first implement a software agent recording face-to-face debates and supporting reviews of the debate for facilitators to reflect on face-to-face discussions. FAJ sometimes conducts "Fishbowl discussion", i.e., the participants and observers of the discussion are divided and the observers take notes and reflect on the discussion. The user interface generated by this agent has a function similar to that of the observer's notes, and we aim to make it possible to look back more exploratorily.

Hylable Discussion analyzes the transitions in the volume of each participant's speech and the tendency of turn-taking on the basis of the results of the auditory scene analysis, i.e., sound localization and sound separation. However, speech recognition is not performed. Therefore, we adopted an approach in which the results of speech recognition by Google Cloud Speech-to-Text from the separated sounds obtained by Hylable Discussion are displayed on a graph of speech volume transitions. The prototype user interface is shown in Fig. 4. On the left is the transition of the amount of speech for each participant, with the results of speech recognition overlaid on top of it. However, it is not possible to display the results of speech recognition of all expressions for a long discussion, so the important remarks that should be displayed need to be selected.

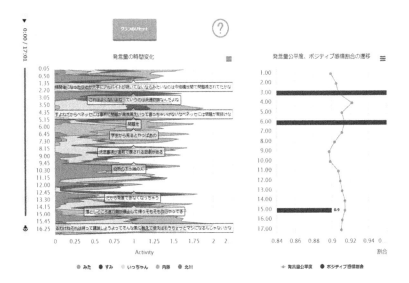

Fig. 4. A review support interface for face-to-face discussions

Through interviews with FAJ facilitators, we learned that facilitators should focus on the process rather than the content of the discussion. The agent auto-matically selects and displays an utterance at the turning-points where the distribution of the amount of utterances changes significantly. Furthermore, the turning-points in the discussion process are represented by overlaid icons corresponding to the emotions estimated from the phonological information. By clicking on the displayed speech recognition results or icons, discussion participants can listen to the corresponding speech at the corresponding time. Since some speech recognition errors are also included, a mechanism is needed that allows the participants to somehow correct the recognition errors.

In the right side of Fig. 4, the transitions of the fairness of the amount of speech and the transitions of the ratio of positive to negative emotions are shown. This also aims to be used as a visualization method for facilitators to understand the discussion process. Furthermore, we are planning to use this interface for not only facilitators but also people who do not participate in a face-to-face debate to understand the content of the debate.

4   Feedback from Facilitators

We conducted an online workshop on our four prototype agents for discussion facilitation on May 10th, 2020 under the collaboration with FAJ. The online workshop was titled "AI × Facilitation: How far has the research gone? Where should we go using this?" (translated from Japanese) [4]. Over 50 Japanese participants, who were mostly FAJ members, listened to the presentation about the four agents and discussed their potential needs.

The feedback from the participants was written in a Google Spreadsheet in Japanese after the presentation. On the agent estimating DDP, a participant wrote "The timing of interventions usually bothers me," which represents a need for this agent. Another participant suggested that the DDP can be used for real-time visualization of discussion status. Furthermore, there was a remark pointing out that debates sometimes need to stagnate.

On the agent providing relevant information, a participant wrote "Textbook-wise, it's good to be able to share the necessary information before the divergence." From this feedback, we need to consider the appropriate timing to provide relevant information. Another participant wrote that such kinds of search tasks are more suitable for artificial intelligence (AI) than human facilitators.

On the agent inviting Twitter users, a participant wrote "It's scary when debate trolls are invited in and we get into a bad discussion." Another participant wrote that actual use is needed to judge whether this prototype agent is useful or not.

On the agent supporting the review of face-to-face debate, multiple participants pointed out the necessity of visual processing for recognizing non-verbal behaviors or emotions of debate participants. Another participant wrote that the user interface for reviewing the debate can be useful in the final stages of consensus building. Furthermore, there was a remark that such a quantitative analysis of the amount of utterance is a suitable task for AI.

5   Conclusion and Future Perspective

We introduced prototypes of three facilitator agents for online debate and one for face-to-face debates. The experiment results showed that the degree of discussion progress (DDP) estimation has a relatively strong correlation with human's subjective estimation in the divergence phase of debate. The experiment results also showed that the accuracy for providing relevant information needs to be improved. Moreover, longer debate experiments are needed, e.g., several days. The experiment results on the invitation agent indicated that we need to consider not only SNS users' interest but also their behavior before inviting them. We also prototyped an agent supporting the review of face-to-face debate while finding the turning-point by calculating the distribution of participants' utterances.

We are planning to improve these facilitator agents in accordance with the feedback on them from the participants in an online workshop organized by FAJ. Especially, to improve the agent for relevant information provision, we are developing a system for gathering social issues and collaborative activities among people from Web articles. As another future work, since we are currently practicing social distancing due to the COVID-19 pandemic, we are also considering how to develop functions for supporting facilitation on online meeting tools.

Acknowledgement. We appreciate Ms. Kayoko HAYASHI and Mr. Shigeru ICHIKI for managing FAJ's online workshop and for providing advices on designing the discussion review support agent. We also thank Dr. Takeshi MIZUMOTO, the president of Hylable Inc., for supporting the use of the Hylable Discussion. Moreover, we appreciate Prof. Takayuki ITO for providing the discussion corpora with COLLAGREE and D-Agree. This work was partially supported by JSPS KAKENHI (17K00461) and JST CREST (JPMJCR15E1).

References

1. Cai, C., Shiramatsu, S.: Estimating Twitter user's interest for inviting potential participants into Web-based debate platforms based on BERT. In: Proceedings of the 2nd International Conference on Artificial Intelligence in Information and Communication, pp. 602–607 (2020)
2. Devlin, J., Chang, M.W., Lee, K., Toutanova, K.: BERT: pre-training of deep bidirectional transformers for language understanding, pp. 4171–4186 (2019)
3. Google: Speech-to-text conversion powered by machine learning. https://cloud.google.com/speech-to-text
4. Hayashi, K., Ichiki, S.: 175th FAJ Chubu Branch Extraordinary Regular Meeting: "AI × Facilitation" (2020). https://www.faj.or.jp/base/chubu/event/2020510aka/. (in Japanese)
5. Ikeda, Y., Shiramatsu, S.: Generating questions asked by facilitator agents using preceding context in web-based discussion. In: Proceedings of the 2nd IEEE International Conference on Agents, pp. 127–132 (2017)
6. Ito, T., Imi, Y., Ito, T., Hideshima, E.: COLLAGREE: a faciliator-mediated largescale consensus support system. In: Collective Intelligence 2014 (2014)
7. Kikuta, Y.: BERT pretrained model trained on Japanese Wikipedia articles (2019). https://github.com/yoheikikuta/bert-japanese
8. Kitagawa, K., Shiramatsu, S., Kamiya, A.: Developing a method for quantifying degree of discussion progress towards automatic facilitation of web-based discussion. In: Lujak, M. (ed.) AT 2018. LNCS (LNAI), vol. 11327, pp. 162–169. Springer, Cham (2019). https://doi.org/10.1007/978-3-030-17294-7_12
9. Matsuoka, M., Mizumoto, T.: Toward a better discussion in English: quantitative perspective of feedback. In: Extended Summaries of the 26th Korea TESOL International Conference, p. 54 (2018)
10. Shibata, D., Moustafa, A., Ito, T., Suzuki, S.: On facilitating large-scale online discussions. In: Nayak, A.C., Sharma, A. (eds.) PRICAI 2019. LNCS (LNAI), vol. 11671, pp. 608–620. Springer, Cham (2019). https://doi.org/10.1007/978-3-030-29911-8_47
11. Shiramatsu, S., Tossavainen, T., Ozono, T., Shintani, T.: Towards continuous collaboration on civic tech projects: use cases of a goal sharing system based on linked open data. In: Tambouris, E., et al. (eds.) ePart 2015. LNCS, vol. 9249, pp. 81–92. Springer, Cham (2015). https://doi.org/10.1007/978-3-319-22500-5_7
12. Xiao, H.: bert-as-service documentation. https://bert-as-service.readthedocs.io/

Author Index

Printed in the United States
By Bookmasters